Do You Love Jehovah?

God Almighty's Infinite Love & Wisdom to Propel You to Greatness

Shirley Cheng

www.DanceWithYourHeart.com

Wappingers Falls, New York

Copyright © 2009 by Shirley Cheng. All rights reserved.

ISBN: 978-0-578-00079-4
Library of Congress Control Number: 2008911394
BISAC: REL070000 – Religion / Christianity / General

www.DanceWithYourHeart.com
Wappingers Falls, New York, United States of America

Front cover of Ezekiel's vision:
"…the likeness of a throne, as the appearance of a sapphire stone; and upon the likeness of the throne was a likeness as the appearance of a man upon it above. And I saw as it were glowing metal, as the appearance of fire within it round about, from the appearance of his loins and upward; and from the appearance of his loins and downward I saw as it were the appearance of fire, and there was brightness round about him. As the appearance of the bow that is in the cloud in the day of rain, so was the appearance of the brightness round about. This was the appearance of the likeness of the glory of Jehovah." (Ezekiel 1:26-28)

Bible Dove Illustration: © James Lee | Dreamstime.com
Dove: © Rbharathi | Dreamstime.com
Throne: © Rossco | Dreamstime.com
Rainbow background: © Roman Smitko | Dreamstime.com

All Bible quotations in this book are from the American Standard Version of 1901, a Public Domain Bible, unless otherwise indicated.
Bible verses from the New International Version are © 1973, 1978, 1984 by International Bible Society.
Bible verses from the Contemporary English Version are © 1995 by American Bible Society.
Bible verses from Holman Christian Standard Bible are © 1999, 2000, 2002, 2003 by Holman Bible Publishers, Nashville Tennessee.
Bible verses from the Amplified Bible are © 1954, 1958, 1962, 1964, 1965, 1987 by The Lockman Foundation.
Bible verses from the English Standard Version are © 2001 by Crossway Bibles, a division of Good News Publishers.

All rights reserved by the author, Shirley Cheng. No part of this publication may be reproduced, stored in a retrieval system, or transmitted in any form or by any means, electronic, mechanical, photocopying, recording or otherwise, without the prior written permission of Shirley Cheng.

Awards Received

Finalist – 2010 International Book Awards – Christianity
Finalist – 2010 International Book Awards – Christian Inspirational
Finalist – National Best Books 2009 Awards – Christianity
Finalist – National Indie Excellence 2010 Awards – Religion
Second Place – 2010 Written Art Awards – Religion/Spirituality
Honorable Mention – Reader Views 2009 Literary Awards – Religion (Eastern/Western)

With all my heart and soul, I dedicate this book to the greatest treasure God has ever bestowed upon me: my beloved and spiritually strong mother, Juliet Cheng, who first brought me the most wonderful news: that Jehovah is our loving Creator and God Almighty. Thank you, Mom, not only for bringing me into this world but also for your endless love and devotion, which are the sunlight and water in my life!

To live in God, we must live in the image of love, for Jehovah is love; and love embraces the entire spectrum of all that is beautiful, precious, and good.

> Make a joyful noise unto Jehovah, all ye lands. Serve Jehovah with gladness. Come before his presence with singing. Know ye that Jehovah, he is God: It is he that hath made us, and we are his; We are his people, and the sheep of his pasture. Enter into his gates with thanksgiving, And into his courts with praise: Give thanks unto him, and bless his name. For Jehovah is good; his lovingkindness endureth for ever, And his faithfulness unto all generations.
> ~*Psalm 100*

Table of Contents

"...our sufficiency is from God; who also made us sufficient as ministers of a new covenant; not of the letter, but of the spirit: for the letter killeth, but the spirit giveth life." (II Corinthians 3:5-6)

The Beginning of Wisdom 7
Jehovah God Almighty, Jesus Christ & the Holy Spirit 15
Great Designs, Greater Designer 17
Purposeful Paradise 29
Jesus, Merely an Ordinary Man? 35
The Christ Jesus: A Mighty Spirit & the Greatest Man 41
Jesus Rocks! But How So? 52
God's Revealing Nature 58
Do You Love Jehovah? 61
Why Do You Love Jehovah? 66
Excused from Future Sins? 70
Act Out Your Faith 73
God Is Love 77
Masterpiece of Love 85
Do You Love Jehovah's Art of Love? 87
The Trinity Mystery 93
The Holy Trinity, the Narrow Path? 95
Prayer of Jesus Christ 110
Trinitarians Argue… 115

The Holy Bible & Its Invaluable Teachings 169
All-Time Best Seller of Infinite Wisdom & Love 171
The Ultimate Life's Manual 174
How Should You Study the Bible?..201
Wisdom—How Should You Cultivate It? 208
Connecting with Jehovah 212
Your Destiny, Designed?..217
Jehovah's Spiritual Image 225
Freedom in Free Will 228
Do Not Be Stupid!...233
Turn from Evil 238
Wash Yourself First 241
Serve Love with Justice 245
Follow the Light 249
Fruitless Worrying or Fruitful Concerns? 256
Do You Eat the Smaller Fish? 260
Our Work Not in Vain! 263
Do Not Destroy the Honor! 267
The Value of Success 269
Life's FAQs: Mysteries, Solved!..272
At Last, an End to All Evil! 310
Your Sacred Mission 320
Personal Experiences 325
Jehovah: Secret to Spiritual Championship: How One Blind
Individual Continues to See...327
A Blind and Disabled Gal...Happy?..335
The Divine Dream of Love & Light..339
Traveling on the Road to Ultra-Ability 343
A Note from the Author...350
Spotlight Reviews...355
About the Author 370

The Beginning of Wisdom

"Happy is the man that findeth wisdom, And the man that getteth understanding. For the gaining of it is better than the gaining of silver, And the profit thereof than fine gold." (Proverbs 3:13-14)

Take a moment to pretend that you do not exist. Imagine that you do not know all the people you love now. Subtract your friends, family, and your associates. Take away the pleasures of your senses: the aroma of newly baked bread, the taste of sweet melon, the sight of a butterfly alighting upon a rose, the warmth of sunlight on your skin, and the melodious songs of birds. Also remove the hobbies and activities you enjoy and any places you have seen and visited. Finally, delete any memories and experiences you have ever had. What is left is utter emptiness; not even darkness exists. You would not even know you did not exist; you would know nothing.

Now replace this void with your life again. Can you not see how much you have in your life? Can you imagine a life without all that you have? Can you not see what a tremendous loss it would be if you had never been gifted with life? Are you grateful to be alive, and grateful to your parents who gave you your life?

If you were an adopted child and after many years you finally found an opportunity to meet your biological parents, would you not want to know the people who gave you your very existence, and thank them for your life? Imagine, then, how much more it is to know the Parent of all parents!

Who is this Parent of all parents? Well, He is unlike any parent out there; He is everything good. He is all virtues: Love, Wisdom, Righteousness, Mercy, Forgiveness, and Power. He is not only the Parent of your parents, but of everything in the universe: all that is visible and invisible; all that is audible and inaudible; all that can be felt, tasted, and smelled; everything intangible and ethereal. All that is good is a part of Him. He is infinite, total, and all-encompassing. He has existed since before the beginning of time. He has no beginning nor has He any end. And His name is Jehovah, the one and only true God Almighty.

Jehovah is the beginning of wisdom, the fulfillment of completeness, and the representation of love. He is the reason why I have written this book: to let you know your Creator so you can have a lasting, fulfilling, and sacred relationship with Him. I know how much joy and peace it can bring a person to know about Jehovah and His greatness, and I have the strong desire to tell you about His glory so you, too, can experience the bliss I enjoy.

Jehovah is the working force behind everything and every order. He is behind all that is good; He is absent from every dark corner. Without

Jehovah, neither your life nor life's virtues would exist.

One other Hero in this book—but more so in our lives—is a Gift from Jehovah that surpasses every essence of life. Whereas God is our Life-Giver, this holy Present is our Life-Sustainer. This Gem is from the depth of Jehovah's heart, and He uses it to forge a lasting connection between Him and us. This Jewel is the one and only begotten Son of God, Jesus, our Messiah, the Savior who works harmoniously in this Father-Son team to provide us with the love and light that will propel us to our greatest heights.

The Christ has received a special mission from his Father, one that is yet to be completed. The mission began two thousand years ago, and when he accomplishes it in God's set time, we will all be witnesses. How will we be a part of this assignment? Do we have our own duties? Exactly, what is this mission? And most importantly, who is Jesus? Soon, you will receive answers to these questions that make up the core of our Christian belief.

> "...the things which are seen are temporal; but the things which are not seen are eternal." (II Corinthians 4:18)

Having the knowledge that there is a Creator, I know life is not about the worldly aspects but all about the spiritual realm. Suffering on Earth strengthens our faith. Challenges and obstacles are exercise machines for our spirits. God has much more prepared for those who can endure the trials and tribulations here, so we can be strong enough to receive an everlasting life of love and happiness under His mighty and just rule. Therefore, we all must concentrate on the spiritual aspects of life: faith, love, values, hope, gratitude, and many other priceless commodities that everyone needs to embrace. If we focus on only the worldly, such as wealth and fame, what we gain will die along with us. On the other hand, if we welcome a life of love and values, we will leave an enduring legacy.

Cultivating the spiritual means that we should do our utmost to live life to the fullest extent possible, all the while keeping in mind our future beyond this world. For if we just live fully for today, for only the pleasures this world brings, our future will be a bleak one—it will not exist at all!

Conversely, if we think only for our future, we will waste our current life. Our world has been blessed with many gifts from Jehovah, so we must focus on His treasures rather than the passing pleasures from His opposing force. God has graciously bestowed life upon each of us so we can enjoy it to its fullest, and this is exactly what I will always do. Why should we resist all the wonders of life just because something negative decides to bump into us? Compared to the entire universe and all the beauty it contains, not to mention the bright future for humankind, our problems are tiny!

Thus, I cannot ignore the strong urge to write this book, to let you know just how much we would be missing if we do not walk on the path of light, to follow Jehovah's guidance and accept His grace. He is why I am not disabled, but ultra-abled. If I do not rejoice in and spread His pivotal and ultimate messages, I will be selfishly concealing from others my secret to ultra-ability, just as a chef deceives when a key ingredient in a culinary masterpiece is kept secret.

> "Every one therefore that heareth these words of mine, and doeth them, shall be likened unto a wise man, who built his house upon the rock: and the rain descended, and the floods came, and the winds blew, and beat upon that house; and if fell not: for it was founded upon the rock." (Matthew 7:24-25)

Let us say you want to build a house. What would the house require to withstand the hostile elements of nature? If you say a strong foundation, you are absolutely correct. Like a house, our lives need to be built upon a strong foundation. To live happily, securely, courageously, freely, with passion, purpose, and plans, that foundation must be God.

Life is worthless without spirituality. Yet, without God, spirituality holds no meaning. So God is the ultimate foundation of a good life. Knowing God should not simply be a desire—it should be a necessity, food that enables us to not only exist but *live*. And the best way to start obtaining knowledge of Jehovah is from His Word, the Bible.

I am far from being a religious scholar. That does not mean I am incapable of realizing and understanding that faith in Jehovah is the cornerstone of spirituality. Like many of God's prophets and Christ's disciples who did not allow the lack of worldly education, wealth, or good health, stop them from accurately knowing God and being His friends, I am a servant who strongly feels that Jehovah's love and messages are too important and holy to be limited to only a privileged few, and that nothing can separate us from obtaining the truths about God, so long as we want to know Him. I am a student of the Bible whose desires for fellowship with God have propelled her to share with you her sheer bliss that is found in only the Bible and in harmony with Jehovah.

To learn and assimilate untainted knowledge, I let Jehovah teach me directly from the Bible—I do not follow the teachings of man, so I do not follow any manmade doctrines, nor do I belong to any sect or denomination. Hence, whatever I have written in this book is gathered from my studying of the Bible; I base my beliefs solely on what the Bible teaches. I will never dispute any Biblical truths, but will always verify what I hear with what the Holy Scriptures say. If what people teach is not confirmed by the Bible, I will question it. So expect to find within the covers of this book questions on subjects to which I have not found satisfactory answers.

I want to learn as much as I can about my Heavenly Father, so sharing my thoughts and what I have learned from studying the sacred writings will help me expand and remember my lessons. In my experience, teaching someone a certain subject I have just learned actually helps my own learning process, assisting me to better understand and remember. But I am by no means a teacher of this utmost important and delicate topic. We have only one Wise Teacher, and He and His greatest teachings are the subject of this small book, which simply acts as a gentle nudge to help you fan the desire to know Jehovah that lies within you—for desires have to first come from deep within you. No one can fire your soul, only you hold the power to create a flicker and fan it.

This volume, just as any other volume, is inferior to God's Word and should not be your primary source of knowledge about God. The Bible is the one and only primary source, so always consult it for guidance and support.

Lastly, this book does not attempt to answer every Bible question you have, although it will definitely cover the key points: Why are you here? What is your purpose? Where will you go after your life on Earth? Where can you find complete and absolute fulfillment? How much success you will experience in obtaining these answers and incorporating the knowledge into your life is solely dependent upon your heart's truthful answer to the fundamental question: Do you love Jehovah?

Friend, our time is quickly passing away and will be gone any minute. We must seize the opportunity right now to live a bright today and welcome an even brighter tomorrow. We must not allow time to slip through the cracks of everyday haste. There are stars we must reach, there are roads we must take, so let us open the doors to our hearts to embrace all that we yearn to experience, to discover, to know, to have. Life's fullness is only found in Jehovah, and the fullness can only be experienced if He lives within you, so do not delay—start your journey to knowing the Great Creator and His most sacred purpose and highest mission for us, in Christ. Once you have Him in your heart, be ready to conquer the highest mountains, cross the deepest oceans, and reach the brightest stars. Do not be surprised if you bump into the silvery moon, for you will celebrate over greater treasures than this.

Jehovah God Almighty
Jesus Christ
The Holy Spirit

"I will extol thee, my God, O King; And I will bless thy name for ever and ever. Every day will I bless thee; And I will praise thy name for ever and ever. Great is Jehovah, and greatly to be praised; And his greatness is unsearchable. Jehovah is righteous in all his ways, and gracious in all his works." (Psalm 145:1-3, 17)

Great Designs, Greater Designer

"I am Jehovah, that maketh all things; that stretcheth forth the heavens alone; that spreadeth abroad the earth..." (Isaiah 44:24)

When we admire a beautiful painting, we are certain that a gifted painter is behind the masterpiece. When we pass by a brick house, we do not doubt that builders must have constructed it. And when we talk on the phone, we are grateful for its invention.

But when we inhale the sweet fragrance of a blossoming rose, rest our eyes upon a rainbow decorating the clearing sky after refreshing spring showers, or look up to soaring eagles amid cloudless skies, why do many of us deny the existence of a Creator of such splendors?

Do these works of art not far surpass the inventions we mere humans have created? Then how could these finely tuned creations, from the microscopic bacteria to our immeasurable universe, have come into existence on their own, by chance?

How could they thrive and continue to flourish? How could living organisms come in such a multitude of varieties, with each reproducing only after its own kind? How could the elements of the universe exist in such harmony, without the planets and stars bumping into one another in a perilous cosmic war? And how could animate beings have the ability to think, to reason, to love, to hate, if they were merely the products of chance?

Consider your own body. Every part serves a marvelously unique purpose. It regulates itself by digesting the food you eat, maintaining a comfortable body temperature, and fighting off invaders with the aide of an army of white blood cells. Do you not agree that your body is a fantastic and complex machine of intelligent design? If so, how could it not have been created by a highly intelligent Designer?

A Purposeless Existence?

When we deny a Designer for the designs, we in turn are taking the creations for granted. Because what purpose could they possibly serve if they all came about by chance, out of thin air? (Where does air itself come from? Surely, not from thin air!) Inventions that do not serve any purpose are valueless.

Computers are built to assist us in personal and business matters. Coats are sewn to keep us warm during the winter. Cars are engineered to allow us to travel farther much faster, more comfortably, and more conveniently. We make things to serve purposes. Would we strenuously create something we do not need?

So should not the natural creations we see all around us—even our own selves—serve a purpose? If they do indeed serve a purpose, then would there not be a designer behind these creations? Again, how could things that come into existence by chance possibly serve purposes?

Yet, many people laugh and shrug, and blithely say, "Things just came into existence on their own." So I guess, next time I come to a house, I can shrug and say, "Oh, it just got built by itself."

> "The fool hath said in his heart, There is no God." (Psalm 14:1)

If you believe in a Creator, you are correct—there *is* a Creator.

Why Know Our Creator?

> "For the invisible things of him since the creation of the world are clearly seen, being perceived through the things that are made, even his everlasting power and divinity; that they may be without excuse: because that, knowing God, they glorified him not as God, neither gave thanks; but became vain in their reasonings, and their senseless heart was darkened. Professing themselves to be wise, they became fools..." (Romans 1:20-22)

Before we begin our journey in learning, or deepening our relationship with and our knowledge about our Creator, let us briefly touch upon the main reasons for our quest. Why do we desire or need to identify that there is a Creator? We have the longing and the duty to know the truth in order to achieve fulfillment. Knowing that we have a Creator satisfies our curiosity about our origins. It answers the most important questions we have about life: From where have we come? What is our purpose? Where will we go?

Knowing our Creator also fulfills our lives. It allows us to live the best life possible and guides us in achieving harmony with the laws of nature and the essence of life. We will have peace of mind, knowing we are moving in the correct direction with the right support. Otherwise, we would be like travelers in the wilderness without maps and a compass to guide us onto the right path to our destination.

Finally, coming to the knowledge of our Creator fulfills our responsibility in rightfully crediting our Designer. Every product in the supermarket displays the manufacturer on its label and packaging; every automobile we drive is emblazoned with its company's name; and every article of clothing we wear bears a tag that shows its brand name. When every manmade product has been credited to its maker, should not the most awesome creation—our universe and all it contains—be especially credited to our Creator as well?

We are grateful for the moment when our children first learn how to talk, for the kisses and hugs we share with our lovers, and for the delectable dishes on our tables; but without our Creator giving us our lives, we would not have had the privilege of enjoying any of these in the first place! So let us thank

Him for honoring us with life, so we may delight in all His creations!

The Designer, Not Nameless!

"I am Jehovah, and there is none else; besides me there is no God." (Isaiah 45:5)

Now that we know we have a Creator, it is time to get to know Him personally. Simply knowing that He exists does not do us much good. In order to build a lasting, fulfilling relationship with Him, we must know Him personally. The first step in getting to know Our Creator is to know His name, just as we should first introduce ourselves when we meet someone new.

Do you know the Creator by name? Would you want to know? Do you not want to know the names of your parents? When you read a good book, are you not curious to know who wrote it? Just as everyone and everything has a name, the Creator deservedly has a name, too. But sadly, many do not know Him by His personal name. Even when some do know His name, they replace it with a generic title, like "the Lord." They even have the audacity to replace every instance of His name with "the Lord" in the entire Bible! Editors have even removed God's name from my own writing! This plague is not merely ignorance: it is a blatant rejection of God's holy name! Why do so many people treat His name so spitefully? Most people do not avoid using or similarly strike the devil's name when they write. Is Satan more honorable than God? Should we respect

Satan more than we honor our Father?

How would you feel if others refused to mention or use your name? If you wrote a book and the publisher took your name off its cover, what would you think? If people who read my books called me "the author," I would not tolerate it—to which "author" do they refer? How could people differentiate this particular "author" from other authors? So a personal name must be used. They should refer to me as Shirley Cheng specifically, so people know about whom they are really talking.

A prayer is like a personal letter you write to a specific person. And like a letter, it needs to be properly addressed to the right recipient. If people only address their letters to me with "Dear Author," that letter will not get to me. So a prayer needs to be addressed to God in His personal name, if only just acknowledging His name in one's heart. To whom would you really be praying if you said, "Dear Lord"? Satan may decide to hear your prayer; after all, he is the lord of this world and of all evil.

For those reasons, we must call our Creator by name and, most importantly, show God respect and honor. God personally told us His personal name in His Holy Scriptures, the Bible. If He did not want it to be known, He would not have shared it—yet He shared it, in both writing and speech, many, many times. How many? The original Hebrew Scriptures mention God's name nearly seven thousand times! All false gods have names, so why should the one and only true God not be called by His name? Which god has ever told you their name but the Almighty One alone? Moreover, regarding His name, God specifically said, "This is my name forever, and this is my memorial unto all generations." (Exodus 3:15)

"That they may know that thou alone, whose name is Jehovah, Art the Most High over all the earth." (Psalm 83:18)

What is God's name? His sacred name is Jehovah (or Yahweh in Hebrew), which means "He Chooses to Become" or "He Who Causes to Be." What a perfect name for this Awesome Creator! Truly, no other could rightfully own this name.

In the original Hebrew Scriptures (the Old Testament), God's name appeared as YHWH (the Tetragrammaton), without any vowels, so we do not know what His exact name is, but "Jehovah" is the widely accepted and recognized English form of this sacred name. Other names in the Bible, such as "Jesus" and "Jeremiah," were developed using the same method, so if we accept the names of Jesus and Jeremiah, we should accept "Jehovah." Therefore, it is the name I will use throughout this book.

Jehovah is the one and only true God. There are millions of false, manmade gods, so referring to Him by name will help identify Him as our Creator. Of course, it is never wrong to call Him "the Lord" as long as we acknowledge His name as well.

As a result of the removal of God's name from most modern Bible versions, many people have automatically thought that I am a Jehovah's Witness just because I use God's name. This is a very sad outcome of man's disrespect of Jehovah. When we do not commemorate, honor, and use the name of God, we are going against His wishes. So while I do not belong to the organization of Jehovah's Witnesses, I am an individual witness to Jehovah.

How should we honor God's name? We must glorify God's name and keep it strictly holy by never using His name, or "God" in vain or disrespectfully. Unfortunately, many have misused His name, either out of ignorance or sheer dishonor. I do not say, "God bless you" when people sneeze, nor do I exclaim, "Oh, my God!" as a common interjection. I also do not swear in God's name; simply asserting "yes" or "no" is enough—for Jesus the Messiah said, "Swear not at all; neither by the heaven, for it is the throne of God; nor by the earth, for it is the footstool of his feet; nor by Jerusalem, for it is the city of the great King. Neither shalt thou swear by thy head, for thou canst not make one hair white or black. But let your speech be, Yea, yea; Nay, nay: and whatsoever is more than these is of the evil one." (Matthew 5:34-37)

The Significance of a Name

> "A son honoreth his father, and a servant his master: if then I am a father, where is mine honor? and if I am a master, where is my fear? saith Jehovah of hosts unto you, O priests, that despise my name." (Malachi 1:6)

When you experienced "love" at first sight, what was one of the first pieces of information you wanted to know about the person who caught your eye? Was it his or her name?

When my mother learned at a very young age that there was a Creator, she was thrilled. When she discovered in the Bible that this God had a personal name, she was even more thrilled. This was not some impersonal force, without a personality, without likes and dislikes, without a purpose or a plan, or without a caring heart. Here was an actual divine Person with a literal name. Now, not only could she put faith in this God, she could put faith in Someone real, Someone who had a formal name that she could call, Someone with whom she could develop a tangible relationship.

When you found out the name of the guy or gal you had a crush on, did you not scribble his or her name multiple times and draw hearts around it? Did you not whisper the name of your love in the dark, and feel his or her closeness just by doing so? And did your heart not skip a beat or two when a friend casually mentioned your significant other's name?

When we possess strong feelings for someone, the way we view and treat that person's name often reflects those feelings. We will not show such interest in a name when it belongs to someone in whom we lack interest, right?

Those who truly want to seek a companionship with God will yearn to know His name, and once known, will cherish that name as the most precious pearl, the grandest prize they have finally won.

I had seen tattoos inscribed with the names of loved ones, jewelry with names woven into their designs, T-shirts bearing the names of the wearers, and everyday items, from mugs to pens and pencils, proudly displaying the names of those who were dear to someone's heart. The popularity of personalized items has boomed significantly through the years. It is little wonder, for giving such gifts makes both the giver and the recipient feel extra special. When people value the names of those they care about so highly, those who are merely mortals that will pass like the wind, should we not treasure and esteem the name of our Life-Granter especially high?

Parents often meticulously pick out their babies' names, sometimes even long before they are even conceived. Like new parents, authors take time to carefully mull over which names to use for the characters in their books. We have named schools, streets, buildings, cities, states, newborns, and even pets after world leaders. Throughout the history of humankind, tribes, clans, and families have fought to preserve their names, making sure they are not soiled. Likewise, individuals and business owners are cautious not to ruin their reputations, for a "good name is better than precious oil." (Ecclesiastes 7:1)

Yes, all of us take special heed to our own names. We appreciate it when others remember our names, and we try to return the same attentiveness to others.

Being the Originator of naming, Jehovah feels strongly about names. After creating Adam, He brought all the animals to Adam to let the man name them, and "whatsoever the man called every living creature, that was the name thereof." (Genesis 2:19) God knows the names of each and every one of us, and even "counteth the number of the stars; He calleth them all by their names." (Psalm 147:4) Should we return His great care by leaving Him nameless?

Should we forget His holy name just as His chosen people have? "How long shall this be in the heart of the prophets that prophesy lies, even the prophets of the deceit of their own heart? that think to cause my people to forget my name by their dreams which they tell every man to his neighbor, as their fathers forgat my name for Baal." (Jeremiah 23:26-27)

When we forget God's name, we are forgetting more than merely a name—we are forgetting God's character, for His name signifies His essence, His ways, His purpose, and His promises. When we honor His name, we honor Him. When we remember His name, we remember Him. When we love His name and take delight in it, we love Him and take delight in who He is—the most special Person in our lives.

Imagine you do not know your best friend's name. Would you be content just to know him or her as "Best Friend"? Or would you rather know his or her name? We have a Creator in the heavens. Would you like to go on living knowing Him as only the Lord, or would you feel a deeper, more fulfilling, and intimate connection with Him if you know His unique name, Jehovah?

> "If we have forgotten the name of our God, Or spread forth our hands to a strange god; Will not God search this out? For he knoweth the secrets of the heart." (Psalm 44:20-21)

Would you want to learn more about Jehovah and His purpose now that we know Him by name? Since He created everything, He has a purpose for His creations, right? Indeed, He does, and in the next chapter, you will learn what His great purpose for our world is, so read on!

Purposeful Paradise

"Blessed are the poor in spirit: for theirs is the kingdom of heaven. Blessed are they that mourn: for they shall be comforted. Blessed are the meek: for they shall inherit the earth. Blessed are they that hunger and thirst after righteousness: for they shall be filled. Blessed are the merciful: for they shall obtain mercy. Blessed are the pure in heart: for they shall see God. Blessed are the peacemakers: for they shall be called sons of God. Blessed are they that have been persecuted for righteousness' sake: for theirs is the kingdom of heaven." (Matthew 5:3-10)

Once upon a time, Jehovah created a paradise—the Garden of Eden—on the newly formed Earth, and in it, He created the first pair of humans: one man, Adam, and one woman, Eve. He told them to be fruitful and multiply and be the masters over the Earth and all the living creatures of the skies, lands, and oceans.

The pair had everything they could possibly ever dream of, all without labor, pain, or fear, for Jehovah supplied all abundantly. They could eat from any of the garden's numerous fruit trees—except for one, the tree of knowledge in its middle. "Of the tree of the knowledge of good and evil, thou shalt not eat of it: for in the day that thou eatest thereof thou shalt surely die," Jehovah commanded them. (Genesis 2:17) Certainly, it was the easiest command to obey!

> **"He hath showed thee, O man, what is good; and what doth Jehovah require of thee, but to do justly, and to love kindness, and to walk humbly with thy God?" (Micah 6:8)**

Yet, such a simple command from their Father they disobeyed without hesitation, when Satan, through a snake, called Jehovah a liar when he told them, "Ye shall not surely die: for God doth know that in the day ye eat thereof, then your eyes shall be opened, and ye shall be as God, knowing good and evil." (Genesis 3:4-5)

Thus, Adam and Eve deliberately (stupidly, I must add) disobeyed Jehovah by taking a route independent of His loving guidance. Like rebellious teenagers, they thought they would gain much more freedom, but in reality, just as teenagers who choose to do drugs and smoke, they ended up harming themselves.

Being always honest and truthful, Jehovah kept His word: He punished Adam and Eve with death, though not an immediate death. He also sent them out of the Garden of Eden, lest they eat from the tree of life that would allow them to live forever. Hence, not only had they lost the right to live in the garden, but they also lost the privilege of immortality, for themselves and for their offspring. So "through one man sin entered into the world, and death through sin; and so death passed unto all men, for that all sinned." (Romans 5:12)

> "There is a way which seemeth right unto a man; But the end thereof are the ways of death." (Proverbs 14:12)

How could eating a fruit earn such a heavy punishment? Some feel that Adam and Eve received a punishment that was way out of proportion to their sin. Was their punishment really too harsh? No, what they got was justified. God did not punish them for eating the fruit; He punished them because they deliberately did not follow His simple command. No matter what the rule was, it was a rule, and a rule should be adhered to, most especially when it comes from God.

God had made a perfect Earth that needed care from perfect people. When Adam and Eve disobeyed an order that should have been easy to follow, they proved that the planet could not be entrusted to their care. If they could not be trusted over a small thing, how could they be trusted with big things?

Also, we need to keep in mind that God specifically told Adam and Eve that they would certainly die if they disobeyed Him. To not punish them the way He warned would make Him a liar. God promises both blessings and curses; He always keeps His word according to what He promises. Enforcing promised disciplines is how He can get His messages and orders taken seriously.

Renewed Earth Paradise

> "...the meek shall inherit the earth...their

inheritance shall be for ever." (Psalm 37:11, 18, King James Version)

If the couple had listened to Jehovah, His purpose for the Earth paradise would have been long ago fulfilled—it would be inhabited by happy, righteous people for eternity. So has Jehovah's purpose for the lovely Earth been ruined? No, His plans are just delayed for a while. At His appointed time, His Kingdom, established in the heavens, will govern our world in the form of a renewed Earth paradise. Right now, however, He is just giving us humans the "freedom" we have chosen, to prove to us that our "freedom" is actually costing us a lot: human government has led to greed, insecurity, pain, and misery. At the same time, Jehovah has been waiting for more people to turn from their old, bad way of living, so when He is ready to fulfill His purpose, there will be a multitude of good people waiting to inhabit the new Earth paradise.

So how can we "quicken" this process? In other words, how can we "help" Jehovah, our Heavenly Father, fulfill His plans for our futures? Remember, God's purpose for the Earth is that it be inhabited by righteous people. So if we want to be a part in fulfilling this purpose, we must turn from our bad ways to embrace an acceptable way of living.

Yet, no matter how hard we try, none of us can become one hundred percent virtuous according to the Holy Scriptures. We can never earn salvation and God's approval on our own, so we can never enter the Kingdom by our own efforts; something has to help bring us closer—much closer to God and the paradise. That something is faith in the "seed of the woman."

After the devil used the serpent to deceive Eve, Jehovah said to the snake, "I will put enmity between thee and the woman, and between thy seed and her seed: he shall bruise thy head, and thou shalt bruise his heel." (Genesis 3:15) Who will be the seed of the woman? What does bruising the head mean? And how would this plan stop the fall of the human race, undo the effects of sin and death, and fulfill God's purpose?

Two millennia ago, this designated seed was born into our world. He was bruised on the heel, died, and on the third day, was raised up. Through his death, he has redeemed the hope for an everlasting life for all of us. Now, it is merely a matter of time before he will return to bruise the seed of the serpent on the head, a wound from which he will never survive. Along with his eternal destruction, any poisonous works Satan has ever planted will be consumed once and for all, and no more evil fruits will bloom again.

The seed of the woman is Jehovah's own beloved Son, Jesus Christ. Faith in the Christ is the only path to Jehovah and the only way to salvation; having faith in him will save us from our sins and bring us to our new home.

"I am the way, and the truth, and the life: no one cometh unto the Father, but by me." (John 14:6)

Who is Jesus? Do you not agree that before we can have faith in someone, we must first know that particular person? How can you properly have faith in someone you do not even know? In the following chapters, you will learn about this Son of God and understand how having faith in him will save us from eternal darkness.

Jesus, Merely an Ordinary Man?

"...behold, a virgin shall conceive, and bear a son, and shall call his name Immanuel." (Isaiah 7:14)

Humans are all sons and daughters of God, but the most special Son of God is Jesus Christ. In what ways is Jesus different than other sons of God? How is he unlike any ordinary man of flesh and blood? Here, I will highlight some of Jesus traits that are unique to him in order to demonstrate his position as the only begotten Son of God.

Jesus' Perfection

The prophet Isaiah wrote that Jesus *shall be* called "Everlasting Father." What does that mean? Should that title not belong to Adam?

God's first human creation, Adam, became the father of everyone else on this planet, including Eve to some extent, since God created her using Adam's rib. He became God's first son as a human, but he lost the sacred relationship with God when he purposely disobeyed His wishes.

Through Adam, sin and death entered all generations of humans. Therefore, not a single person who has ever lived is perfectly sinless, no matter how virtuous he or she might be.

In order to clean away our sins, Jehovah required a being who was not tainted by imperfection. There was no way He could find such perfection in true flesh and blood, so He used the Spirit Being of Jesus Christ and turned him into an earthly, flesh-and-blood man to cleanse us. Hence, Jesus became our "Everlasting Father," whose death and resurrection brought us life, whereas Adam brought us death: "For as in Adam all die, so also in Christ shall all be made alive." (I Corinthians 15:22)

Jesus' perfection proves to us that he was no ordinary man—for I stress that no human can ever be perfect—so Jesus must have been a Spirit whom God sent down to us. Although Jesus as an earthly being needed to be perfected by passing Satan's numerous tests, he was perfect prior to his coming to Earth, so he was able to beautifully pass any and all temptations.

"Everlasting Father" also means "Father of the Age" that is coming, which is actually the most accurate translation. The Christ will be the Father to everyone during the upcoming age—the brand-new world after our current system of human governance is completely consumed by fire, leaving no root or seed.

Jesus' Power to Forgive

While on Earth, Jesus performed many miracles, most not unique to him; prophets before his arrival performed the same miracles, including raising the dead and curing people's illnesses. But there was one power Jesus exercised that was unique to him: the forgiving of sins. No other being besides Jehovah could ever forgive sins, but Jehovah gave this authority to Jesus. This further shows us that Jesus is the one and only beloved Son of God.

Jesus Is Known by Spirits

After casting out demons from the possessed, Jesus forbade the demons to speak, "because they knew him." (Mark 1:34) If Jesus were merely an ordinary servant of God, why would it be such a big deal if the demons spoke of his identity?

There had been occasions when the demons did cry out, as in Mark 3:11: "And the unclean spirits, whensoever they beheld him, fell down before him, and cried, saying, Thou art the Son of God." And Jesus responded by charging them much "that they should not make him known." (Mark 3:12) Note that not only did they proclaim his identity but also fell down before him.

Once, the demons, through their possessed victim, pleaded to Jesus, "What have I to do with thee, Jesus, thou Son of the Most High God? I adjure thee by God, torment me not." (Mark 5:7) Would these demons be afraid of Jesus if he were initially a mortal man? Clearly, all of these demons knew who Jesus was: the extraordinary Son of God.

While testing Jesus, Satan said, "If thou art the Son of God, command that these stones become bread." (Matthew 4:3) Obviously, Satan meant that Jesus was no ordinary man or simply a prophet when he used the "Son of God" title to challenge Jesus.

Jesus' Supernatural Death

Immediately after Jesus died, "the veil of the temple was rent in two from the top to the bottom; and the earth did quake; and the rocks were rent; and the tombs were opened; and many bodies of the saints that had fallen asleep were raised; and coming forth out of the tombs after his resurrection they entered into the holy city and appeared unto many." (Matthew 27:51-53) When the centurion and those who witnessed the earthquake, and "the things that were done, feared exceedingly, saying, Truly this was the Son of God." (Matthew 27:54)

If these witnesses thought that Jesus was any ordinary human with no spiritual beginning, what would be the point of their exclaiming that this was God's Son? Would they have even said that in the first place? And why would they fear exceedingly?

Jesus' Prehuman Existence

Jesus was born after John the Baptist, yet John said, "He that cometh after me is become before me: for he was before me." (John 1:15) Further, he called

Jesus "the only begotten Son" of God. (John 1:18) These two revelations in the fourth Gospel clearly show us that John knew not only that Jesus' title as the "Son of God" is unique and far different from any other son of God, but also of his prehuman existence. Let us examine what the Gospel of John has to say regarding Jesus' prehuman existence.

"In the beginning was the Word, and the Word was with God," begins the Gospel of John. Jesus is God's chief Spokesperson, so this is why Jesus is called the Word. "And the Word became flesh, and dwelt among us (and we beheld his glory, glory as of the only begotten from the Father), full of grace and truth." (John 1:14) This meant that Jesus came into this world from heaven, and whomever receives him, he will give the "right to become children of God" and salvation. (John 1:12) Jesus himself said, "I am come down from heaven, not to do mine own will, but the will of him that sent me. For this is the will of my Father, that every one that beholdeth the Son, and believeth on him, should have eternal life; and I will raise him up at the last day." (John 6:38, 40) Exactly, how did Jesus descend from heaven to become a human man so he could carry out his mission?

Jesus' Miraculous Birth

One day, some two thousand years ago, God's great messenger, the angel Gabriel, visited a home in the city of Nazareth, where Mary, a virgin betrothed to a poor carpenter named Joseph, lived. The angel greeted her and announced, "Fear not, Mary: for thou hast found favor with God. And behold, thou shalt conceive in thy womb, and bring forth a son, and shalt call his name JESUS. He shall be great, and shall be called the Son of the Most High: and the Lord God shall give unto him the throne of his father David: and he shall reign over the house of Jacob for ever; and of his kingdom there shall be no end." (Luke 1:30-33)

Imagine Mary's shock when the great angel gave her such startling news: that she would conceive as a virgin, for the Holy Spirit would come upon her, and that "the holy thing which is begotten shall be called the Son of God"! (Luke 1:35) Truly, she must have been an exceedingly faithful woman to be given the highest honor, that of carrying the Son of God in her womb and giving birth to the world's light! This was how the Word became flesh and entered this world to save us from death.

If Jesus were just an ordinary son of God like the rest of us, the Bible would not have used the "Son of God" title so profusely and with such emphasis. It is used frequently to set this "Son of God" apart from any other son of God and indicate that he is unique.

Since Jesus was not a human but a spirit, could he be an angel? No, for the Bible says, "For unto which of the angels said he at any time, Thou art my Son, This day have I begotten thee? and again, I will be to him a Father, And he shall be to me a Son?" (Hebrews 1:5)

Next, we will probe deeper into Jesus' special position as the Son of God, as well as his grand mission on Earth.

The Christ Jesus: A Mighty Spirit & the Greatest Man

"Behold, the Lamb of God, that taketh away the sin of the world!" (John 1:29)

Who is Jesus Christ? What does "Christ" mean?

At least twice when Jesus was living on Earth, God openly proclaimed from the heavens that Jesus is His Son, whom He approves.

God's Son? What does that mean?

Well, we all should know by now that God can create anything and everything He wants, and He has the right to designate the positions, purposes, and roles each of His creations has or plays. For instance, He created millions of angels to be His personal messengers and servants. So He could rightfully designate a special creation to be His "Son."

Before Jehovah made our Earth and everything and everyone on it, He first created Someone very special, a Spirit Being who is godly and possesses godly powers given by God Himself. As a matter of fact, this Creation is God's very first, and became God's Partner in creating everything else, including our Earth and humankind, for "all things were made through him; and without him was not anything made that hath been made." (John 1:3) This Spirit, although supreme in power and status, is still a Creation, and is therefore inferior to God.

This Creation, God has chosen, is His beloved Son, and we know him by his name, Jesus.

Thus, before coming to Earth as an earthly man by means of a virgin birth, Jesus lived in heaven with his Father, God. And after he died and was resurrected by God, he returned to his Father's side in heaven.

Jesus said that anyone who had seen him had seen his Father, for he diligently follows God in His footsteps—whatever his Father does, he does likewise. So through Jesus, we can clearly see that God is a loving, kind, yet powerfully righteous, justice-seeking Supreme Being.

> "All authority hath been given unto me in heaven and on earth." (Matthew 28:18)

All things have been committed to Jesus by his Father; Jehovah has given him many obligations and powers, such as healing and forgiving people, and raising the dead; in turn, Jesus had some powers given to his followers.

> "And he that overcometh, and he that keepeth my works unto the end, to him will I give

authority over the nations: and he shall rule them with a rod of iron, as the vessels of the potter are broken to shivers; as I also have received of my Father." (Revelation 2:26-27)

Therefore, Jesus is godly, God-like, the "Son of God," which also means the "nature of God," but he is not God, for there is only one true God: Jehovah.

Jesus' Grand Coming

Since we now have a deeper knowledge of Jesus, the man whom we should embrace, the next step is to obtain a better understanding of his purpose for us humans.

Why did Jehovah send His Son down to the wicked Earth? What is so important about Jesus' coming down from his heavenly home to become a man of flesh and blood?

Hundreds of years before Jesus' arrival, the prophet Isaiah foretold of his great birth and purpose: "For unto us a child is born, unto us a son is given; and the government shall be upon his shoulder: and his name shall be called Wonderful, Counsellor, Mighty God, Everlasting Father, Prince of Peace. Of the increase of his government and of peace there shall be no end, upon the throne of David, and upon his kingdom, to establish it, and to uphold it with justice and with righteousness from henceforth even for ever." (Isaiah 9:6-7)

Yes, Jesus came to our Earth to deliver us from the wickedness and the resulting imperfection and death we inherited through the first man, Adam.

Jesus saved us in primarily two ways: by spreading the good news of Jehovah's forthcoming Kingdom, wherein he will be the Prince of Peace, and by having his own blood cleanse us of our sins so we can enter into the Kingdom. So Jesus' coming to Earth was so much more than simply arriving as flesh and blood; he was sent down so Jehovah can wash away our sins using his blood. Indeed, he had to die for us, and die he did, when the Jewish religious leaders impaled him (*staurotheto* in Greek). So not only did Jesus die but he also died a most agonizing and painful death by being affixed alive to a *stauros* (Greek word for a pole or stake, not a cross) with nails through both wrists and ankles, and being left upright under the blazing sun.

Jesus' Teaching of the Kingdom of God

Picture a paradise filled with happy people who do not have a care in the world, for they do not need to toil under the hot sun for life's necessities. They have nothing to fear; no doors need to be locked, no children will be abducted, and no parent will pass away, leaving their children behind, for there are no such things as death, diseases, or danger—all forces of evil have been abolished. To top it off, the entire paradise is ruled by a loving Father-Son team, a King and a Prince who are the light for Their people; no sunlight or moonlight is necessary, for Their light of love and justice is more than sufficient.

Sound like a utopia, a fantasy world of which you can only dream? Of a certainty, it will be a utopia, but not a fantasy; it will be a dream come true forever. Such a kingdom will soon exist, governed by the Almighty King Jehovah, who will temporarily entrust His Kingdom to His Son Jesus as the Prince of Peace; we can rest assured that love and justice will be served on end. Jesus will bring loving yet firm care to people in this Kingdom, which is Jehovah's promised paradise at last fulfilled, as he judges people in accordance to his Father's standards.

This Kingdom of God is one reason why Jesus came to our world. He wisely used his time to proclaim the good message, not only focusing on how wonderful the heavenly government will be, but on how we can enter it.

How can you be privileged enough to step into this Kingdom, let alone live in it for eternity? In order to call this paradise home, you must be a true follower of Jehovah and Jesus. You must model yourself after Jesus' ways while he lived among people. Granted, we cannot be as perfect as he, but if we truly desire to follow in his footsteps, we will receive the strength from God to do so with our utmost ability. How should we follow him? Since this chapter is solely dedicated to Jesus and his purpose in coming, turn to the section titled "The Ultimate Life's Manual" to see how you can follow his teachings.

Besides spreading the word to multitudes of people, Jesus was also compelled to perform miracles whenever his heart was moved by people's illnesses and distress. His supernatural powers gave people a glimpse of what is to come. He gave sight to the blind, hearing to the deaf, and speech to the mute. He enabled the crippled to walk, raised the dead, cast out demons from the possessed, and even forgave sins.

Combining his superpowers as the Son of God with his infinite teachings and exemplary example as a perfect human being, Jesus attracted many followers. But as with anything good, especially such purity as Jesus' goodness, he also attracted quite a few enemies—enemies of the worst kind, for they hated him enough to have him wrongly killed. Yet, they could kill him for only three days; Jehovah raised him up on the third day, fulfilling Jesus' second reason for coming to Earth: washing away our sins using his innocent and flawless blood.

Jesus' Great Sacrifice

How could Jesus' blood wash away our sins? To understand this, we need to know how God's system of the sacrifice works. The books of Exodus and Leviticus in the Bible extensively talk about sacrificing livestock, such as cattle and sheep, to cleanse the people of their sins so God could forgive them. Animals used in the sacrifice must be without any defects, and priests must perform specific steps during the sacrifice, including pouring out their blood upon the altar for atonement.

> "...thou shalt offer thy burnt-offerings, the flesh and the blood, upon the altar of Jehovah thy God; and the blood of thy sacrifices shall be poured out upon the altar of Jehovah thy God; and thou shalt eat the flesh." (Deuteronomy 12:27)

Why is the pouring out of blood necessary? What is important about blood? Jehovah answered this question in the Bible: "For the life of the flesh is in the blood; and I have given it to you upon the altar to make atonement for your souls: for it is the blood that maketh atonement by reason of the life." (Leviticus 17:11) Blood is the life, so when you pour out the life of a perfect sacrifice, you cleanse your own life.

Hence, in order to wash away the sins of a great multitude, God chose His Son, who is absolutely flawless; no other man who has ever lived could be perfect enough for the job. Ultimately, the life—Jesus' blood—was poured out as a ransom to redeem our own blood.

> "For such a high priest became us, holy, guileless, undefiled, separated from sinners, and made higher than the heavens; who needeth not daily, like those high priests, to offer up sacrifices, first for his own sins, and then for the sins of the people: for this he did once for all, when he offered up himself. For the law appointeth men high priests, having infirmity; but the word of the oath, which was after the law, appointeth a Son, perfected for evermore." (Hebrews 7:26-28)

The sacrifice for salvation had to be perfect for another reason. In Jehovah's perfect justice system, the restitution has to be of equal value as the original: "He that smiteth a beast mortally shall make it good, life for life. And if a man cause a blemish in his neighbor; as he hath done, so shall it be done to him:

breach for breach, eye for eye, tooth for tooth; as he hath caused a blemish in a man, so shall it be rendered unto him." (Leviticus 24:18-20) So when Adam was a perfect human being, another perfect human being had to be sacrificed to set things right.

Even so, after an explanation of God's sacrificial system, you still may not comprehend it fully; you may find it too extreme for God to have sacrificed Jesus, and to me, it was. But as mere creations, do we have the capacity to completely understand Jehovah and His ways? Jehovah Himself best said it: "For my thoughts are not your thoughts, neither are your ways my ways. For as the heavens are higher than the earth, so are my ways higher than your ways, and my thoughts than your thoughts." (Isaiah 55:8-9)

Jesus was willing to let his Father sacrifice him in ransom for our sins. Imagine a purely innocent being suffering for our wickedness! What unconditional love Father and Son showed—the love Jehovah showed for us, and the love Jesus showed for his dear Father: "That the world may know that I love the Father, and as the Father gave me commandment, even so I do." (John 14:31) Try to find a better love story!

This is why Jesus is called Christ, or the Messiah, which means "the Anointed One." "Jesus" (Yeshua) in Hebrew means "Jehovah Is Salvation." He is the agent Jehovah has assigned to be our Savior, to save us from sins and death!

> "I am the resurrection, and the life: he that believeth on me, though he die, yet shall he live; and whosoever liveth and believeth on me shall

never die." (John 11:25-26)

Happiness Is When Love Is Served

What else has Jesus' life on Earth accomplished? What lessons have you learned from his way of living?

Some people think that being completely virtuous can take happiness and freedom from you. Jesus lived a perfect life, obeying Jehovah's commands to his very death. Did obeying his Father's wishes make him unhappy? No, Jesus was quite a social, happy, loving person who was never gloomy. If he had been miserable, he would have given up being so righteous long before his execution. And he would not have allowed people to impale him if he had not thought it worthwhile to die for Jehovah and for us. Hence, the way he lived shows us the truth: being under Jehovah's rulership and listening to His commands will not take away happiness, but will only add to our happiness, with the kind of happiness that will truly last, not the passing happiness the worldly bring. Truly loving someone makes the lover glad; selfish love may make the lover glad for a little while, but then it will no longer be fruitful.

Jesus loves his dear Father without bounds. His life on Earth tells us that the truth is proven by his own obedience.

Jesus' Future

It is only a matter of time before Jehovah fulfills His promise of paradise. When that day comes, humankind will be eternally ruled by Him and His Son, who will be His entrusted King for one thousand years, acting as a righteous Judge, before returning the Kingdom to his Father.

Currently, Jesus is the King in Their heavenly Kingdom. After Jehovah resurrected Jesus from the dead, He "made him to sit at his right hand in the heavenly places, far above all rule, and authority, and power, and dominion, and every name that is named, not only in this world, but also in that which is to come: and he put all things in subjection under his feet, and gave him to be head over all things to the church, which is his body, the fulness of him that filleth all in all." (Ephesians 1:20-23) What a glorious reward Jehovah has bestowed upon His dearest Son, who no doubt deserves all the honor and glory!

Both Father and Son are keeping a close eye on us down here, noting who are good and who are evil. And when the final day of our world comes, each one of us, alive or dead, will be judged according to our own deeds throughout our lifetime. Rest assured that we will each receive the fairest judgment.

How can we survive this impending Judgment Day? Simply knowing that our sins have been washed away is not enough for us to enter the Kingdom; Jesus would not have been down here teaching about the Kingdom of God and how to get in if all he needed to do was be sacrificed. He completed his great mission, and now we must complete ours: to have faith in Jehovah and Jesus.

So the next question is: exactly, how should we embrace Jesus and his Father? Is believing in Them all we need to do? What does "believing" actually imply? You will discover the answer later in this book, so keep reading.

Jesus Rocks! But How So?

"I am the good shepherd: the good shepherd layeth down his life for the sheep." (John 10:11)

Jesus was a great person, we all know that. But what are the specific characteristics that made him so wonderful, besides the fact that he died for us? Certainly, someone who died in order to save sinners would possess fantastic qualities: "Greater love hath no man than this, that a man lay down his life for his friends." (John 15:13)

Below is a partial list of the traits that made Jesus so great, in no particular order because all of his acts of perfection are of equal value. May we learn from his ways and adapt them into our daily living.

Jesus was…

• Resistant: He overcame all temptations, even when he was physically weak from hunger.
• Truthful: He lived by what he taught. He did

not say one thing and do another.

• Obedient: He obeyed his Father's commands to his very death, and continually does so.

• Diligent: He wasted no time while on Earth. He spent every chance he got preaching the good news.

• Merciful: He did not condemn sinners. Rather, he befriended them in order to draw them closer to God and the Kingdom, and rejoiced whenever he could turn a sinner from wicked ways.

• Peaceful: He did not approve of human systems, yet he did not revolt. Instead, he put his faith in his Father's future Kingdom to take care of every existing problem.

• Straightforward: He preached with frankness, without using force, trickery or treachery to convince people to believe in him and follow his commands.

• Unassuming: He performed miracles that were necessary to 1) back up his words, 2) heal the sickly and feed the hungry, and 3) offer a sample of what is to come after our system of things ends. He did not perform miracles to show off, to credit himself, or to quench people's curiosity. Rather, his miracles were to glorify God.

• Honest: He took no credit for himself. He clearly stated and showed that he was simply God's servant, doing God's will.

• Courageous: He was not deterred by human power, nor did he let humans influence him. He was not afraid to defend God's teaching and prove others wrong, even when it meant that he had to offend the evildoers and lose his life. When someone committed a wrong, he confronted them face to face, instead of simply talking about how bad they were behind their back. He challenged wrongdoers physically if he had to without harming anyone—for example, he overturned the tables and drove those who were selling oxen, sheep, and doves, out of the temple because they were turning God's house of prayers into a thieves' nest.

- Laudatory: Just as he was not hesitant to openly proclaim someone's wrongdoing or hypocrisy, he likewise openly and promptly declared someone's faithfulness.
- God-fearing: He feared no human, only God.
- Knowledgeable: His teachings were clear and succinct, not sugar-coated or constructed to appeal to worldly senses. He also made his teachings interesting and memorable by using stories to illustrate his points. His parables also helped discern his true followers from the rest. Above all, his teachings were meant to benefit us, not trap us or make our lives difficult, unlike the rituals and traditions religious hypocrites forced on others. For instance, Pharisees imposed strict sabbath rules that Jesus disobeyed by healing the ill on that day, pointing out, "Which of you shall have an ass or an ox fallen into a well, and will not straightway draw him up on a sabbath day?" (Luke 14:5)
- Loving: He put others' interests and well-being above his own. He would not refuse to drink from the cup God gave him because of his love for his Father and people. So, like an innocent lamb, he was slaughtered without uttering a single word. He "loved his own that were in the world, he loved them

unto the end." (John 13:1)
- Witty: He was very sharp-minded, and always had the right words to say at the right time. Pharisees and the scribes could never win an argument with him!
- Meek and humble: He embraced everyone, from the poor to the sickly, with plenty of love: "When thou makest a feast, bid the poor, the maimed, the lame, the blind: and thou shalt be blessed; because they have not wherewith to recompense thee: for thou shalt be recompensed in the resurrection of the just." (Luke 14:13-14)
- Gracious: He gave every person the chance to change and repent, to hope for an everlasting life of happiness, and he offered the opportunity to be his brother or sister.
- Thorough: He delivered both good and bad news, blessings and curses—blessings if people followed God's laws, curses if they abandoned God's ways. He gave people plenty of warning, so no one could say, "I was not warned!" He warned people not to threaten them, but to fully inform them of the consequences beforehand.
- Prioritized: Despite his hectic schedule, he made sure to spend some time alone so he could pray to God and replenish his strength in mind, body, and spirit. He did not let his duties hinder him from taking precious time to spend with his closest Person, God.
- Law-abiding: Even though he is the Son of God, he still obeyed manmade laws, including paying his double-drachma tax.
- Submissive: Even though he is the master

over all people, he showed servility by washing his disciples' feet: "If I then, the Lord and the Teacher, have washed your feet, ye also ought to wash one another's feet. For I have given you an example, that ye also should do as I have done to you." (John 13:14-15)

- Approachable: He was an easy-going, outspoken person who loved children and respected women and the elderly.
- Resilient: When his persecutors insulted, beat, and spat on him, he neither flinched nor fought back but only let them continue. He also did not defend himself when Pontius Pilate questioned him about the false charges against him, which amazed the governor. He knew that when God is for him, what else matters?
- Wise: He identified the root of all problems: evil acts start with evil thoughts from the heart.
- Compassionate: He lamented and wept over Jerusalem that killed the prophets: "How often would I have gathered thy children together, even as a hen gathereth her own brood under her wings, and ye would not!" (Luke 13:34)
- Selfless: He had no place to properly lay his head as he traveled all about, devoting himself to spreading God's messages.
- Assuring: He told people not to worry about daily necessities, for God knew what they needed and would provide for them. He also assured his disciples not to be concerned about what to say in defense when they were persecuted, for the Holy Spirit would put the right words into them when the time came.

- Thoughtful: Although in agony while hanging upon a pole, Jesus still had great consideration and care for Mary, his mother, to whom he said, "Woman, behold thy son!" and to John, his loved disciple: "Behold, thy mother!" Hence, "the disciple took her unto his own home" from that hour onward so Mary could be cared for. (John 19: 26-27)

God's Revealing Nature

"The heavens declare the glory of God; And the firmament showeth his handiwork. Day unto day uttereth speech, and night unto night showeth knowledge." (Psalm 19:1-2)

How can you start knowing God? By reading the Bible? Sure, that is a great place to start, but what of those who cannot read? What if a young child wants to learn about God? How can people start their revelation about God without first learning how to read?

Pretend that you need to learn about a contemporary sculptor. You go to the library to find books about him, but since he is still not very well-known, no book has been written about his life. How will you get to know him? Why, you can visit any exhibitions that have his sculptures on display! By examining his works, you will be able to learn something about his character.

The revelation of God starts in learning about His creations. His splendid works are everywhere, so anyone can become His pupil and easily access His lessons without receiving any formal education first. I was such a pupil when I was four years old, during my first and only year of walking. I was receiving shots of Western medicines combined with massage therapy, and these treatments had enabled me to run and dance with the wind for the first time in my life. I explored a world I had never really fully experienced before: the world outside hospital walls.

I happily picked wildflowers, captivated by their brilliant shades of red. Their soft petals between my fingers delighted me, and their fragrances soothed my spirit with every breath I took. Besides enjoying the flowers, I chased after bugs of all kinds, catching bumble bees, butterflies, houseflies, moths, caterpillars, and, yes, even spiders. None scared me — I was too enthralled by these fascinating creatures to be frightened. As a matter of fact, anything that moved, anything colorful, anything smaller than I, was mine for me to study.

Then one day, my mother told me about God. She called Him our Heavenly Father, who created everything and everyone. *Ah-ha*, I thought, *so those insects and flowers my senses relish have a Creator!* So before knowing about God's existence, I already knew about His magnificent works.

What have I learned about God, just by getting to know His creations? Well, I had seen a very wide range of creatures, of all shapes and sizes. Some crawl, some swim, and some can even fly. Along with the awesome world of fauna, is the plant life, vibrant with the entire spectrum of colors, from red roses and pink tulips to yellow dandelions and white lilies of the valley; from the mellow blue of conifers to the eye-popping hues of lichens. And I must not forget the puffy white clouds in the blue sky, the bolts of lightning zigzagging across an inky backdrop on stormy nights, and the luminous full moon that shines like a guiding beacon during the darkest hours. Finally, I have felt some of the most powerful elements of the intangible: love and hatred, happiness and sadness, wisdom and foolishness, hope and dread, fear and bravery.

So what have I learned about God through His handiwork? I have learned He is supremely intelligent, wise, creative, masterful, and above all, He is infinitely loving. How about you? What have you learned just by studying God's inventions? What has nature revealed to you?

Do You Love Jehovah?

"If I speak with the tongues of men and of angels, but have not love, I am become sounding brass, or a clanging cymbal. And if I have the gift of prophecy, and know all mysteries and all knowledge; and if I have all faith, so as to remove mountains, but have not love, I am nothing. And if I bestow all my goods to feed the poor, and if I give my body to be burned, but have not love, it profiteth me nothing." (I Corinthians 13:1-3)

Do you believe in God? If you answered "Yes," your answer would match about half of the human population, because Christians, Muslims, and Jews, all believe in the same God, Jehovah (though Muslims use the name Allah for God).

While I do not doubt the depth or strength of their belief, I do have to wonder: if so many people believe in God, why do we experience so many manmade problems in life? If we believe in God, that means that we should know His principles for living in a good way, so we ought to be able to live well, right? Apparently, believing in God is not enough; or perhaps, we are not grasping what belief actually is.

What *does* believing in God mean? Many would say that it is accepting that God exists and that

He is the Creator of everything. Period.

If that is the case, then let us put Satan under the spotlight. Do you not agree with me that he believes in God? He was an angel living in heaven who regularly spoke with God! So he is not only a believer, as any of us are who have never seen or spoken with God, he is a spirit who witnessed God in person, face to face. So why is Satan still so evil when he believes in God?

Believing in God actually means much more than simply accepting His existence and creation. How much more? Exactly, what should believing in God mean?

When people tell me, "I believe in God," I often ask myself, *But do they love God?*

It all lies in love—loving God. This is why Satan has chosen to be evil even though he believes in God—Satan does not love God; he loves himself much more, and that has driven him to do evil and to spread evil to others.

Truly believing in God means we must love God. The most important commandment, as put by Jesus Christ, is to love God with all your heart, strength, and mind.

How should we show God we love Him? How should we show our parents we love them? How do we show people we love them? Is it by making them happy? How do we make them happy? We make them happy by doing what they like, what meets with their approval. Therefore, we must show our love for God by doing what He wants from us.

What does God want from us? Why does it matter to Him?

When you were growing up, your parents or guardians must have given you a set of Do's and Don't's. But what does it matter to them, whether you follow their rules? Because following their rules is for your own good. That is why laws are made, to establish order and to protect everyone's interests.

Think about it: God is not at all dependent upon us. After all, He created us, so what can we do for Him? Not much—not for His survival, certainly.

> "Jehovah, what is man, that thou takest knowledge of him? Or the son of man, that thou makest account of him? Man is like to vanity: His days are as a shadow that passeth away." (Psalm 144:3-4)

Jehovah wants us to follow His guidance for our own good, not really for His own good (but it does make Him very happy—He is happy when His creations are happy); by following his guidance, we show love for not only Him, but ourselves, as well.

Why is it important to listen to your Heavenly Father? Here, I will cover the three top reasons why heeding God is vital to our lives.

- It shows that you are returning your Heavenly Father's love—the number one reason why it is a good idea to pay heed to what Jehovah says.

I have heard people posing the question, "Why was God so terribly angry in the Old Testament?" Well, let me ask you this: Would you not be upset if your children constantly did things that were downright evil, after you repeatedly told them not to do so? Only an uncaring parent would not mind what bad deeds their children committed. So God was truly loving when He got angry when His creations harmed one another, shedding innocent blood.

What else can we learn from the people's rebellion in the Old Testament? It showed that His children did not care about His feelings; they did not return His love after He had so painstakingly created them after His own spiritual image. All they were interested in were their own desires, getting whatever they wanted at all costs and even taking pride in the wrongs they did.

So show that you love your Parent back by obeying His wishes. Do not grieve your dear Heavenly Father with your selfish ways.

• Listening to God is best for you. God created us human beings, so He obviously knows what is best for us, yet since the beginning of our world, countless people have not followed His advice. Jehovah is so much more knowledgeable than the earthly parents, who cared for us from birth; He is the only one who knows our every need and how to meet it. Yet, not many of us want to listen to Him — we think that somehow, we are wise enough to do things our way.

• You receive support. When we listen to another's advice, we are being supported at the same time. Talking to God through prayers and receiving His insights through the Bible will not only help you live a better life, but strengthen the bond between you and your Creator.

If all human beings listened to God's loving words, imagine what a beautiful world this would be for each and every one of us! Even now, having God close to our hearts and doing what He loves, brings us spiritually closer to Him, thus breathing energy into our spirits so we can build a better life for all.

Personally, it makes me very happy when I pay attention to His words in the Bible. It gives me a sense of security and support, as I know I am doing what is best for me, that whatever I am doing could not be wrong because it has been laid out by the most Supreme Being ever, and above all, that I am not alone—I have Him to guide me.

Parents should be their children's best source of support on Earth. My mother is my number one confidant and best friend. But the ultimate support comes from Jehovah, the Parent of all parents. When I listen to Him, it means I love Him, I trust Him, and I will not feel as if I must deal with things on my own. Who could give better advice than the One who gave us life?

Having faith, therefore, is really loving God and His Son. And loving Jehovah and Jesus is the only thing we need to do to be saved, to receive eternal salvation. This is what exercising faith in Jesus is all about—it is all about love!

So the next time someone asks you, "How should I believe in God?" give them this answer: "Love God. Love what God loves and hate what God hates."

Why Do You Love Jehovah?

"We love, because he first loved us." (I John 4:19)

  Why do you love Jehovah? That is the next most pivotal question after, "Do you love Jehovah?" Your answer to this second question determines whether you truly do love God; it confirms your love. How so? Let us examine the story below to find out.

  A mighty king once ruled over a vast land. His decisions were just and fair, and he gave lavishly to those who served him well. Everyone worshipped him, treating him with utmost respect and honor.
  "The people love me," he said one day, and smiled.
  "But do you know why they love you?" his closest advisor asked.
  The king hesitated, then asked, "How should I find out?"
  "Pretend to be weak."
  The king thought about this. The easiest way

to pretend to be weak was to feign illness, he decided. So revealing his ruse only to his trusty advisor, he stayed in his room and did not come out for days. Word quickly spread that the mighty king was ill. Truth—or what people believed to be the truth—soon grew into rumors that he was dying.

Whenever the "ill" king called upon his subjects, only a few showed up at his bedside. Those who did come treated him with impatience and haughtiness that had never before been present.

After a month, the king had a message delivered to all of his subjects: everyone was to come to the palace for a special announcement from the king. Most thought that the king planned to give his farewell speech, and gathered outside under the king's balcony on the appointed day.

To everyone's surprise, a radiant king with rosy cheeks walked out to stand before them. "When I was healthy and full of vigor," he told them, "you showered me with praise. But when I needed you the most, I saw only your backs. I know now that your 'love' was just a pretense; you loved what I gave you, not who I am." And he promptly dismissed the gathering of his subjects and sent them away forever.

Would you love Jehovah if He did not give riches? Do you love Jehovah simply for the great promises He offers you and your children? Or do you love Him because He is your loving Heavenly Father? If your love for Him is only for the gifts He promises to give you, you do not have love for Him; but if you love Him from the depths of your heart because He is your Creator, then you truthfully love

Him, and that is the key to any crown you will win in your journey of fulfillment and completeness.

> **"There is no fear in love: but perfect love casteth out fear, because fear hath punishment; and he that feareth is not made perfect in love." (I John 4:18)**

Do not let your worship of God be toward the paradise that will soon come, nor toward the everlasting life for your children. Do not let it be fear that governs your love. Although we must be God-fearing, we must also have the strong desire to do what is good, not because we fear Him but because we love Him. We should put His wishes above all else. We should take His advice above all others'. And we must be led by Him, not by anyone else.

Moreover, we should love Jehovah because He first loved us. We are simply returning His gracious love, not doing something spectacular or sacrificial, such as the way that Jesus loved us.

Above all else, we are not loving Jehovah without regarding His qualities and traits. Are we loving someone who is unloving, selfish, greedy, and envious? No, far from it. Jehovah has the most admirable and praiseworthy characteristics anyone can possibly possess and exhibit. We are attracted to His qualities more than anything else. His love, longsuffering, lovingkindness, grace, honesty, sincerity, faithfulness, trustworthiness, righteousness, mercy, kindness, gentleness, warmth, wisdom, zeal, determination, modesty, understanding, affection, courage, power, charm, devotion, intelligence, openness, diligence, loyalty, majesty, sense of humor, wit, creativity, happiness, joy, serenity, passion, and practicality, among all other existing virtues, are what draw us to Him. Each of His traits is fully realized and of the highest caliber, not merely a fraction or partially complete.

I do not know about you, but I am so proud to have Him as our God, to have the highest privilege of calling Him Father! We would be insane *not* to love Him. Do you not also think that it would be rather hard to resist loving someone so charming? Yes, Jehovah is our ultimate Gold Medal, our highest goal!

Excused from Future Sins?

"Not every one that saith unto me, Lord, Lord, shall enter into the kingdom of heaven; but he that doeth the will of my Father who is in heaven." (Matthew 7:21)

Since Jehovah sacrificed His dearest Son to cleanse us of our sins, does that mean that, once we accept that Jesus Christ is His Son, we can continue with our sinful living? Absolutely not! Accepting Jesus Christ is forever embracing him within our hearts. Once he is in our hearts, we must let this Treasure guide us in striving to live a sin-free life, and never forsake it. Granted, we will never be sinless, but if we truly, strongly want to follow Jehovah and Jesus' commandments and do what is right in God's eyes, we will have the strength to commit as few sins as possible.

Unfortunately, many people think that since their sins have been cleansed and that Jehovah is most forgiving, they have the right to continue being bad, claiming that Jehovah is too good and forgiving to punish them. They do not know or choose to ignore the fact that Jehovah is a lover of justice, so He is not a pushover. He will never be "too good" to punish the wicked who refuse to turn to the path of light. He is forgiving only when the evil have truly repented.

Many also think that if they say they have faith, they will automatically be saved without having to do anything to prove their faith. Quite the contrary is true.

How can you tell if someone is faithful? They demonstrate their faith through their actions. If someone says he or she is faithful, but does not show it in his or her works, then that person is faithless. For example, there are folks who claim to have faith in God, yet they worry all the time. Is that the behavior of a faithful person?

Those who will receive salvation are those who work hard from their hearts to show they do indeed have faith. They are the ones who "come of the great tribulation, and they washed their robes, and made them white in the blood of the Lamb." (Revelation 7:14)

If you only say you believe in Jehovah without the works to back up your words, you are faithless and a liar. It is better to say you do not have faith than it is to lie and say that you do.

Plenty of people perform righteous deeds in front of others, tricking people into believing they are among the faithful. Behind closed doors, their actions tell a completely different story. These people are faithless, for they do not fear that Jehovah will most certainly see them. How could they claim to have faith in God when they think the Almighty One lacks the power to see everything they do?

> **"The sacrifice of the wicked is an abomination to Jehovah; But the prayer of the upright is his delight." (Proverbs 15:8)**

Beware that you do not become a religious hypocrite. Let all of your words and actions be clean, not just half good and half bad. If even deeds that are ninety-nine percent good cannot earn us salvation, how can we expect half-good deeds to earn it! Remember, salvation is a gift freely given to us sinners by Jehovah; it is not something we rightfully earned. In order to keep this free gift and show that we value and appreciate it, we must let our actions reveal that we are worthy of this gift. Otherwise, Jehovah will withdraw this gift from us.

I must also stress here: do not do good for the sake of this reward of salvation; do good for the sake of Jehovah. Do good because you love God and do good because your heart yearns for it. Do not do good grudgingly or forcefully, for if you do, your good deeds will not last long. People who hate their jobs will eventually fail in their work. Do not consider doing good a job you are stuck with, but a hobby you cannot live without doing. And just as if you were enjoying your work without aiming for a promotion, you will be unexpectedly promoted, and what a promotion it will be!

Act Out Your Faith

"What doth it profit, my brethren, if a man say he hath faith, but have not works? can that faith save him?" (James 2:14)

A man named Jordan had two good friends, Jim and Bruce. One day, he asked them to help him with some carpentry work for the following month. Both of them agreed, saying that they would do a great job. When the day arrived, both friends showed up as promised. But by the end of the day, Jordan and Bruce wound up doing most of the work, even cleaning up after the mess Jim made.

Steven constantly told his wife, Judy, how much he loved her and how beautiful she was, while their neighbor, Tom, rarely said "I love you" to his wife, Julie. Yet, both couples seemed happily married. One day, Judy became extremely ill and had to rest in bed for days. She was dismayed when Steven not only failed to state his love for her but also treated her roughly, nearly making her cry a few times. Meanwhile Julie also fell ill, but her suffering was not as great, for she had a doting husband who looked after her every need. She recuperated more quickly in her happiness.

Linda was a regular church goer. She even taught Bible studies every Friday evening. She also enjoyed volunteering in her community and donating to educational institutions and charities. People viewed her as a model citizen. But if they had a hidden camera in her home, they would have been appalled to see that she did not show the same kind of love and care toward her grandmother, who seldom had enough to eat.

It was discovered that Vincent, a man known for his strict moral teachings, was having an extramarital affair. Soon, it was also discovered that he physically abused his only child. Everyone was shocked, for they had always viewed him as Mr. Virtuous, whose teachings reviled the exact sins he had committed.

What do all of these fictional characters have in common? All of them illustrate the fact that actions prove faith, whereas words only claim faith.

What else can you learn from the third story? While Linda's actions in her community are highly admirable, she showed her true nature at home. Could Linda's actions outside of her home be truly honest when she cannot even show love to the person closest to her, one who needs her care the most? This story demonstrates that true love starts at home. If you cannot love the people who are closest to you, how can you truly care for strangers?

"But if any provideth not for his own, and specially his own household, he hath denied the faith, and is worse than an unbeliever." (I Timothy 5:8)

What are the two most important commandments in life? Jesus supplied: "Thou shalt love the Lord thy God with all thy heart, and with all thy soul, and with all thy mind, and with all thy strength. The second is this, Thou shalt love thy neighbor as thyself. There is none other commandment greater than these." (Mark 12:30-31) Many claim to love God, while they do not care much for their fellow humans. How can you truly love God, the Great Creator you cannot see, when you cannot love those you see every day?

We can show our love to God only by loving His creations. If we love God, we automatically love others; if we love others, it means we love God. The two go hand in hand; we cannot do one without doing the other.

How do you behave at home? Are you doing good in secrecy, without letting the world know about it? (Yet, God will record your every good done behind closed doors.) Your actions at home are vastly more important than your actions performed beyond its walls. But that does not mean you should treat your family with love while treating outsiders horribly! If you are good at home, you ought to be the same outside, and vice versa.

Lastly, doing good does not mean speaking badly is acceptable. Speaking is also an important action. A word spoken rashly is wrong, and should be avoided. One of my biggest pet peeves is people speaking without thinking first, and inadvertently saying something that is either hurtful or untrue. Doing good does not give people the excuse to speak badly.

Do you speak with words or actions? How well do your actions speak for you?

God Is Love

"Jehovah, Jehovah, a God merciful and gracious, slow to anger, and abundant in lovingkindness and truth, keeping lovingkindness for thousands, forgiving iniquity and transgression and sin; and that will by no means clear the guilty, visiting the iniquity of the fathers upon the children, and upon the children's children, upon the third and upon the fourth generation." (Exodus 34:6-7)

Who is God? The apostle John answered that question with just three words: "God is love." Jehovah is not only a loving God, He represents love itself.

What does love mean to you? What rightfully constitutes love? The apostle Paul supplied a most wonderful definition of love:

"Love suffereth long, and is kind; love envieth not; love vaunteth not itself, is not puffed up, doth not behave itself unseemly, seeketh not its own, is not provoked, taketh not account of evil; rejoiceth not in unrighteousness, but rejoiceth with the truth; beareth all things, believeth all things, hopeth all things, endureth all things. Love never faileth..." (I Corinthians 13:4-8)

How has Jehovah shown His love? What has He done for us? Well, for starters, He gave us our very existence. If we did not exist, we would not be around to laugh, to weep, to dance, or to sing. We would not experience love or hate, happiness or sorrow. We would not delight in making merry music, bringing a smile to a stranger's face, or admiring the dawn of morning's first rays. Above all, we would not have the great honor to be called God's children.

After creating us, has Jehovah left us empty-handed? No, He lovingly provides for our physical, mental, and spiritual needs. He created this wonderful planet that gives us everything we could ever need. Its natural resources are too numerous to count, and the nutritious fruits and vegetables it yields are delightful to look at, smell, feel, and taste.

Besides providing us nourishment for our physical survival, Jehovah has also abundantly supplied spiritual foods to help us truly *live*. Material foods sustain our existence, whereas His loving guidance keeps us spiritually healthy. We exist on food, but we live on His Word of wisdom: His Bible.

Has Jehovah set us upon a boring home, with nothing productive or interesting to do? Not at all. He has granted us not only life's necessities but also life's pleasures, from wildlife companions of every kind to our own creativity and imagination so people from all walks of life, from artists to zoologists, can explore His wondrous world to their hearts' content.

Why has Jehovah bestowed so many treasures and riches upon us? Jehovah loves us not because we are good, but because He is love. Are we innocent, righteous, and lovable beings who deserve His infinite love and grace? No, time and time again we prove that we are unworthy of His love, and that many of us do not love Him, yet this Father unfailingly devotes His whole soul to our well-being. This is no mere momentary devotion: it will last to time indefinite. He even makes it possible for all of us to receive immortality by laying down His most precious Son—His only begotten Son—as ransom, so whosoever have faith in Jesus "should not perish, but have eternal life." (John 3:16) He sacrificed His most beloved Creation, One who is absolutely sinless and perfect, just so the wicked can be cleansed and drawn near to Him. Many consider this sacrifice and salvation God's grandest show of love for us. While Jesus' death is God's greatest personal sacrifice, I feel that God's most sterling love is shown in the granting of our existence. We would not be privileged to receive His gift of salvation if He had not created us in the first place!

But Jehovah let Jesus die only for three days, not for eternity, you may be thinking. Indeed, that is true, but it is not a matter of how long Jesus died for us—that is unimportant; the point is that he died for us. He went through both physical and spiritual sacrifice for our sake. While on Earth, Jesus, as a man who possessed every physical property of a real, flesh-and-blood human being, had suffered a great deal. Can you imagine being impaled with long nails driven through your wrists and ankles while you are alive, and left there to die slowly under the blazing sun?

> "God is love; and he that abideth in love abideth in God, and God abideth in him." (I

John 4:16)

Would we be able to return such an overwhelming love to God? With a mere man, nothing is possible, for everything a man has is given to him by God—nothing comes from himself. But with God, everything is possible, for He is the Originator of everything. Therefore, when you love God to the best of your human ability, He will give you the capacity and might to love fully and infinitely, in the way defined by the apostle Paul.

Return God's love by loving others. I quote the apostle John: "If a man say, I love God, and hateth his brother, he is a liar: for he that loveth not his brother whom he hath seen, cannot love God whom he hath not seen. And this commandment have we from him, that he who loveth God love his brother also." (I John 4:20-21) If you love others, it means you love God; but if you hate others, it means you hate God. When we love, we come from God and we are one with Him, for love comes from God. When we have no love, we have no God in our heart and we do not belong to Him.

Love is the seed for all that is righteous; nothing that is good comes from any element but love, and nothing is good without love. Everything is based on and determined by love. Love is the wisest of all wisdom, the meekest of all humility, and the smartest of all intelligence. Your IQ identifies only superficial intelligence; your real intelligence is measured by the amount of love you have and give—and the more you give freely, without reproach, without expecting anything in return, and without feeling as though you have sacrificed in any way, the smarter you are.

Put love at the number one spot on your list. Make it your priority to be more loving, to show more love to your fellow humans, to animals, and the environment. In other words, to all of God's creations—never leave one out! Love those who need your love the most first; start from your home or with those nearest to you, and spread it outward. What kind of love is it when you only love outsiders and not your own family? Do not search far and wide to give your love; find those to whom you can give your love in your surroundings.

Love others equally. Treat paupers the way you would treat kings. Show no less kindness and respect toward the sickly, the poor, and the elderly than you would toward the wealthy, the handsome, and the healthy.

It tends to be easy to maintain relationships, from friendships to marriages, when the days are bright. True love is tested when people face mountains in life. We laugh together, but can we always endure together? Marriages fall apart when one partner gets ill, grows old and gray, or becomes less attractive, causing the other partner to abandon their marriage vow. If you can endure hardships, hand in hand, you know you have true love. True love is brightest when days are darkest.

A loving person is an understanding person who treats everyone with equality. A loving person will embrace the sickly, the poor, and the not-so-pretty as they were siblings. They will lend a helping hand to those in need and will not expect any monetary or material benefits in return. Instead, they will desire the good feeling that only loving others can bring.

A loving person seeks spiritual gifts, not the spotlight. A loving person embraces others and does not care about opinions or rumors, for when the loving people know they are good, they have nothing to worry about. Only the guilty worry about what others whisper behind their backs.

A loving person is filled with compassion for others and understands what others need. The loving will not question the actions of the good but will honor and respect others even when they cannot understand them.

Above all, the loving love honestly. They do not express their love falsely; they do not use love to get what they want. They love with real love. The loving love for the sake of love, not for rewards. They simply love love. They love because they love the lovely feeling and the virtue of loving others. They love because they are glad to be alive, they love because they have the privilege to love, and they love because God made us so we can love.

> "If thine enemy be hungry, give him bread to eat; And if he be thirsty, give him water to drink: For thou wilt heap coals of fire upon his head, And Jehovah will reward thee." (Proverbs 25:21-22)

Love without boundaries: do not love only those you like, but also your enemies, meaning that you show no hatred toward them and you do not plan vengeance in your heart, even while you hate the bad they did. For Jesus said, "If ye love them that love you, what thank have ye? for even sinners love those that love them. And if ye do good to them that do good to you, what thank have ye? for even sinners do the same. And if ye lend to them of whom ye hope to receive, what thank have ye? even sinners lend to sinners, to receive again as much. But love your enemies, and do them good, and lend, never despairing; and your reward shall be great, and ye shall be sons of the Most High: for he is kind toward the unthankful and evil. Be ye merciful, even as your Father is merciful. And judge not, and ye shall not be judged: and condemn not, and ye shall not be condemned: release, and ye shall be released: give, and it shall be given unto you; good measure, pressed down, shaken together, running over, shall they give into your bosom. For with what measure ye mete it shall be measured to you again." (Luke 6:32-38)

    Fight evil with love and justice, not with evil — let evil be done by evildoers only. Remain loving at all times, just as Jehovah has used love to wash the dirt from sinners. Listen to the wise counsel of the apostle Peter: "Finally, be ye all of one mind, having compassion one of another, love as brethren, be pitiful, be courteous: Not rendering evil for evil, or railing for railing: but contrariwise blessing; knowing that ye are thereunto called, that ye should inherit a blessing. For he that will love life, and see good days, let him refrain his tongue from evil, and his lips that they speak no guile: Let him eschew evil, and do good; let him seek peace, and ensue it." (I Peter 3:8-11, King James Version) But be careful that, by showing love to the evil people, you not sacrifice the good people; do not let it be an excuse to take love away from the good. Love justly and fairly. Protect the good from the bad; do not let the bad take advantage of your care and misuse it to harm the good, or fool you into leaving the good. Love involves justice, so make sure that, in your love for the wicked, you do not reward them for their evil deeds, promote what they do, or praise them.

Leave final judgment in the hands of God. Yet, do not be a mere bystander—if you find your neighbor doing wrong, promptly censure him as the Bible says: "Thou shalt not hate thy brother in thy heart: thou shalt surely rebuke thy neighbor, and not bear sin because of him." (Leviticus 19:17) If you know that what your friend does is wrong, yet you do not say so and remain silent, you will become a partner in his sin. Correcting your friend will do your friend good and show your love, for love seeks justice. In the long run, your friend will thank you, for only true friends have the power from God to defeat manmade barriers to save the soul, whereas false friends are only interested in preserving the surface, dragging others into eternal darkness along with them.

Masterpiece of Love

"Stand still, and consider the wondrous works of God. Dost thou know the balancings of the clouds, The wondrous works of him who is perfect in knowledge?" (Job 37:14, 16)

Mighty eagles soaring in blue skies; green grasses bedecked with colorful wildflowers; the bright sun unfailingly rising every morning to give us warmth and light—what do these natural phenomena we see and experience daily tell us about their Creator?

Jesus Christ, when accused of casting demons out of their victims with the powers of Satan, said in response, "Every kingdom divided against itself is brought to desolation; and every city or house divided against itself shall not stand." (Matthew 12:25) So if he used Satan's power to drive away demons, would not the evil forces have fallen apart?

What does this have to do with the question opening this chapter? It, as a matter of fact, has everything to do with it.

Think about the vast universe, with its myriad stars and planets, and then imagine that its creator is Satan. Would the stars and planets exist in such impeccable harmony? Would the plants and animals that inhabit our green and blue planet have thrived and been so fruitful for so long if their creator were the devil? Would there be the possibility of love, joy, peace, and happiness? And would there be an innate conscience in humankind to know right from wrong and to seek infinite wisdom? No, I dare say. If an evil creator were the originator of everything, the universe would have been a complete mess, if not crumpled by now. There would not be balance, there would not be elements of the righteous; creations would not stand and survive, but would perish while fighting one another.

A painting reflects the character of its painter; a piece of writing offers a glimpse of its author's personality. Likewise, just by observing Jehovah's awesome world, we can conclude that He is the greatest force of Love. From love, all wondrous elements bloom. From Jehovah comes beauty, harmony, and serenity in all we see, feel, hear, smell, and taste. We get to wake up each morning to the cheerful calls of birds; we get to wipe tears from strangers' faces; and we get to dance under a refreshing rain. Do you not agree that these wonders are signs of love?

Do You Love Jehovah's Art of Love?

"Rejoice always; pray without ceasing; in everything give thanks: for this is the will of God in Christ Jesus to you-ward." (I Thessalonians 5:16-18)

Are you unconditionally grateful for your life? Sure, you may be grateful when the sun is shining and the sky is blue, but what if black clouds roll in and the sky decides to cry? Would you cry also, or would you be grateful that you had the privilege of experiencing the sunshine and blue sky in the past, and be grateful that you can now take a nice shower under the refreshing rain?

If you can be grateful for both your sunny days and your dark days, if you can be grateful while at your lowest, most primitive level—while you have only yourself left in life—you will be able to face any challenges that come your way. What is there to fear if you fear no losses?

Appreciate today and its riches. Be thankful for the gems that sparkle; focus on the gifts God has bestowed upon you. Do not let any dust or dirt tarnish the value of these diamonds, for the dirt itself cannot touch or harm the treasures—only you have the power to ultimately soil the gems, so handle them with grace and appreciation. Thank God for each day that passes and its riches. Instead of waiting for disaster to strike in order to be thankful for what little is left after its devastation, love and appreciate everything and everyone right now.

When you are given life, hold on to it tightly yet delicately; cherish what has been given to you: your privilege to enjoy dawn's first rays, your power to give words of comfort to a stranger, and your fortune in receiving warm embraces after a good cry. If you allow your mishaps to cloud these treasures—or do not realize the true value of challenges—you will make your situation worse than it is already, losing every good thing you do have. And watch out for the thieves who try to belittle your gifts; they are the people who refuse to recognize the worth of life.

Start everything with appreciation. Before you start anything new, say anything new, or go anywhere new, first appreciate every aspect of your current state. This appreciation will act like a cushion if you ever fall back to where you started, your original state. So if you are thankful for now, when you return to now, you will be thankful that you have not lost anything and will be extra grateful for anything you have gained, even the tiniest amount.

Appreciate challenges and setbacks. Take a moment to reflect on life and your past. What parts of life have taught you lessons, have made you wiser, have made your spirit stronger? Were they not challenges? Life gives us many treasures to be thankful for, and the gifts that make you stronger are challenges. Challenges are life's vaccines: they equip your soul with the necessary antidotes to battle future storms. I have received many of these vaccines; the obstacles have left numerous scars in all shapes and sizes on my body, but these marks have made me stronger and more invincible as I wait for the next high mountain to scale. I relish the taste of victory each and every time I battle and win. If there were no challenges, how could I name myself a victor? If there were no darkness, how could the stars appear so bright?

So next time when you see a butterfly fluttering among wildflowers or hear a songbird's song, smile. You are privileged to be in this life. There are millions of less fortunate souls, and think of those infinite souls that have never been born to know this, to experience all this… I know I am one lucky gal!

Loving life unconditionally goes hand in hand with gratitude—being grateful for your life, unconditionally. Many people have asked me, "What inspires you?" I have always given my four-letter answer: life. Once when I gave this answer, the lady laughed and said that, while I love life, many people *complain* about life. How true! I often hear people say, "Life is unfair," and they grumble against God. I will never call my life unfair. If I do, then I suppose it would also be unfair to the sun, for it cannot provide us with water. It would also be unfair to the flowers, for they cannot sing.

When things go wrong in people's lives, or when they do not get what they want, they start complaining about life. But does life ever complain about you? No matter how many times you have made a mistake, has the sun ever left your side? Have the birds ever stopped singing to you? Why do you not return that unconditional love?

Value life as is, in its purest form. Love the purity of life, which I do. What do I mean by the purity of life? Well, when you think about it, most problems in life, except for natural disasters and some diseases, are caused by humans. When you brush away those manmade problems, what is left is life in its purest form. And this is what I am madly in love with. Yes, call me a lovesick gal! But let me ask you this: what would you have missed if your existence had never existed? I know I am able to laugh; I am able to weep. Without my life, I would be able to do neither of these.

To love and accept life is to love and accept God. When you love someone, what they do, what they say, even the places they visit and their personal belongings, become more interesting and significant to you. Worshipping the ground they walk on no longer seems so farfetched. To a parent, their child's drawing is much more precious than any famous masterpiece. To a lover's ears, the name of their beloved one is music. You would more likely take the advice of someone you trust than that of a stranger. A simple gift from a friend is more valuable than an expensive present given by your least favorite person. I remember the pretty doll my mother gave me for my fourth birthday when we were in China. I loved it dearly. It was so much more special because it was from my mother's heart. The gift, even if bedecked in real gold and silver, would not mean much to me if it came from someone else. So how you feel about someone will be reflected in your feelings for what the person does, says, or gives.

Show your love for God by loving life. Love all His creations and His gifts to you. Be serious about life, for its value is immeasurable. But also have a grand time, for life is all about the bliss.

The Trinity Mystery

"Jehovah our God is one Jehovah." (Deuteronomy 6:4)

The Holy Trinity, the Narrow Path?

"Trust in Jehovah with all thy heart, And lean not upon thine own understanding: In all thy ways acknowledge him, And he will direct thy paths. Be not wise in thine own eyes; Fear Jehovah, and depart from evil." (Proverbs 3:5-7)

Have you heard of the "Holy Trinity"? Anyone who has heard of Christianity will have heard of this term, for it is the central doctrine in mainstream Christianity. But do you know what it actually means?

The Athanasian Creed, the formal statement of the Holy Trinity, states:

The Holy Trinity consists of the Father, the Son, and the Holy Spirit, where the Father is God, the Son is God, and the Holy Spirit is God, but They all point to one God, not three individual Gods. This Godhead is Jehovah, and "They" are three Persons, one substance, and They all co-exist, and are co-equal and co-eternal. In other words, it teaches that Jesus Christ is actually God Almighty.

Is this doctrine true? Is Jesus really God

Almighty?

Is "Holy Trinity" the teachings of the Christ? Jesus founded the one and only true religion called Christianity (which simply affirms the Old Testament and fulfills God's promise to establish a new covenant); therefore, what he taught two thousand years ago is the absolute truth, the one and only path that will lead to salvation and the wonderful Kingdom of God. Jesus once said, "For narrow is the gate, and straitened the way, that leadeth unto life, and few are they that find it." (Matthew 7:14) So it is extremely important to see whether this doctrine is the narrow path that leads to the true knowledge of Jehovah. If we cannot even understand who God is, how can we properly have faith in Him?

What did Jesus say regarding who God is and who he himself is? Would we not all agree that whatever Jesus taught is the ultimate truth, and no one should alter any of his teachings in any way?

Let us examine the facts from the Bible to answer these questions, to help us identify the true God Almighty.

On the evening of the Passover, Jesus prayed to Jehovah three times before he was betrayed by Judas to be wrongly executed.
- Would Jesus really pray to himself if he were truly God as stated in the doctrine of the Holy Trinity? People say we are crazy when we talk to ourselves, so what do they say about praying to oneself?
- This also shows that Jesus worships Jehovah. Would God worship Himself?

In his prayers, Jesus bravely said to Jehovah, "Father, if thou be willing, remove this cup from me: nevertheless not my will, but thine, be done." (Luke 22:42)
- If Jesus and Jehovah were one God, how could the wills (wishes or desires) of one Being conflict regarding one subject?

Regarding the exact time of his second coming on Earth, Jesus told people: "But of that day and hour knoweth no one, not even the angels of heaven, neither the Son, but the Father only." (Matthew 24:36)
- How could one single God know and not know one piece of information at the same time?
- How could the all-powerful God Almighty possibly not know anything, let alone the most important date of our world?

Jesus said, "Whosoever shall speak a word against the Son of man, it shall be forgiven him; but whosoever shall speak against the Holy Spirit, it shall not be forgiven him, neither in this world, nor in that which is to come." (Matthew 12:32)
- If Jesus and the Holy Spirit were indeed one single God in the Trinity, then why would Jesus indicate otherwise? How could it be acceptable to blaspheme one and not the other if both were indeed the same God?

Before Jesus began preaching God's messages, Satan tested him in various ways. The devil took him "unto an exceeding high mountain, and showeth him all the kingdoms of the world, and the glory of them," and he said to him, "All these things will I give thee, if thou wilt fall down and worship me." (Matthew 4:8-9) Of course, Jesus refused, saying, "Get thee hence, Satan: for it is written, Thou shalt worship the Lord thy God, and him only shalt thou serve." (Matthew 4:10)

• Would God need to be tempted to sin, let alone by Satan of all people? Such insane nonsense! James 1:13 specifically says: "God cannot be tempted by evil."

• Would Satan really ask Jesus to bow down to him if he were God? It is true that Satan is stupid, but he cannot be *that* stupid, to ask God to worship him, can he? Would Satan ask God to worship him just to receive control of the world He already owns? God owns absolutely everything, even though our world is ruled by Satan under God's permissive will.

When Jesus broke a few loaves of bread to feed about five thousand men, besides women and children, he looked up toward the heavens and gave thanks. "And he commanded the multitudes to sit down on the grass; and he took the five loaves, and the two fishes, and looking up to heaven, he blessed, and brake and gave the loaves to the disciples, and the disciples to the multitudes." (Matthew 14:19)

• If Jesus were God, why would he look up at the heavens? Would God need to look toward Himself? (But wait a minute, God is already Himself, so does it mean He was confused about where He was?)

When the mother of the sons of Zebedee requested that each of her sons sit on either side of Jesus in his Kingdom, Jesus answered, "...to sit on my right hand, and on my left hand, is not mine to give; but it is for them for whom it hath been prepared of my Father." (Matthew 20:23)
• Enough said!

In a letter to Timothy, the apostle Paul wrote: "...there is one God, one mediator also between God and men, himself man, Christ Jesus..." (I Timothy 2:5)
• How could one be between oneself and others? A mediator is always a totally different person, not a part of the person being mediated.

Before his death, Jesus cried with a loud voice, "Eloi, Eloi, lama sabachthani?" which is, being interpreted, "My God, my God, why hast thou forsaken me?" (Mark 15:34)
• Jesus called Jehovah his God. Would he call himself "My God"?
• Would Jesus really ask himself why he had forsaken himself?

A ruler once called Jesus "Good teacher," but Jesus answered, "Why callest thou me good? none is good save one, even God." (Mark 10:18)
• Jesus indicated that only God is good—no one else, not even himself—so how could he be God?

Once, a wild demon-possessed man cried out before Jesus, saying, "What have I to do with thee, Jesus, thou Son of the Most High God? I adjure thee

by God, torment me not." (Mark 5:7)
- The unclean spirit clearly knew that Jesus was the Son of God, not God, the Son; and his plea was "I adjure thee by God," which obviously differentiated Jesus from God. If Jesus were really God Almighty, then why would the man say, "I adjure thee by God"? Remember, all the demons knew who Jesus was, so no mistaken identity occurred.

Jesus said this about God: "He is not the God of the dead, but of the living." (Mark 12:27)
- Jesus did not say that he, himself, is the God of the living.
- Jesus referred to God always using the third person, such as "He" and "Him," and never with the first person, such as "I" or "me."

Jesus said, "For as the Father hath life in himself, even so gave he to the Son also to have life in himself" and "I live because of the Father; so he that eateth me, he also shall live because of me." (John 5:26; 6:57)
- Jesus lives because of his Father, who gave him life. Would God need anyone to give Him life?

In Genesis 2:24, it says, "Therefore shall a man leave his father and his mother, and shall cleave unto his wife: and they shall be one flesh." Does that literally mean that man and woman will be glued into one flesh after marriage? Of course not—thank goodness! It simply means that they will be united spiritually.

This "one" idea was referred to by Jesus as well, when he talked about himself and Jehovah God. In one of his prayers to his Father, he wished to have his followers be one just as he and God are one: "Holy Father, keep them in thy name which thou hast given me, that they may be one, even as we are." (John 17:11)
- This clearly shows that Jesus and Jehovah are two separate Beings, just as his followers are separate beings from Jesus and Jehovah. Would Jesus have asked his followers to be one body? (Can you imagine that?)

Jesus said, "…the Father is greater than I." (John 14:28)
- Jesus plainly indicated that he and Jehovah are not equal, so he cannot be God Almighty.

What does Jehovah Himself say about who Jesus is?
Jehovah said, "…behold, I will bring forth my servant the Branch." (Zechariah 3:8) And "Behold, my servant, whom I uphold; my chosen, in whom my soul delighteth…" (Isaiah 42:1) Also, as we already know, God calls Jesus "my Son."
- Yes, Jehovah calls Jesus His servant. Would God call Himself "my servant"?
- Would God call Himself "my Son"?

Jehovah told Moses about Jesus: "I will raise them up a prophet from among their brethren, like unto thee; and I will put my words in his mouth, and he shall speak unto them all that I shall command

him." (Deuteronomy 18:18)
- Jehovah *raised* up Jesus, and *put* His words into his mouth, so Jesus can speak whatever He *commands* him to say. If Jesus were God, would he need to raise himself up, put his own words into his mouth, and command himself to speak what he, himself, wanted himself to speak?

In Isaiah 11:2, it says: "The Spirit of Jehovah shall rest upon him," where "him" refers to Jesus. Also in Isaiah 42:1, Jehovah said: "I have put my Spirit upon him."
- Why would God need to put the Holy Spirit on Jesus if Jesus were God already?

A similar example: After Jesus was baptized by John the Baptist, the "Spirit driveth him forth into the wilderness" to be tempted by Satan. (Mark 1:12)
- Jesus drove himself out into the wilderness?

An even better example: Just prior to Jesus being sent out into the wilderness, the heavens parted, and the Spirit descended on him like a dove. A voice came out of the sky: "Thou art my beloved Son, in thee I am well pleased." (Mark 1:11)
- Would Jesus call himself his own beloved Son? Certainly, most of us love ourselves; God does not need to make this proclamation that He is pleased with Himself into a showy display with all the special effects. Would God be so conceited?

God said to Jesus: "Thou art my son; This day have I begotten thee." (Psalm 2:7)

• Self-explanatory.

A passage from Hebrews also proves that Jesus is not God: "For every high priest, being taken from among men, is appointed for men in things pertaining to God, that he may offer both gifts and sacrifices for sins: who can bear gently with the ignorant and erring, for that he himself also is compassed with infirmity; and by reason thereof is bound, as for the people, so also for himself, to offer for sins. And no man taketh the honor unto himself, but when he is called of God, even as was Aaron. So Christ also glorified not himself to be made a high priest, but he that spake unto him, Thou art my Son, This day have I begotten thee." (Hebrews 5:1-5)
• In this analogy, Jesus Christ is compared with a human priest; just as a priest's duty and honor are appointed by God, not by oneself, so Jesus' honor is appointed by God, not by himself. If Jesus were God, he would automatically be honorable from the start, and would need no one to appoint honor to him.

In Isaiah 11:2-3, it says: "And the Spirit of Jehovah shall rest upon him, the spirit of wisdom and understanding, the spirit of counsel and might, the spirit of knowledge and of the fear of Jehovah. And his delight shall be in the fear of Jehovah…"
• How could God fear Himself?

In the vision concerning the end time of our world, the prophet Daniel saw "with the clouds of heaven one like unto a son of man, and he came even to the ancient of days, and they brought him near before him. And there was given him dominion, and glory, and a kingdom, that all the peoples, nations, and languages should serve him: his dominion is an everlasting dominion, which shall not pass away, and his kingdom that which shall not be destroyed." (Daniel 7:13-14)

- The "son of man" is Jesus Christ, and the "ancient of days" is obviously Jehovah. It is apparent from this passage that they are separate Beings, and that God's Kingdom will be *given* to the "son of man," not that it was his to start with. If the "son of man" were God, why would the Kingdom be *given* to him? Surely, God is already the King of His Kingdom, is He not? Therefore, He does not need His own Kingdom to be given to Him.

Trinitarians say that the "ancient of days" refers to God, the Father, while at the same time that Jesus has existed with the Father from the very beginning. How could the Son have the same beginning as the Father when only the Father is "ancient"?

The Gospel of John is especially good at distinguishing between the Father and the Son. Let us examine some of its passages.

In Jesus' days, the Jewish religious leaders who wanted to persecute him also thought that Jesus was equal to God, but Jesus rebuked them: "Verily, verily, I say unto you, The Son can do nothing of himself, but what he seeth the Father doing: for what things soever he doeth, these the Son also doeth in like manner." (John 5:19)

Jesus said, "I can of myself do nothing: as I hear, I judge: and my judgment is righteous; because I seek not mine own will, but the will of him that sent me." (John 5:30)

Jesus said the same thing on another occasion: "For I am come down from heaven, not to do mine own will, but the will of him that sent me." (John 6:38)

Regarding his teaching, Jesus said, "My teaching is not mine, but his that sent me. If any man willeth to do his will, he shall know of the teaching, whether it is of God, or whether I speak from myself. He that speaketh from himself seeketh his own glory: but he that seeketh the glory of him that sent him, the same is true, and no unrighteousness is in him." (John 7:16-18)

About the witness of him, Jesus said, "In your law it is written, that the witness of two men is true. I am he that beareth witness of myself, and the Father that sent me beareth witness of me." (John 8:17-18)

Concerning his glory, Jesus said, "If I glorify myself, my glory is nothing: it is my Father that glorifieth me." (John 8:54)

In regards to whom to believe, Jesus said, "Let not your heart be troubled: believe in God, believe also in me." (John 14:1)

- If Jesus were God, would it be necessary for him to say believe *also* in him? It would be the same if I were to say, "Believe in Shirley Cheng; believe also in me." What would others think? I cannot imagine!

About what he spoke, Jesus said, "I spake not from myself; but the Father that sent me, he hath given me a commandment, what I should say, and what I should speak." (John 12:49)

Regarding the power and authority Jesus can exercise, John the Baptist said, "The Father loveth the Son, and hath given all things into his hand." (John 3:35)

Before returning to his Father's side in heaven, Jesus said to Mary from Magdala, "Touch me not; for I am not yet ascended unto the Father: but go unto my brethren, and say to them, I ascend unto my Father and your Father, and my God and your God." (John 20:17)

Even after he was back at his Father's side in heaven, Jesus still called Him "my God," as in: "He that overcometh, I will make him a pillar in the temple of my God, and he shall go out thence no more: and I will write upon him the name of my God, and the name of the city of my God, the new Jerusalem, which cometh down out of heaven from my God, and mine own new name." (Revelation 3:12)

The book of Micah prophesied the birth of Jesus, whose actual origin is "from of old, from everlasting," and foretold that "he shall stand, and shall feed his flock in the strength of Jehovah, in the majesty of the name of Jehovah his God: and they shall abide; for now shall he be great unto the ends of the earth." (Micah 5:2, 4)

- Again, Jehovah is *his* God, not Jehovah is *he*. This fact is supported by the apostle Paul, who plainly stated that Jehovah is "the God and Father of our Lord Jesus Christ." (Romans 15:6) No, you cannot get any clearer than this.

Finally, one *extremely* important question: could God really die? Would God really die? If people were to believe Jesus is God, then they are saying that God died, which is the biggest, most serious blasphemy! God "who only hath immortality, dwelling in light unapproachable; whom no man hath seen, nor can see" cannot die! (I Timothy 6:16) Also, would God really sacrifice Himself? Do you not agree with me that Jehovah is much too supreme to be sacrificed for anything? Trinitarians think too highly of us humans when they dare claim that God Almighty would actually die for us. Who are we? Are we not but like the vapor that will be gone tomorrow? Would it not make much more sense to sacrifice His perfect Creation for the sins of His imperfect creations, instead of sacrificing Himself?

Lastly, Jesus was resurrected *by* God. To be resurrected, one must be completely dead, and it would require someone else to do the raising up.

The doctrine of the Holy Trinity has caused people to call virgin Mary the "mother of God"! Does that mean that Joseph is therefore God's adoptive father? (So who is His biological father?) What insults! God has no mother; He is the beginning and the end; He has no beginning and no end.

So from this handful of simple examples (and there are more apparent ones in the Bible), we can clearly see that Jehovah and Jesus are indeed two separate Spirits, not one God; therefore, it completely destroys the "Holy Trinity" idea in its physical sense.

The apostle Paul said, "God is not a God of confusion," so clearly, God will not cause confusion among people about something as fundamental as His true identity. (I Corinthians 14:33) If He did indeed belong in a Trinity, He would have mentioned it at least once in His holy word, the Bible.

I will never dare blindly dispute true Bible teachings. If Trinitarians can satisfactorily answer the questions I have posed in this chapter, I will very happily accept the Holy Trinity doctrine. But until now, I have not come upon any text or reasoning that can answer the questions I have posed in this chapter; everything I have read either conflicts with everything else, goes in circles, or greatly distorts God's splendid image. The idea of Jehovah and Jesus being two separate Spirits, on the other hand, is not confusing and is supported throughout the Bible.

However, I must admit, I like to use "Holy Trinity" in the spiritual sense—that the Father, the Son, and the Holy Spirit are one, spiritually. I always say my mother and I are one, but that does not mean that we are actually one fleshly person.

In conclusion, Jehovah is the one and only true God Almighty, the only One who should be worshipped. The Christ Jesus is His beloved Son, as God indicated several times in the Bible. Jehovah is

Almighty, whereas Jesus is Mighty, second in line to Jehovah.

What about the Holy Spirit? The Holy Spirit is God's active force, which He uses to perform any and all tasks. For instance, He used the Holy Spirit to impregnate the virgin Mary so she could have Jesus. God freely gives His Holy Spirit to anyone He chooses. If the Holy Spirit were God, that would suggest God literally gives away pieces of Himself.

The Holy Spirit of God is like the rays of the sun. When we say the sun kissed our hair, it does not literally mean that the sun itself actually kissed our hair; it means that the rays of the sun reached us to warm our hair, just as if God's Holy Spirit, not God Himself, were to come down upon us.

God possesses the Holy Spirit—it is a part of Him. The Holy Spirit is not God, just as my hair is not me. People possess properties; the properties are not the people. The Bible says "God is love." Does that mean love is God? If love is God, then numerous people are also God, for many possess love.

Whom should we worship? Jesus clearly worships Jehovah, so we should follow his example. The Bible indicates that "the head of every man is Christ; and the head of the woman is the man; and the head of Christ is God," and that we "are Christ's; and Christ is God's," therefore we must worship the One sitting in the highest seat. (I Corinthians 11:3; 1 Corinthians 3:23)

Do not give glory to Satan—you indeed give glory to Satan if you believe that Jesus is God; therefore Satan even had the power to ask God to worship him!

Prayer of Jesus Christ

"I will pray with the spirit, and I will pray with the understanding also: I will sing with the spirit, and I will sing with the understanding also." (I Corinthians 14:15)

I will ask this question again: if Jesus were God Almighty, would he really pray to himself? Throughout the gospels, Jesus prayed to Jehovah. Here, we will examine Jesus' longest prayer, which takes up John 17. I have included two versions of his prayer—one original, and one altered in a way that conveys what it would actually mean if Jesus were indeed praying to himself. The latter version is quite hilarious, do you not agree? But this is really what the prayer would mean if Jesus were God, as the Trinitarians proclaim.

Original prayer found in John 17, World English Bible:

Jesus said these things, and lifting up his eyes to heaven, he said, "Father, the time has come. Glorify your Son, that your Son may also glorify you; even as you gave him authority over all flesh, he will give eternal life to all whom you have given him. This is eternal life, that they should know you, the only true God, and him whom you sent, Jesus Christ. [Author's note: Notice that Jesus calls his Father, not "we," the "only true God.") I glorified you on the earth. I have accomplished the work which you have given me to do. Now, Father, glorify me with your own self with the glory which I had with you before the world existed. I revealed your name to the people whom you have given me out of the world. They were yours, and you have given them to me. They have kept your word. Now they have known that all things whatever you have given me are from you, for the words which you have given me I have given to them, and they received them, and knew for sure that I came forth from you, and they have believed that you sent me. I pray for them. I don't pray for the world, but for those whom you have given me, for they are yours. All things that are mine are yours, and yours are mine, and I am glorified in them. I am no more in the world, but these are in the world, and I am coming to you. Holy Father, keep them through your name which you have given me, that they may be one, even as we are. While I was with them in the world, I kept them in your name. Those whom you have given me I have kept. None of them is lost, except the son of destruction, that the Scripture might be fulfilled. But now I come to you, and I say these things in the world, that they may have my joy made full in themselves. I have given them your word. The world hated them, because they are not of the world, even as I am not of the world. I pray not that you would take them from the world, but that you would keep them from the evil one. They are not of the world even as I am not of the world. Sanctify them in your truth. Your word is truth. As you sent me into the world, even so I have sent them into the world. For their sakes I sanctify myself, that they themselves also may be sanctified in truth. Not for these only do I pray, but for those also who believe in me through their word, that they may all be one; even as you, Father, are in me, and I in you, that they also may be one in us; that the world may believe that you sent me. The glory which you have given me, I have given to them; that they may be one, even as we are one; I in them, and you in me, that they may be perfected into one; that the world may know that you sent me, and loved them, even as you loved me. Father, I desire that they also whom you have given me be with me where I am, that they may see my glory, which you have given me, for you loved me before the foundation of the world. Righteous Father, the world hasn't known you, but I knew you; and these knew that you sent me. I made known to them your name, and will make it known; that the love with which you loved me may be in them, and I in them."

The altered version:

Jesus said these things, and lifting up his eyes to heaven, he said, "Me, the time has come. Glorify My Son, that My Son may also glorify Me; even as I gave Me authority over all flesh, I will give eternal life to all whom Me have given Me. This is eternal life, that they should know Me, the only true God, and I whom I sent, Jesus Christ. I glorified Myself on the earth. I have accomplished the work which I have given me to do. Now, Myself, glorify me with my own self with the glory which I had with Me before the world existed. I revealed My name to the people whom I have given me out of the world. They were Mine, and I have given them to me. They have kept My word. Now they have known that all things whatever I have given me are from Me, for the words which I have given me I have given to them, and they received them, and knew for sure that I came forth from Me, and they have believed that I sent me. I pray for them. I don't pray for the world, but for those whom I have given me, for they are Mine. All things that are mine are Mine, and Mine are mine, and I am glorified in them. I am no more in the world, but these are in the world, and I am coming to Me. Holy Me, keep them through My name which I have given me, that they may be one, even as we are. While I was with them in the world, I kept them in My name. Those whom I have given me I have kept. None of them is lost, except the son of destruction, that the Scripture might be fulfilled. But now I come to Me, and I say these things in the world, that they may have my joy made full in themselves. I have given them My word. The world hated them, because they are not of the world, even as I am not of the world. I pray not that I would take them from the world, but that I would keep them from the evil one. They are not of the world even as I am not of the world. Sanctify them in My truth. My word is truth. As I sent me into the world, even so I have sent them into the world. For their sakes I sanctify myself, that they themselves also may be sanctified in truth. Not for these only do I pray, but for those also who believe in me through their word, that they may all be one; even as Me, Me, am in me, and I in Me, that they also may be one in us; that the world may believe that I sent me. The glory which I have given me, I have given to them; that they may be one, even as we are one; I in them, and I in me, that they may be perfected into one; that the world may know that I sent me, and loved them, even as I loved me. Me, I desire that they also whom I have given me be with me where I am, that they may see my glory, which I have given me, for I loved me before the foundation of the world. Righteous Me, the world hasn't known Me, but I knew Me; and these knew that I sent me. I made known to them My name, and will make it known; that the love with which I loved me may be in them, and I in them."

Trinitarians Argue...

"And if the blind guide the blind, both shall fall into a pit." (Matthew 15:14)

Any theories need reasoning to back them up; without reasoning, a theory will not attract many followers. So, as with any theory, the doctrine of the Holy Trinity has reasoning behind it. Yet, Trinitarians do not call their doctrine a theory but a fact. In this chapter, I will cover Trinitarians' main arguments and let you decide for yourself how reasonable or unreasonable their arguments are.

We are created in God's image. We are endowed with the precious commodities of logic and common sense sufficient for our use in our daily lives and in our understanding of the basic facts of God. We are commanded to love God with our minds, so that means we have the necessary reasoning capacity for understanding God as best we can, in order to draw as close to Him as possible.

God gave us the Bible so we can learn the truths, not to confuse us. Remember, He is not a God of confusion. Yet, we are required to study the

Scriptures with both faith and reasoning. We need to exert some effort in obtaining the truths, and utilize our God-gifted intelligence, logic, and common sense as the essential tools to help us learn and absorb His lessons.

How logical are the Trinitarians' arguments? Let us see what your common sense tells you after you finish reviewing this section.

But before I present the arguments, I would like you to first study the Athanasian Creed, which defines the doctrine of the Holy Trinity.

The Athanasian Creed

Whosoever will be saved, before all things it is necessary that he hold the catholic faith. Which faith except everyone do keep whole and undefiled, without doubt he shall perish everlastingly. And the catholic faith is this: That we worship one God in Trinity, and Trinity in Unity, neither confounding the persons, nor dividing the substance.

For there is one Person of the Father, another of the Son, and another of the Holy Spirit. But the godhead of the Father, of the Son, and of the Holy Spirit, is all one, the glory equal, the majesty co-eternal.

Such as the Father is, such is the Son, and such is the Holy Spirit. The Father uncreated, the Son uncreated, and the Holy Spirit uncreated. The Father incomprehensible, the Son incomprehensible, and the Holy Spirit incomprehensible.

The Father eternal, the Son eternal, and the Holy Spirit eternal. And yet they are not three eternals, but one Eternal.

As also there are not three incomprehensibles, nor three uncreated, but one Uncreated, and one Incomprehensible. So likewise the Father is Almighty, the Son Almighty, and the Holy Spirit Almighty. And yet they are not three almighties, but one Almighty.

So the Father is God, the Son is God, and the Holy Spirit is God. And yet they are not three gods, but one God.

So likewise the Father is Lord, the Son Lord, and the Holy Spirit Lord. And yet not three lords, but one Lord.

For as we are compelled by the Christian verity to acknowledge each Person by Himself to be both God and Lord, so we are also forbidden by the catholic religion to say that there are three gods or three lords.

The Father is made of none, neither created, nor begotten. The Son is of the Father alone, not made, nor created, but begotten. The Holy Spirit is of the Father, neither made, nor created, nor begotten, but proceeding.

So there is one Father, not three fathers; one Son, not three sons; one Holy Spirit, not three holy spirits.

And in the Trinity none is before or after another; none is greater or less than another, but all three Persons are co-eternal together and co-equal. So that in all things, as is aforesaid, the Unity in Trinity and the Trinity in Unity is to be worshipped.

He therefore that will be saved is must think thus of the Trinity.

Furthermore, it is necessary to everlasting

salvation that he also believe rightly the Incarnation of our Lord Jesus Christ. For the right faith is, that we believe and confess, that our Lord Jesus Christ, the Son of God, is God and man; God, of the substance of the Father, begotten before the worlds; and man of the substance of his mother, born in the world; perfect God and perfect man, of a rational soul and human flesh subsisting. Equal to the Father, as touching His godhead; and inferior to the Father, as touching His manhood; who, although He is God and man, yet he is not two, but one Christ; one, not by conversion of the godhead into flesh but by taking of the manhood into God; one altogether; not by confusion of substance, but by unity of person. For as the rational soul and flesh is one man, so God and man is one Christ; who suffered for our salvation, descended into hell, rose again the third day from the dead. He ascended into heaven, He sits at the right hand of the Father, God Almighty, from whence He will come to judge the quick and the dead. At His coming all men will rise again with their bodies and shall give account for their own works. And they that have done good shall go into life everlasting; and they that have done evil into everlasting fire.

This is the catholic faith, which except a man believe faithfully, he cannot be saved.

Arguments

An argument with Trinitarians may start like this:

Trinitarians: When a human has a son, is that son a human, too?

Your answer: Yes.

Trinitarians: Then God has a Son, so this Son is God, too.

My dispute: A human's son is not the same human as his parent. If a son stole from a store, would the police arrest his father? Just because God has a Son does not make that Son the same God as his Parent. Just because I am begotten by my mother, Juliet, does not mean I am the same being as Juliet.

Trinitarians: 1 Corinthians 12:4-6 supports the Holy Trinity doctrine: "Now there are diversities of gifts, but the same Spirit. And there are diversities of ministrations, and the same Lord. And there are diversities of workings, but the same God, who worketh all things in all."

My dispute: Does this passage indicate any attributes of the doctrine? No, it only affirms that there are one God, one Lord, and one Spirit.

It is crucial to note that no verse in this section uses "Father," as in the Trinitarian formula. Instead, it uses "God." If this passage could have any remote resemblance to the creed, then it should have, at the very least, used "Father." Since it mentions one God, one Lord, and one Spirit—not one Father, one Lord, and one Spirit—it should be obvious that the Lord and the Spirit are not the same Beings as God, since They are identified separately and distinctly. Otherwise, it would be superfluous to say that the Lord and the Spirit are God when God has been singly and additionally pointed out.

This passage distinguishes between the two Beings of God and Christ: "For though there be that are called gods, whether in heaven or on earth; as there are gods many, and lords many; yet to us there is one God, the Father, of whom are all things, and we unto him; and one Lord, Jesus Christ, through whom are all things, and we through him." (I Corinthians 8:5-6)

Trinitarians also often use these two verses to prove their doctrine:

"The grace of the Lord Jesus Christ, and the love of God, and the communion of the Holy Spirit, be with you all." (II Corinthians 13:14)

"Go ye therefore, and make disciples of all the nations, baptizing them into the name of the Father and of the Son and of the Holy Spirit." (Matthew 28:19)

Again, I ask the same question: do these verses indicate that the Father, the Son, and the Holy Spirit possess the attributes as described in the doctrine of the Trinity?

Just because a passage refers to three different objects does not mean all three objects belong in a Trinity. Abraham, Isaac, and Jacob are often mentioned together in the same verse, as well as the apostles Peter, John, and James. Are these two sets of three people two Trinities?

Trinitarians: The Father and the Son are co-eternal.

My dispute: Yes, Jesus is eternal! But Trinitarians seem to confuse the facts about eternity.

Being "eternal" does not mean "without a beginning or an origin." "Eternal" simply means forever. Jesus will live endlessly, like his Father, but he has a beginning, whereas God does not.

Jesus is God's only *begotten* Son. Do you not agree that anything that is begotten has a start that begins after its parent? So when Jesus is begotten, he has a beginning that begins after God's beginning. God is the beginning Himself, meaning that He has no beginning, so how could Jesus and God be co-eternal in the sense that they have the same origins?

Augustine of Hippo said, "Thy years are one day, and Thy day is not daily, but today; because Thy today yields not to tomorrow, for neither does it follow yesterday. Thy today is eternity; therefore Thou begat the Co-eternal, to whom Thou saidst, 'This day have I begotten Thee.'"

Is this how the Bible explains it? No, God's Word states that our one thousand years is a day to God. It also informs us that He took six days to create our world and rested on the seventh. Hence, God notes the passage of time—a different time from us, but a time nonetheless. Therefore, all of His creations are younger than He, including His only begotten Son.

Also, let us not forget that Jesus died. God can never die. This is another reason why the Father and the Son do not share the same immortality.

Trinitarians: Since Jesus emptied himself and became a perfect human man, he was inferior to his Father, just as the Athanasian Creed says: "Equal to the Father, as touching His godhead; and inferior to the Father, as touching His manhood." This was why Jesus prayed to the Father, and why Jesus did not know the day and hour of the end of our current system of things. And this was how Jesus could die and be tested by Satan.

My dispute: Does this mean that if the Father chooses to become a human man Himself, He would lose His powers as God Almighty? Even if He became a human, how could He ever possibly not know, or forget, specific information, such as the day and hour of the end of our world? To say that Jesus could lose such powers as God Almighty means he is not God Almighty! Jehovah's powers will never be limited. No matter what form Jehovah is in, and no matter where He is, He will always be all-powerful and all-knowing. If He turns Himself into a squeaky mouse, He will still be all-knowing; if He turns Himself into a tiny bacterium, He will still be all-powerful — He will still know everything, including when the last day will arrive. How could He possibly lose power or be less knowing if He becomes a human? To say Jesus is God Almighty and that he lost power because he was a human is nothing but insulting to Jehovah!

Even if Jesus did somehow lose godly powers and forgot the time of the last day, he would have told people about it. He would not simply have said that only the Father knows the day and hour of the last day. Would Jesus have given us the false impression that he was not God if he was indeed God? Could he act so deceptively?

If they call Jesus God Almighty, they are saying that God Almighty died and was tested by evil. Let me repeat: God cannot die, and God cannot be tested by evil; not God Almighty—not one hundred percent of Him, not fifty percent of Him, not one percent of Him. If Jesus, one part of God Almighty, was able to die and be tested by evil, he is not God Almighty, who is eternal and immortal and cannot be tempted by evil.

What if Jesus, being God with limited abilities as a real human, failed one of the tests from Satan? Would that mean that God Almighty was overcome by Satan?

Lastly, would it not be rather silly and ridiculous for Jesus to pray to God if he were God?

Trinitarians: Jesus is God Almighty because he is glorious, for the Bible says, "Worthy is the Lamb that hath been slain to receive the power, and riches, and wisdom, and might and honor, and glory, and blessing." (Revelation 5:12)

My dispute: John 7:39 says "Jesus was not yet glorified" prior to his death and resurrection. He was glorified by God only after he was resurrected: "God highly exalted him, and gave unto him the name which is above every name..." (Philippians 2:9) So Jesus *received* glory from his Father. Jesus *earned* his glory. On the other hand, Jehovah God Almighty was glorious from the very beginning; He has never *earned* His glory—He does not need to, ever. Therefore, no one is exactly like Him, for He is the only Being who is glorious from the beginning, unlike Jesus, who was *glorified*. Hence, Jesus is not God Almighty, for only God Almighty is glorious from the start. Just because Jesus *earned* glory does not make him God Almighty. Moreover, Jesus' glory is different from that of Jehovah, whose glory no one can possibly match one hundred percent.

But I must add here that the specific glory Jesus earned is for our benefit, and, above all, is to glorify God; he indeed was glorious prior to his coming on Earth—his Father glorified him long ago, for God loved him before the foundation of the world. So Jesus is not God Almighty, for Jehovah Himself does not need to be glorified again for our sake.

Trinitarians: When Jesus was a man, he was called Son of Man, so that made him one hundred percent man. Jesus is also called Son of God; would that not therefore make him one hundred percent God?

My dispute: There is one major flaw in this argument. Being one hundred percent God would make Jesus into another God Almighty. Just because Jesus was as one hundred percent human as all of us does not mean that we could call him Abraham, David, or Jeremiah.

Trinitarians: Here, Jesus is said to be the image of God and the firstborn of all creation, so he must be God: "…who is the image of the invisible God, the firstborn of all creation; for in him were all things created, in the heavens and upon the earth…" (Colossians 1:15-16)

My dispute: I will show you, step by step, that the passage in question actually disproves the theory that Jesus is God. Let us examine the following verses in Colossians 1, and I will dissect each verse's meaning with you.

> Verse 15: ...who is the image of the invisible God, the firstborn of all creation;
> 16: for in him were all things created, in the heavens and upon the earth, things visible and things invisible, whether thrones or dominions or principalities or powers; all things have been created through him, and unto him;
> 17: and he is before all things, and in him all things consist.
> 18: And he is the head of the body, the church: who is the beginning, the firstborn from the dead; that in all things he might have the preeminence.

The first part of verse fifteen tells us that Jesus is like the invisible God, exhibiting the same spiritual traits of Jehovah. Note that Jesus is the *image* of God, not that he *is* God. An image is a reflection or representation of someone or something, not the original. God is love, God is the image of love; does that mean love is God? Even we mere mortal beings are created in God's image; do not tell me that because of this, we are all God! The Bible also informs us that whom God foreknew, He "also foreordained to be conformed to the image of his Son, that he might be the firstborn among many brethren." (Romans 8:29) Does that mean Christians are Jesus just because God has chosen that they conform to the image of His Son?

Verse fifteen further indicates that Jesus is the

first and the most distinct of Jehovah's creations. This is supported by both Revelation 3:14: "...the faithful and true witness, the beginning of the creation of God" and Hebrews 1:6: "And when he again bringeth in the firstborn into the world he saith, And let all the angels of God worship him." Note that this Hebrews verse indicates that Jehovah *brought* Jesus into the world.

"Firstborn" has two meanings in the Bible: 1) the first one to be born, and 2) the most important or preeminent. Let us substitute both meanings into the segment "firstborn of all creation."

The first one born of all creation (all creation's first one to be born).

The preeminent of all creation (all creation's preeminent).

If both meanings hold true, it means that Jesus is Jehovah's first creation, and His most important creation.

This verse could not be about God Almighty because Jehovah is not the first one born—He has existed from the very start; He was not born or created. Since He was not created, He is outside of creation, and cannot be the preeminent of all creation.

Trinitarians will then argue that if the apostle Paul really meant that Jesus was created, he would have used a better Greek word for "firstborn." I counter this by using Isaiah 7:14 as an example. Isaiah used a word that means both "virgin" and "young woman," who does not necessarily have to be a virgin. If Isaiah 7:14 really refers to a virgin birth, one that does not involve sexual intercourse, Isaiah should have used a word that only means "virgin."

But most Christians, including Trinitarians, believe that Isaiah 7:14 means "virgin." So why do Trinitarians accept an ambiguous word for "virgin" in Isaiah 7:14 but cannot accept an ambiguous word for "firstborn" in Colossians 1:15? One cannot pick and choose to one's own liking.

How did the Trinitarians arrive at the conclusion that "firstborn of all creation" means "creator of all creation"? Would they say that "the firstborn of the flock" means "the creator of the flock"? I would assume not. You cannot change a word (firstborn) into another word with a completely different meaning (creator) in order to fit your doctrine.

Verses sixteen and seventeen inform us that Jesus is indeed a creator of all things. But how can Jesus be the creator of everything when we know Jehovah is the only Creator? If you read Genesis, you will see that Jehovah said: "Let us create man in our image..." What does it mean? It means that Jehovah had a partner or an agent in creating humans. When Jehovah and Jesus share a complete spiritual oneness, they are one. Of course, God does not need to have a partner. But can He have the freedom and desire to choose to exchange ideas and talk about His plans with His special Son? Who else would be great enough to be His partner other than the one He has specially created?

God often executes His plans and works through agents, such as the time He brought Israel out of Egypt through Moses, so it should not be considered out of the ordinary that He used an agent—Jesus—in creation.

How often have you used "let us" in a group situation without actually referring to absolutely everyone? Often, when we use "let us," such as in "let us work on this project," we are not instructing everyone to perform the same work. One person may be the brainstormer, one can take notes, one can get the necessary materials, while many may do the actual labor; still others may end up not participating at all. Jehovah was most likely the Mastermind behind every creation and Jesus might have only assisted his Father.

In John 1:1, it says: "In the beginning was the Word and the Word was with God..." Jesus is known as the Word because he is Jehovah's chief Spokesperson. As you can see, Jesus has been with God from the beginning of creation, so Jesus can create everything else alongside his Father. This is supported in Hebrews 1:2: "...Son, whom he appointed heir of all things, through whom also he made the worlds." Note the word "through." The world was created *through* Jesus, not *by* Jesus. Hence, this further indicates that Jesus acted more like a partner or a tool than the actual Creator of the world, just like the computer on which I am typing this book. My book is written by me, through my computer. Yes, I am aware of the fact that some translations use "by" instead of "through," and that can be correct, too, and does not contradict any teaching in the Bible.

But here, Trinitarians will protest, "How could Jesus be a creation when he is the creator of 'all things'?" Do Trinitarians not understand that "all other things" is implied in this sentence? If they pick on this wording, then what do they say about "Jehovah is greater than all gods" in Exodus 18:11? Clearly, "all gods" excludes Jehovah; likewise, "all things" excludes Jesus.

Lastly, verse eighteen says that because Jesus was the first one to rise from the dead as an immortal being, he has received the highest status or importance among all things. Jesus was glorified after his resurrection. If this verse does refer to God Almighty, why would God have needed to be the firstborn of the resurrected in order to receive preeminence? God Almighty has been preeminent from the start—He does not need to prove to us or to do something (especially not die!) in order to seek glory from anyone!

In conclusion, the Bible passage we just studied refers to Jesus only, not Jehovah, because "firstborn" cannot possibly describe Jehovah—He is not a creation of any kind. When you read verse fifteen and sixteen as one sentence, you can see that Jesus is Jehovah's first and most important creation and also His Partner in creating all creations. Simply put, the entire section definitively refutes the doctrine of the Trinity.

Trinitarians: Jesus was not created, but existed from the very beginning as God Almighty, as the Athanasian Creed states: "The Son is of the Father alone; not made nor created, but begotten."

My dispute: If Jesus is not created, then how is he the "begotten" Son of Jehovah? Something that is begotten is created. Mothers beget their children by creating them in their wombs and giving birth to them. Even if Jehovah literally gave birth to Jesus, Jesus would still be created or made.

What if Jesus begets a son? Would his son be called Almighty God?

A "son" always proceeds from the parent. If Jesus has existed with Jehovah from the very beginning as the Trinitarians claim, then why is "Son" used to describe Jesus? Would "Twin Brother" not be much more suitable?

Trinitarians: The Athanasian Creed has, "And in the Trinity...none is greater or less than another, but all three Persons are co-eternal together and co-equal."

My dispute: Why did Jesus say that his Father is greater than he? Even if Jesus became less than the Father after emptying himself, he would have said so, instead of leaving the impression that his statement would remain true indefinitely.

Trinitarians: This sentence proves that Jesus could not be Jehovah's partner in creation: "I am Jehovah, that maketh all things; that stretcheth forth the heavens alone; that spreadeth abroad the earth (who is with me?)..." (Isaiah 44:24)

My dispute: The Bible tells us that Jehovah alone led Jacob (Israel): "Jehovah alone did lead him, And there was no foreign god with him." (Deuteronomy 32:12) Yet, we know that Jehovah used Moses to lead the nation out of Egypt. Jehovah was "alone" in the sense that He was the Director, the Boss, and He had no equal—and still does not and never will. When you study Isaiah 44:24 and Deuteronomy 32:12 in context, you can see that this is the intended meaning—Jehovah was alone, as the one and only true God, without any match, in both situations. In the same way, Adam was described to be "alone" before God made Eve. Was Adam really alone? No, God was with Him, as well as the animals, and let us not forget the angels. Adam was "alone" because he was the only human being.

When Jehovah created the world, He was truly alone, even though His angels witnessed and rejoiced over His creations. He alone created the world by Jesus, just as He alone led Israel "by the hand of Moses and Aaron." (Psalm 77:20)

One last example: King Solomon was the one who built God's temple. Did he do the construction alone? No, he hired workers for the job, but he was credited to be the builder because he directed the work.

Trinitarians: John 1:1 indicates that Jesus is God Almighty: "In the beginning was the Word, and the Word was with God and the Word was God."

My dispute: Back during Jesus' days, the Greek word for god simply meant Powerful One (any mention of "god" in the old manuscripts is capitalized—false gods and the only true God were written the same way). Any high-ranking or powerful human could be called god. Even Satan was called the god of the world. Therefore, Jesus is God in this sense; this was why Jesus allowed his disciple Thomas to exclaim, "My God!" Still, Jehovah is the one and only true God.

There are other literal translations that have: "the Word was a God," meaning that Jesus is godly, but not God Almighty himself. Since I am not literate in Greek, I cannot examine the syntax and determine how the phrase should be translated. I have read arguments from both Trinitarians and anti-Trinitarians, and I cannot say who is correct when I cannot study Greek myself. However, the Bible as a whole supports that Jehovah is the one and only God Almighty, where as Jesus is his Son, therefore inferior to Him as long as God lives. Thus, I believe the translations that render "Word was a God" or "Word was divine" are most accurate.

Trinitarians: The following Bible passages prove that our doctrine is supported.

John 5:18: "For this cause therefore the Jews sought the more to kill him, because he not only brake the sabbath, but also called God his own Father, making himself equal with God."

John 10:33: "The Jews answered him, For a good work we stone thee not, but for blasphemy; and because that thou, being a man, makest thyself God."

My dispute: Are Trinitarians who use these two "proof" texts blind? Do they not see Jesus' sharp rebuttal immediately following the Jews' accusation and false assumption?

Study Jesus' responses:

John 5:19-23: "Jesus therefore answered and

said unto them, Verily, verily, I say unto you, The Son can do nothing of himself, but what he seeth the Father doing: for what things soever he doeth, these the Son also doeth in like manner. For the Father loveth the Son, and showeth him all things that himself doeth: and greater works than these will he show him, that ye may marvel. For as the Father raiseth the dead and giveth them life, even so the Son also giveth life to whom he will. For neither doth the Father judge any man, but he hath given all judgment unto the Son; that all may honor the Son, even as they honor the Father. He that honoreth not the Son honoreth not the Father that sent him."

If Jesus and God were co-equal as the Trinitarians claim, then why did Jesus say that he cannot do anything on his own but only follows what his Father does?

Jehovah and Jesus are like a commander and a soldier. In a battlefield, soldiers act only when they are given a command telling them what to do; they follow their commander's lead. Even though both the commander and the soldiers may end up doing the same thing, that does not make them equal. When one has to take orders from another, that one is not equal to the commander, unless that person becomes a commander himself.

Also, does equality prove exact substance or entity? Judah said to Joseph: "…though you are equal to Pharaoh himself." (Genesis 44:18, New International Version) Does it mean that Joseph is Pharaoh? Just because two people are "equal" does not mean they are the same being. People all over the world are fighting for equality—are we fighting to be the same person?

John 10:34-38: "Jesus answered them, Is it not written in your law, I said, ye are gods? If he called them gods, unto whom the word of God came (and the scripture cannot be broken), say ye of him, whom the Father sanctified and sent into the world, Thou blasphemest; because I said, I am the Son of God? If I do not the works of my Father, believe me not. But if I do them, though ye believe not me, believe the works: that ye may know and understand that the Father is in me, and I in the Father."

Trinitarians: John 10:38 proves that Jesus still supported the doctrine. What Jesus said was: "...the Father is in me, and I in the Father."

My dispute: Jesus said "Ye shall know that I am in my Father, and ye in me, and I in you" to his disciples. (John 14:20) Does that make his disciples one God Almighty?

If Trinitarians claim that Jesus supports their doctrine, then they are really calling all of us God Almighty!

The apostle Paul wrote, "Now he that planteth and he that watereth are one: but each shall receive his own reward according to his own labor." (I Corinthians 3) Here, Paul spoke of oneness in spirit, not literal physical unity. When we work together in harmony, when we have a common purpose, we become one.

Some of the earliest Christians described in the book of Acts were also one: "And the multitude of them that believed were of one heart and soul..."

(Acts 4:32) All Christians should be one with God—one with Him spiritually—but it does not make us all one God Almighty!

Trinitarians: Jesus' other name is "Jehovah."

My dispute: Regarding His name, Jehovah specifically said, "This is my name forever, and this is my memorial unto all generations." (Exodus 3:15) Did Jehovah ever say that His other name is "Jesus"? Did Jesus ever say that his name is "Jehovah"? If both answers are "No," then we should not name Them whatever we *think* They are named. Certainly, I would not want others to call me "Samantha" when my birth certificate indicates otherwise! Since the Bible is inspired by God, it should be the one and only authority on Jehovah, His divine name, and His characteristics.

Jehovah is an ultra-loving Parent, more loving than the best human parents on Earth. Would this Father with His enormous love let His little children guess about something as critical and basic as His own name? Would He leave us wondering who "Jesus" is and who "Jehovah" is, and whether they are one and the same? If He had, how would His children know whom they could call on during dark nights, and whom to thank during sunny days?

One of parents' first responsibilities is to teach their children their names. They would not leave their children thinking, "What's mommy's name? What's daddy's name? Are both of them called Philip?" Fulfilling a fundamental duty of parenthood, Jehovah has clearly made His name known to us, not only once or twice, but nearly *seven thousand* times. He has also revealed His Son's name to us: Jesus. Is there anything baffling in the way God's Word presents their names? No, it openly and plainly presents both names. So how could any of us confuse their names, and call Jesus "Jehovah" and vice versa? We have absolutely no excuse! If Jehovah's other name is Jesus, would He have not said so? We all should know the answer.

Quite frequently, Jesus began his statements with, "I tell you the truth," or something of a similar nature, depending on which Bible version we use. God never lies, and when Jesus is the image of God, it means Jesus never lies, either, and will always tell the truth, as he often stated. If Jesus were Jehovah, would he not have said so? We should know the answer to this as well.

A donkey and a horse are two different animals, so they have two different names. When a male donkey and a female horse mate, they beget a mule. A mule is a different animal from its parents, so it has a different name. The Father and the Son are two different Persons, as the Trinitarians agree, so do they not deserve two different names? And when they become one in the Trinity as described by Trinitarians, should the resulting one God have a different name apart from the second Person in the Godhead? The Father, the Son, and the combining God all cannot have the same name.

Jehovah is the name of the Father, God Almighty, and Jesus is the name of God's Son. What can be simpler?

"Whosoever shall call on the name of Jehovah

shall be delivered." (Joel 2:32) Yes, knowing who is who is vital to our salvation—we need to call on the right name to be saved. On the great day of Jehovah, will people still stubbornly refuse to acknowledge God's personal name?

Trinitarians: This talks about two Jehovahs: "Then Jehovah rained upon Sodom and upon Gomorrah brimstone and fire from Jehovah out of heaven." (Genesis 19:24)

My dispute: No, it does not. "Then Jehovah rained upon Sodom and upon Gomorrah brimstone and fire" refers to Jehovah doing the action, and "from Jehovah out of heaven" simply emphasizes that fact and further tells us from where Jehovah rained brimstone and fire upon the cities. The New International Version clearly illustrates this point: "Then the LORD rained down burning sulfur on Sodom and Gomorrah—from the LORD out of the heavens."
Study Genesis 18:19: "For I have known him, to the end that he may command his children and his household after him, that they may keep the way of Jehovah, to do righteousness and justice; to the end that Jehovah may bring upon Abraham that which he hath spoken of him." As in many other verses, Jehovah here partially spoke in third person, calling Himself by name. He also emphasized whom He was talking about by mentioning Abraham's name in the second half of the verse. Do we have two Jehovahs and two Abrahams here?

Trinitarians: In the Old Testament, God indicated that He will come on the day of Jehovah. But in the New Testament, we see that Jesus is the one who will come on that day. Therefore, Jesus is God.

My dispute: The Old Testament says, "Behold, I will send you Elijah the prophet before the great and terrible day of Jehovah come." (Malachi 4:5) But in the New Testament, we learn that Jesus indicated that it was John the Baptist who has already come before the day of Jehovah: "Elijah indeed cometh, and shall restore all things: but I say into you, that Elijah is come already, and they knew him not, but did unto him whatsoever they would. Even so shall the Son of man also suffer of them. Then understood the disciples that he spake unto them of John the Baptist." (Matthew 17:11-13) Therefore, according to Trinitarian logic, John is literally Elijah.

Jehovah is the Director and Supervisor of the events on His great day. As on many other occasions, He has appointed an agent to fulfill the mission; and this time, for the most important period in our lives, this agent is His own Son. Jehovah Himself will be present to oversee Jesus' work throughout the day, I am sure.

Trinitarians: Jesus *is* Jehovah, for the Bible says, "This is his name whereby he shall be called: Jehovah our righteousness." (Jeremiah 23:6)

My dispute: Then Jerusalem is also Jehovah, for the Bible says, "Jerusalem shall dwell safely; and this is the name whereby she shall be called: Jehovah our righteousness." (Jeremiah 33:16)

Trinitarians: Revelation 7:17 tells us that the Lamb, Jesus Christ, "is in the midst of the throne" in heaven, so he must be God.

My dispute: Jesus said, "He that overcometh, I will give to him to sit down with me in my throne, as I also overcame, and sat down with my Father in his throne." (Revelation 3:21) The one who will endure to the end for Jesus will sit down on Jesus' throne, just as Jesus sat down on his Father's throne; will that make the faithful person Jesus just because he will sit on the Christ's throne?

Apparently, along with entrusting His entire Kingdom to His Son, Jehovah is also sharing His throne with Jesus. This is more evident in Revelation 22:1, which describes the throne as "the throne of God and of the Lamb." But God's kingship will last forever and ever, and "his servants shall serve him; and they shall see his face; and his name shall be on their foreheads." (Revelation 22:3-4) Amen!

Trinitarians: Jesus is greater than Moses because he is the builder of the house, whereas Moses was the house. God is the builder of everything, so Jesus is God.

My dispute: God is the builder of everything, and we are the builders of our houses: "For every house is builded by some one; but he that built all things is God." (Hebrews 3:4) So does that mean we are God?

God exercises His will as the Builder of all things in mainly two ways: 1) He created us—if He had not created us, we would not have had the opportunity to build our houses. 2) He allows us to build our houses—all activities occur under God's permissive will.

Trinitarians: Both God and Jesus are called Lord, Savior, King of kings, Lord of lords, "the First and the Last," among other titles, so Jesus must be God.

My dispute: King Artaxerxes is called king of kings in the Bible. (Ezra 7:12) God Himself called King Nebuchadnezzar "king of kings." (Ezekiel 26:7) Are these two kings God Almighty?

Many people share the titles "Lord" and "Savior," including Lord Byron, one of my mother's favorite poets. No one has the title "God Almighty" but Jehovah alone. He is our Almighty King of kings, our ultimate Savior, and highest Lord above all lords: "I, even I, am Jehovah; and besides me there is no saviour." (Isaiah 43:11)

Trinitarians: This proves that Jesus is God: "Have this mind in you, which was also in Christ Jesus: who, existing in the form of God, counted not the being on an equality with God a thing to be grasped, but emptied himself, taking the form of a servant…" (Philippians 2:5-7)

My dispute: Does it *really*? As a matter of fact,

this passage *disproves* that Jesus is God. Ask yourself this: if Jesus were God, would he need to *grasp* at equality with God? Would you need to *grasp* at equality with yourself?

Second, if Jesus were God, why did the apostle Paul need to use "in the form of God"? Someone in "the form of" someone else is not that person. Is there any verse in the Bible that says Jehovah is "in the form of God"? The actual person never has to be in "the form of" himself. Would I need to say "I'm in the form of Shirley Cheng" to describe myself? Only a reflection, a representation, an impostor is in "the form of." For example, God was in a pillar of cloud as He guided the Israelites, but it does not mean that God was actually a real cloud. We cannot say, "Oh, that's God!" whenever we see a cloud in the sky. If anyone tells you, "She is coming in the form of Shirley Cheng," watch out—that will not be me!

If Jesus and Jehovah are the same God Almighty, then why is Jesus described throughout the Bible as "the form of," "the nature of," and "the imprint of" God? Never do we see Jehovah being described as "the form of," "the nature of," or "the imprint of" God. If they were one and the same, then the same descriptions would be applied to both of them: Jesus exists in the form of God, and Jehovah exists in the form of God.

If Jesus is God, such "in the form of" descriptions are unnecessary. We are humans; it is rather silly to say we are in the form of humans, unless we were originally nonhumans.

If Jesus were God, Paul would have used "existing as God," not "existing in the form of God."

If Paul did not say that Jesus *is* God, we should not, either.

Note that Jesus took the form of a servant. In other words, he became a servant in nature, just as he is an image of God.

Another major flaw exists in the way Trinitarians understand this Bible passage. When they say that Jesus is God Almighty just because he existed in the form of God, they are really saying that Jesus existed in three Persons! Let us just say, if you were in the form of a cloud, would you not have the key characteristics of a cloud? Yes, you would: you would be puffy, cotton-like, and able to float above Earth. What is the fundamental characteristic of God? According to Trinitarians, He exists as three Persons in one. Therefore, based on this belief, to be in the form of God, one has to be three Persons in one. Trinitarians cannot claim that God is made of three Persons while at the same time that Jesus, even though in the form of God, only consists of one Person. If Paul wrote that Jesus existed as *a part of* God, then the doctrine of the Trinity would work out. But since Paul said that Jesus was in the form of God, Trinitarians have some explaining to do, for we all know that Jesus is only one Person.

We should apply this logic to other similar descriptions, like "in the image of" and "the nature of." For example, each human individual is only one person, even though we are all created in the image of God. As I wrote previously for another argument, an image is a replica of the original. So when Trinitarians say that Jesus is God just because he is the image of the invisible God, as stated in Colossians

1:15, they are actually saying that Jesus is made of three Persons. We are made in the image of God, so where are the other two persons?

Some Trinitarians go so far as to claim that we indeed are Trinities ourselves. Each of us has a body, a soul, and a spirit, so they say that these components compose the Trinity. Let me ask you: without the spirit, would your body still be a person? Without your body, could your soul continue to live on as an individual? Without even one element, would you be able to exist as a creature? Does each component have a mind of its own, able to think and reason? No, you are a person only when your body, spirit, and soul are together in one package. Then and only then can you function as a human being. Later in this book, you will learn more about the three components of yourself, and you will be able to conclusively determine that you are definitely not a Trinity of any kind.

Trinitarians: God in fullness dwells in Jesus, making Jesus God: "For it was the good pleasure of the Father that in him should all the fulness dwell." (Colossians 1:19)

My dispute: We, in our entirety or fullness, live in houses; does that make our houses us? When the Holy Spirit dwells in Christians, does that mean Christians are literally the Holy Spirit? Just because God lives in Jesus does not make Jesus God. That verse is just one of numerous Scriptures that refer to the God-Jesus spiritual unity.

Trinitarians: The Jews wanted to stone Jesus because he claimed to be God by saying, "Verily, verily, I say unto you, Before Abraham was born, I am." (John 8:58)

My dispute: Did Jesus really claim to be God? Before I prove Trinitarians wrong, *again*, let us carefully study Exodus 3, which tells of the summoning of Moses by Jehovah to deliver His people from slavery.

> Verse 13: And Moses said unto God, Behold, when I come unto the children of Israel, and shall say unto them, The God of your fathers hath sent me unto you; and they shall say to me, What is his name? What shall I say unto them?
> 14: And God said unto Moses, I AM THAT I AM: and he said, Thus shalt thou say unto the children of Israel, I AM hath sent me unto you.
> 15: And God said moreover unto Moses, Thus shalt thou say unto the children of Israel, Jehovah, the God of your fathers, the God of Abraham, the God of Isaac, and the God of Jacob, hath sent me unto you: this is my name forever, and this is my memorial unto all generations.

Many names throughout the history of humankind have specific meanings, especially during Biblical times, and people often give a name to someone, something, or some place, based on their characteristics and qualities. For example, God changed Abram's name to Abraham, which means "father of many," for he was to become the father of many nations. God also changed Abraham's wife's name from Sarai to Sarah, meaning "princess," for "she shall be a mother of nations; kings of peoples shall be of her." (Genesis 17:16)

When Moses asked for God's name, he was actually asking for what His name signifies, not just what His name is. By knowing the meaning of God's name, the Israelites would be able to understand God's nature and receive confirmation of the deliverance He promised. So God answered Moses in two ways: "I am" and "Jehovah."

"I am" is the nature of God; it has meaning as "He chooses to become," or "He who causes to be," which is what "Jehovah" means. "I am" is His unique characteristics, whereas "Jehovah" is His actual name.

The New International Version has a footnote that says, "Or I will be what I will be" for "I AM THAT I AM." Similarly, other Bible translations have:

• "I AM WHO I AM and WHAT I AM, and I WILL BE WHAT I WILL BE." (Amplified Bible, translation)

• "I AM WHAT I AM, or I WILL BE WHAT I WILL BE." (English Standard Version, footnote)

• "I am the eternal God. So tell them that the LORD, whose name is " I Am," has sent you," and "LORD: The Hebrew text has " Yahweh," which is usually translated " LORD" in the CEV. Since it seems related to the word translated " I am," it may mean " I am the one who is" or " I will be what I will be" or " I am the one who brings into being." (Contemporary English Version, translation and footnote, respectively)

• "The Hebrew words are like the name "Yahweh." This Hebrew name for God, usually called "LORD," shows that God always lives and is always with his people." (New Century Version, footnote)

• "I AM THAT WHICH I AM." (Young's Literal Translation, translation)

• "Or I AM BECAUSE I AM, or I WILL BE WHO I WILL BE." (Holman Christian Standard Bible, footnote)

Now let us see why Trinitarians say that Jesus claimed to be God. Trinitarians stumble because Jesus used "I am" in his reply to the Jews' question: "Thou art not yet fifty years old, and hast thou seen Abraham?" (John 8:57)

What Jesus meant was that he existed before Abraham was even born, so he had seen Abraham even though the man died a long time ago. The Contemporary English Version has "I tell you for certain that even before Abraham was, I was, and I am." And the New Living Translation has this footnote: "Or before Abraham was even born, I have always been alive; Greek reads before Abraham was, I am."

Jesus was not claiming to be God when he used "I am." He was not even using it as a title or name—he was simply properly answering the Jews' question!

An alarming number of people throughout history have used "I am"! Do not tell me that we all have claimed to be God. Even the wicked city, Nineveh, is said to say, "I am, and there is none besides me." (Zephaniah 2:15) Babylon said the same thing: "I am, and there is none else besides me." (Isaiah 47:10) Can we say that Nineveh and Babylon are both God Almighty just because they said, "I am"?

Just because "I AM" is related to "Jehovah," does not make every instance of "I am" God! Many names, such as Jeremiah, Joshua, and Elijah, include a part of Jehovah's name; it would be outrageous and absurd to say these men were Jehovah!

But wherever Jesus used "I am," as in "I am he," Trinitarians say that Jesus meant that he was God! Please, as a Chinese proverb says: Do not try to find bones in an egg!

If Jesus claimed to be God, would he not have simply said, "I am God Almighty, Jehovah"?

If Jesus could not even use "I am" without giving Trinitarians the wrong notion, then what else could he have possibly used? "I am" is a main, practical way to identify oneself, and it is often the only way. Try having a conversation without using "I am" next time. That ought to be fun, eh?

Trinitarians: If Jesus did not claim to be God, then why did the Jews want to stone him?

My dispute: Why did they want to kill Jesus? Were any of their actions justified? Can we trust those who executed an innocent man? They even called Jesus a sinner because he healed on the sabbath, and accused him of being possessed by demons! Surely, their opinions cannot be taken seriously as Biblical truths! To count on their words and actions will be the same as counting on the devil.

Let us not forget that the Jews had been looking for any chance to kill Jesus for quite some time, even though they knew they could never find a good reason to do so. Once, people in Nazareth even wanted to "throw him down headlong" from "the hill whereon their city was built" only because he told the truth that offended them. (Luke 4:29) So Jesus saying that he had existed before Abraham was born was the last thing from this perfect man they could possibly bear.

Finally, if the Jews truly believe that Jesus used "I am" to indicate that he was God Almighty, they would not have experienced any problem finding witnesses against him to lawfully execute him, especially when Jesus had just said, "I am he" before his capture. Their trouble in finding true witnesses who could agree with one another proved to us that they could not find any fault with him, that he did not claim to be God.

Trinitarians: Only God can forgive sins, so when Jesus can forgive sins as well, it means that he is God.

My dispute: Forgiveness of sins is the sole power of God, but He gives others the authority to forgive sins as He wishes. He gave Jesus "all authority," which includes the authority to forgive sins. In turn, Jesus passed this authority to his own disciples after his resurrection. After giving them the Holy Spirit, he said to them, "Whose soever sins ye forgive, they are forgiven unto them; whose soever sins ye retain, they are retained." (John 20:23)

Trinitarians: Jesus could resurrect himself, so

he must be God: "No one taketh it away from me, but I lay it down of myself. I have power to lay it down, and I have power to take it again. This commandment received I from my Father." (John 10:18)

My dispute: Jesus played a crucial role in his death and resurrection. He was willing to die for us, willing to obey his Father to his very death, so his fate rested in his hands. We all know that God resurrected Jesus, but it was Jesus who fulfilled his mission; if he had not loved God to the end, he would have failed in his mission, thus we would not be saved.

We say that the Jews killed Jesus even though we know as a fact that the Romans physically performed the execution; the Jews played a vital part in Jesus' death, just as Jesus played a huge part in his own resurrection.

What Jesus said is similar to what I often say: we are the artists of our lives. We hold the power to create our destiny. What happens to us tomorrow will be the result of the decisions we make today. But this power and authority we have is from God. Likewise, God gave Jesus the power to lay down his life and take it again. No one can take away that power, except God, who gives any authority to anyone He wishes at any time.

Trinitarians: Verses that talk about God in the Old Testament are quoted in the New Testament to describe Jesus, so it means that Jesus is God indeed. One such occurrence is found in Hebrews 1:10: "In the beginning, O Lord, you laid the foundations of the earth, and the heavens are the work of your hands."

My dispute: Various verses from the Old Testament have been quoted to accommodate situations in the New Testament. When this is done, it does not mean that the same verses in two different passages are talking about the same event or person. For example, "When Israel was a child, then I loved him, and called my son out of Egypt" from Hosea 11:1 is quoted in Matthew 2:15: "…that it might be fulfilled which was spoken by the Lord through the prophet, saying, Out of Egypt did I call my son." As you can see, in Matthew, this verse takes on a different meaning: the reference to Jesus leaving Egypt.

Sometimes, a prophecy or passage in the Old Testament fulfills or refers to two unrelated events, one in the near future or from the past and one that is far more distant. Hence, the verse from Psalm 102:25 transferred to Hebrews 1:10 now describes the upcoming establishment of the new world, which is created by Jesus' sacrifice.

Trinitarians: Only God is to be worshipped, but people also worshipped Jesus and were not rebuked, so Jesus is God.

My dispute: Yes, Jesus was indeed worshipped! Do you know who else were also worshipped without being rebuked? Jehovah's servant Daniel: "Then the king Nebuchadnezzar fell upon his face, and worshipped Daniel, and commanded that they should offer an oblation and sweet odors unto him," (Daniel 2:46) and King David, the man after God's heart: "And all the assembly blessed Jehovah, the God of their fathers, and bowed down their heads, and worshipped Jehovah, and the king." (I Chronicles 29:20)

Do you know what else? Jesus told the faithful servants in the church in Philadelphia: "Behold, I give of the synagogue of Satan, of them that say they are Jews, and they are not, but do lie; behold, I will make them to come and worship before thy feet, and to know that I have loved thee." (Revelation 3:9) Yes, Jesus will make false worshippers worship the righteous!

When King David, Daniel, and faithful servants could be worshipped, why could Jesus not be worshipped as well, especially when he is above them all? Since God is glad to fully live in Jesus, He must desire that His beloved Son be honored as He.

But does worshipping Jesus make him God? No, it does not, just as it does not make David or Daniel God.

However, the worship we have for Jehovah is unique to Him only. We have more than enough Scriptural proofs that show us Jehovah is the only true God, as Jesus says, so only the true God deserves our most special worship from the deepest part of our hearts.

Trinitarians: The Holy Spirit possesses personal characteristics; it can talk and grieve, and is said to be a "him." He must be God.

My dispute: Ladies and gentlemen, I introduce to you Wisdom:

"Doth not wisdom cry? and understanding put forth her voice? She standeth in the top of high places, by the way in the places of the paths. She crieth at the gates, at the entry of the city, at the coming in at the doors. Unto you, O men, I call; and my voice is to the sons of man. O ye simple, understand wisdom: and, ye fools, be ye of an understanding heart. Hear; for I will speak of excellent things; and the opening of my lips shall be right things. For my mouth shall speak truth; and wickedness is an abomination to my lips. All the words of my mouth are in righteousness; there is nothing froward or perverse in them. They are all plain to him that understandeth, and right to them that find knowledge. Receive my instruction, and not silver; and knowledge rather than choice gold. For wisdom is better than rubies; and all the things that may be desired are not to be compared to it. I wisdom dwell with prudence, and find out knowledge of witty inventions." (Proverbs 8:1-12, King James Version)

Enough said. Let those who are friends with Lady Wisdom proclaim the truth!

God uses His Holy Spirit to do absolutely everything. When an angel could make even a donkey talk, described in the book of Numbers, then Jehovah can most certainly make His active power talk as well.

Trinitarians: Isaiah 48:16 proves our Trinity doctrine: "Come ye near unto me, hear ye this; from the beginning I have not spoken in secret; from the time that it was, there am I: and now the Lord Jehovah hath sent me, and his Spirit."

My dispute: Actually, it does not. Let me include the surrounding verses in Isaiah 48 before I explain why this does not prove the doctrine.

> Verse 12: Hearken unto me, O Jacob, and Israel my called: I am he; I am the first, I also am the last.
> 13: Yea, my hand hath laid the foundation of the earth, and my right hand hath spread out the heavens: when I call unto them, they stand up together.
> 14: Assemble yourselves, all ye, and hear; who among them hath declared these things? He whom Jehovah loveth shall perform his pleasure on Babylon, and his arm shall be on the Chaldeans.
> 15: I, even I, have spoken; yea, I have called him; I have brought him, and he shall make his way prosperous.
> 16: Come ye near unto me, hear ye this; from the beginning I have not spoken in secret; from the time that it was, there am I: and now the Lord Jehovah hath sent me, and his Spirit.
> 17: Thus saith Jehovah, thy Redeemer, the Holy One of Israel: I am Jehovah thy God, who teacheth thee to profit, who leadeth thee by the way that thou shouldest go.

At first glance—even after carefully examining the sixteenth verse, as I did—it does seem to prove the Trinity doctrine, does it not? So how did I arrive at my conclusion that it does not? Well, allow me to give you a few facts about the old Hebrew manuscripts first:

- The Hebrew manuscripts contain no vowels.

- There are no spaces between letters.
- Punctuation marks are absent, as well as the division of verses and chapters.

For example, the verse in question may look like this: cmynrntmhryths...

How did translators manage to translate that segment, let alone the entire Bible? I will tell you: the translation process must have been divinely led!

Much of chapter forty-eight in Isaiah is obviously the speech Jehovah gave through the prophet Isaiah, even though there are no quotation marks. If you read a novel that is written in first person point of view, without any quotation marks around any of the characters' speeches, how would you be able to discern what is said by whom? Fortunately, most books nowadays all have the necessary quotation marks to set dialogue apart from narration. However, some versions of the most important book in our history—the Bible—do not have quotation marks. For instance, the American Standard Version, from which I am quoting, does not. Therefore, it appears as though the entire sixteenth verse is God's speech. It gives the impression that God, the Son (Jesus) said, "And now the Lord Jehovah hath sent me, and his Spirit," thus seemingly proving the Trinity.

After the Trinity doctrine has been disproved again and again by the Bible, how could one single verse proclaim Trinity, out of the blue? I knew it could not, so I thought hard about it. Then it dawned on me: the last part of verse sixteen is not a part of what God said. Rather, it is a part of the main narration spoken by the prophet.

American Standard Version is not the best Bible translation to study. I have compared several versions, and found that most have the quotation marks, and many of them have placed the marks in the right places. Yes, it is extremely important to always compare several versions as you study the Bible!

This is how Isaiah 48:14-17 should read:

"Assemble yourselves, all ye, and hear; who among them hath declared these things? He whom Jehovah loveth shall perform his pleasure on Babylon, and his arm shall be on the Chaldeans. I, even I, have spoken; yea, I have called him; I have brought him, and he shall make his way prosperous. Come ye near unto me, hear ye this; from the beginning I have not spoken in secret; from the time that it was, there am I."

And now the Lord Jehovah hath sent me, and his Spirit. Thus saith Jehovah, thy Redeemer, the Holy One of Israel: "I am Jehovah thy God, who teacheth thee to profit, who leadeth thee by the way that thou shouldest go."

Clearer? I thought so. Problem resolved.

One last note about the Bible: We need to be careful about which Bible versions to trust when many have been translated in accordance with certain religious bias. Once in a while, translators even dare add their own words into their translation in order to support their doctrine! For example, I read that one such spurious addition may be 1 John 5:7 in the King James Version: "For there are three that bear record in heaven, the Father, the Word, and the Holy Ghost: and these three are one." Although I cannot verify this claim—I would have to examine every manuscript with my own eyes—I just wanted to bring this up in case this allegation is true. If this is indeed so, I have to ask: if the Bible clearly supported their doctrine, why would Trinitarians have to add anything to it? I suppose that since the Bible does not support the doctrine, they resorted to tampering with the Holy Scriptures, a grave sin! Suspects who tamper with evidence are often proven guilty.

What if the verse is true? Does it prove the Trinity? No, in fact, it does not. We already know that the Father and the Son are one, and that the Holy Spirit is God's active force, so, yes, they are all one. So whether the statement is original or spurious, it will not cause any problem for our understanding of God. If it is true, it would simply affirm God's oneness with His Son; if it is false, then whoever added those words would bring trouble upon their own head.

Trinitarians: The Trinity is a mystery. Who could really understand God fully?

My dispute: So after all their arguments, Trinitarians can only weakly conclude, "It's a mystery"! Simply put, Trinitarians believe in a mystery.

God's identity is not a mystery! Whatever God wants us to know, whatever is necessary, He Has made known to us. He and Jesus have already clearly revealed their identities to us. God clearly said that Jesus is His beloved Son and that we ought to listen to him. What more do you want God to say? Do you want God to literally say, "I am not Jesus, Jesus is not me; we are separate Beings just as you and your parent are"?

Jesus said, "Ask, and it shall be given you; seek, and ye shall find; knock, and it shall be opened unto you: for every one that asketh receiveth; and he that seeketh findeth; and to him that knocketh it shall be opened." (Matthew 7:7-8) If we truly have the heart to know God, He will make Himself known to us. Of course, we, mere creations, cannot fully understand our Creator, but we can at least know the basic fundamental truths about Him, and His Bible clearly supplies all the information we need. If He felt that we needed to know more, God would have provided it. Therefore, whatever is given to us in the Bible is just what He wants us to know. "The secret things belong unto Jehovah our God; but the things that are revealed belong unto us and to our children for ever..." (Deuteronomy 29:29)

Proverbs 30:6 warns us, "Add thou not unto his words, Lest he reprove thee, and thou be found a liar." Has Jehovah told us that Jesus is God, and that They belong in a Trinity? If not, then it is wrong to add anything to His teachings or His identity. If God did not say, "Jesus is Me," then we should not put the words into His mouth. If someone teaches something that Jehovah did not explicitly teach, then I have to question it.

How logical are the Trinitarians' arguments you have read? What does your God-gifted common sense tell you?

My final disputes for you to mull over: If the Bible truly taught the idea of the Trinity, then how come nowhere did it use "God, the Son" or simply "God" but only "Son of God" to describe Jesus? The Bible does not use "God, the Holy Spirit," either.

If Jesus is God, why did Jesus say that all authority has been *given* to him by God? God by His very nature does not need anyone to *give* Him anything, let alone any authority. If you do not have the absolute and total authority from the beginning, you are not God.

If the Holy Spirit is God, why does only the Father know the date of Jesus' second coming? God is all-knowing. To not know even a smallest detail disqualifies anyone from being God.

If Jesus is God, why did Jesus call only his Father "the only true God"? Why is only God "good," but not Jesus himself?

If Jesus is God, why did God call him "my servant"? How could he be the *heir*?

Jesus is the Anointed One: "…Jesus of Nazareth, how God anointed him with the Holy Spirit and with power: who went about doing good, and healing all that were oppressed of the devil; for God was with him." (Acts 10:38) Does the Bible say that God anointed Himself? Would God need to be anointed with the Holy Spirit and power? Does God need to be *with* Himself? How can you be with yourself?

After Jesus' millennium rule, he will return the Kingdom back to his Father so "that God may be all in all." (I Corinthians 15:28) If Jesus were God Almighty, then would everything not *already* be with

God, without Jesus needing to *return* the Kingdom to *God*? Contemporary English Version translates this passage very clearly: "Christ will rule until he puts all his enemies under his power, and the last enemy he destroys will be death. When the Scriptures say that he will put everything under his power, they don't include God. It was God who put everything under the power of Christ. After everything is under the power of God's Son, he will put himself under the power of God, who put everything under his Son's power. Then God will mean everything to everyone." (I Corinthians 15:25-28) How much clearer a distinction between Jesus and God can you possibly need?

And the big question: Why did neither Jehovah, Jesus, the Holy Spirit, nor any of the Bible writers, plainly say that God consists of three Persons? It would be extremely easy to state such an exceptionally important fact if it were true, do you not think so? In fact, the Word of God explicitly tells us, "Jehovah our God is one Jehovah." (Deuteronomy 6:4) Jehovah is one Being, not three Persons in one Being, just as Abraham was "one" before God made him many (good thing Trinitarians do not take this to mean that Abraham himself became "many persons"!). (Isaiah 51:2)

The Deuteronomy verse is the ultimate, concrete revelation of God's identity: one God as one Being and one Person.

Back in Moses' days, the concept of Trinity had long been well established in various pagan religions, so the singular nature of God was stressed. It has been the fundamental truth about God among the

Jews to this date, and should be ours as well. After all, Christianity is not a new religion, and God's nature has not changed since the Old Testament was written, and He will always remain the same. If we were to believe in the Trinity, we would be worshipping a different God, not the God of Abraham, Isaac, and Jacob.

Jehovah: God of Truth

When you read the Bible, it is not hard at all to tell that Jehovah has a remarkably down-to-earth, upfront personality. If He did belong in a Trinity, would He not have referred to it at least once in His Scriptures? His honesty is flawless. He tells us everything we need to know. Our problem lies in the fact that we lack appreciation of God's sacred and holy qualities and values; we do not have the capacity to realize the extent of God's honesty and openness. We instead turn what He says into something that tickles our imagination.

In the Bible, He told us that He was in the pillar of fire that guided Israel during the night and the pillar of cloud that guided them during the day, in the wilderness. He did not hide the fact that He regretted creating humans or crowning Saul as Israel's first king. He wrote about the weaknesses of Biblical heroes, pointed out the clean and the unclean, and told us exactly what He wants from us.

Therefore, when Jehovah said "My Son," He figured that we would take it literally, in its normal sense. Instead, we have managed to distort "Son of God" into "God, the Son." If Jesus were God the Son,

Jehovah would have said, "My Son is a part of me." Would He really cloak something as vital as His identity and make us play guessing games among ourselves only to arrive at the wrong conclusion, especially when He knows of our weaknesses and sinful nature? Most, if not all, of godly principles are stressed repeatedly in the Bible, in multiple books and chapters, far more than just once. So would it be in God's character to not explain His identity even once? The answer is an absolute "No!" Instead, Jehovah repeatedly and clearly identified Himself.

Please, please read what Jehovah said, *carefully* with heart:

"I am Jehovah, and there is none else; besides me there is no God." (Isaiah 45:5)

"...there is none besides me: I am Jehovah, and there is none else." (Isaiah 45:6)

"I am Jehovah; and there is none else." (Isaiah 45:18)

"...there is no God else besides me, a just God and a Saviour; there is none besides me." (Isaiah 45:21)

"Look unto me, and be ye saved, all the ends of the earth; for I am God, and there is none else. By myself have I sworn, the word is gone forth from my mouth in righteousness, and shall not return, that unto me every knee shall bow, every tongue shall swear. Only in Jehovah, it is said of me, is righteousness and strength; even to him shall men come..." (Isaiah 45:22-24)

"To whom will ye like me, and make me equal, and compare me, that we may be like?" (Isaiah 46:5)

"I am God, and there is none else; I am God,

and there is none like me." (Isaiah 46:9)

How much clearer do you want Jehovah to identify Himself? *He* is Jehovah, not *They* are Jehovah. *He* has no equal, not *They* have no equal. He Himself has no equal; there is *no one* like Him. There is *none* else other than Himself. To say that God has *three* Persons, equal to one another, makes Jehovah's statements about Himself null and void. Jehovah said, "I have not spoken in secret, in a place of the land of darkness; I said not unto the seed of Jacob, Seek ye me in vain: I, Jehovah, speak righteousness, I declare things that are right." (Isaiah 45:19) Let us take heed to what this truthful, open, upfront Almighty tells us.

Next, please carefully read what Jesus said about himself: "If God were your Father, ye would love me: for I came forth and am come from God; for neither have I come of myself, but he sent me. Why do ye not understand my speech? Even because ye cannot hear my word. Ye are of your father the devil, and the lusts of your father it is your will to do. He was a murderer from the beginning, and standeth not in the truth, because there is no truth in him. When he speaketh a lie, he speaketh of his own: for he is a liar, and the father thereof. But because I say the truth, ye believe me not. Which of you convicteth me of sin? If I say truth, why do ye not believe me? He that is of God heareth the words of God: for this cause ye hear them not, because ye are not of God." (John 8:42-47) I understand Jesus' speech. How about you?

Furthermore, Jesus said, "I have spoken openly to the world; I ever taught in synagogues, and in the temple, where all the Jews come together; and in secret spake I nothing." (John 18:20) Everything we need to know, he has made known to us.

I know I am repeating myself, but I need to stress this: the very life of our faith is dependent upon knowing God and His Son accurately. If we cannot identify the true God, then how can we properly worship the true God?

I will never say that it would be illogical for God to exist as a Trinity. After all, God is above all and is too awesome for us to comprehend fully, and to put Him on the same level as His creations and understand Him solely in our own human terms is wrong. What I am saying is that if God indeed belongs in a Trinity, then I want to learn it from the Bible, not from man. Since I cannot find the doctrine of the Trinity in the Bible, I must question it as a curious student who desires to know God to the best of her ability. Right now, my faith is in Jehovah God Almighty and Jesus Christ, the Son of God, not God, the Son.

If Trinitarians would call Jesus "Mighty God," their doctrine would work out. But since they call Jesus "Almighty God," their doctrine simply cannot stand. The Bible disproves their doctrine again and again. Do not just take my word for it—read it and see for yourself. Plenty more arguments against the Trinity creed can be established from God's Word.

Trinitarians will then argue: how could Jesus be "Mighty God" when Jehovah said that there is no one like Him?

If you read other parts of the Bible, you will learn that Jehovah calls Himself God Almighty.

Indeed, there is no one like Him—no one could so deservedly be called God Almighty. Just because Jesus is known as Mighty in the book of Isaiah does not make him the one and only true God we should devote ourselves to and worship.

Moreover, as we have already covered, powerful men were called gods in the past. Even Jehovah Himself called Moses God: "And Jehovah said unto Moses, See, I have made thee as God to Pharaoh; and Aaron thy brother shall be thy prophet." (Exodus 7:1) When Jesus is above all men, does he not especially deserve such a title?

So What?

By now, you may be thinking, "What is the big deal? Can we not go on with our lives, believe in God, without knowing the nature of God and Jesus?"

Would you invite strangers you had just met into your house? Would you entrust your keys to them? Would you randomly pick someone from the street to baby sit your child? Would you instantly marry your blind date? If you take care to get to know and develop a relationship with a person prior to trusting that person, would you not take care in knowing God in order to establish a loving relationship with Him?

If I marry, it would be for love only—no more and no less. I do not care if the man is richer than King Solomon or handsomer than King David; if I do not know him intimately, I will not say, "I do." If you want to marry someone for money, fine. You will get what you want (money), but you will not get what you need: love.

If you develop a relationship with Jehovah without knowing Him, how fulfilling or lasting would the relationship really be? How could you completely love Him?

Moreover, receiving salvation and an eternal existence is based on our acceptance of Jesus and an accurate knowledge of his Father: "This is life eternal, that they should know thee the only true God, and him whom thou didst send, even Jesus Christ." (John 17:3) How could we accept the right person if we do not know who he is? If I ask you to deliver a letter to a guy named Mark, would you not want to know his last name and address in order to deliver it to the right Mark? Thus, for the same reason, we need to pinpoint who is the true God and who is our Redeemer. It is not only for our salvation, but most of all to show our fullest gratitude to the right Person.

Salvation is not something we can instigate. Salvation is a beautifully wrapped present given to us freely by God. We do not gain or earn it; all we can do is humbly accept it and gratefully keep it. But we first need to know from whom we are accepting this gift. If you receive a gift with no sender's name or address attached, how would you be able to thank the giver? How would you be able to know the gift's true value without knowing the caliber of the sender? If you receive a gift box containing only two coins, what would you think? Perhaps, "What a cheap gift!"? But what if you found out those coins were given to you by a poor widow? Would you then not feel deeply touched?

Conclusion

To conclude this arduous chapter, I would like to recapitulate the doctrine of the Holy Trinity.

Holy Trinity consists of the Father, the Son, and the Holy Spirit, where the Father is God (God, the Father), the Son is God (God, the Son), and the Holy Spirit is God (God, the Holy Spirit), yet They all point to one God, not three individual Gods. One ultimate description is three Persons, one substance, meaning that each Person has a unique, distinct personality and traits, but all three Persons are of one substance, and one Godhead as a whole. All three Persons co-exist and are co-equal and co-eternal.

I would like you to pretend that we are not talking about God here, but an ordinary human. What would come to mind when this Trinity doctrine applies to a human individual?

Three persons, three personalities, yet one substance, one individual... Yes, it sounds like multiple personality disorder! People who have this disorder exhibit two or more completely different personalities, including different wishes, desires, attitudes, as though two or three people reside within one individual.

When Trinitarians say that Jehovah belongs in a Trinity, they really say God has multiple personality disorder!

What causes Trinitarians to misinterpret the Bible? What could have caused the problem called the Holy Trinity?

The root of their problem lies in the fact that Trinitarians do not have spiritual understanding of the Bible. They do not understand that two different Persons can be one, *spiritually*. This spiritual oneness is what makes them stumble and fall. Why could they not understand that totally different, separate beings could be one spiritually? What do they think about the Bible passage where it says that when a man and a woman become husband and wife, they will be one flesh? Certainly, they do not think that a married couple would literally become one body!

However, some say that when the Bible mentions a married couple's oneness, it is primarily referring to their physical unity during intimacy, not the spiritual aspect. If this is the case, then does it mean that the pair is not considered as one during much of their marriage? Flies, cats, and dogs all can share this oneness during mating, so would these pairs of creatures not be one flesh as well? Accepting intimacy as the primary reference to the "one flesh" concept would also make this oneness less unique to a couple, for prostitutes experience this kind of physical oneness with their clients more often than most married people. If everyone can effortlessly achieve such oneness just by having sexual relations, the Bible would not have emphasized the significance of such a union. Uniting physically can be quite easily done, but uniting spiritually takes a deep, heart-to-heart connection.

Can we achieve ultimate oneness without the physical intimacy? All Christians are said to be one body. Do not tell me they have to be in an orgy to be one! Hence, any Biblical reference to oneness primarily implies spiritual harmony.

Of course, physical oneness is also beautiful

and special when in a God-approved relationship, but it is not the primary importance of marriage. A married couple does not need to have sex in order to be one flesh, and having sex without love does not make them one. It is love that binds two into one.

If Trinitarians cannot grasp this most basic yet vital concept of spiritual oneness, how could they understand the rest of the Bible upon which spirituality lives?

As imperfect humans, we cannot achieve total and all-encompassing spiritual oneness. Perhaps this is why Trinitarians cannot understand the extent of the seamless and perfect spiritual unity Jehovah and Jesus share. They show their love for each other in astounding deeds, not just in speech, though their words are abundantly filled with their love; take, for example, the heartfelt prayer of Jesus in John 17. This Father-Son team is the epitome of true unconditional love, and is the most wonderful example after which we should model ourselves. Granted, most of us can never achieve such oneness in our current state. When Jehovah's Kingdom comes, I believe it will be quite possible for many to accomplish such a seemingly impossible feat. But we have to start loving now, and the best place to do so is in loving Almighty Jehovah and His Mighty Son.

The Holy Bible
Its Invaluable Teachings

"Every scripture inspired of God is also profitable for teaching, for reproof, for correction, for instruction which is in righteousness. That the man of God may be complete, furnished completely unto every good work." (II Timothy 3:16-17)

All-Time Best Seller of Infinite Wisdom & Love

"Finally, brethren, whatsoever things are true, whatsoever things are honorable, whatsoever things are just, whatsoever things are pure, whatsoever things are lovely, whatsoever things are of good report; if there be any virtue, and if there be any praise, think on these things." (Philippians 4:8)

What book was most influential in your life? When I was asked this, many of the two thousand titles I have ever read swam through my head at lightning speed, yet my heart instantly singled out one among them. It is an all-time runaway international best seller, translated into over two thousand four hundred languages. Not a single book has ever come close to matching the number of copies sold or freely distributed, nor has any book ever been as studied, discussed, assimilated, criticized, loved, or hated. No wonder, for I know it is a masterpiece that has not only greatly influenced my life but is the cornerstone of every person—past, present, and future.

The book is like a history textbook; when

studied with faith and reasoning, it will guide us in making the right choices today to positively affect our futures. Each nonfictional character depicted in its pages is significant, no matter how small or how major the role each plays, and by studying their life stories, we can apply the same principles that helped them climb high mountains, or avoid the same temptations that brought them to their ruin.

From the story of a man sacrificing his own life to save the lives of sinners, I discovered what unconditional love is all about. From the tale of a mere shepherd boy defeating a giant with only a stone and a sling, I learned what great miracles faith can perform. Between its covers, I have also learned how to remain hopeful when all around me seems hopeless; I have learned how to love strangers as my own family members; I have learned how to overcome challenges with the powers with which I am gifted; and above all, I have learned how to return the unconditional love I have been blessed with from the day I was an embryo. Hence, the course of my life has been solely dependent on absorbing its knowledge, and it has led me to a life filled with immeasurable happiness, love, peace, and hope.

Reading, as you can see, has changed my life in every sense of the word. For without the knowledge of words, how could I personally read, study, and apply the infinite wisdom found in this best seller? How could I have known of the existence of the wondrous treasures that hunger to be found and cherished? How could I have made a lasting, positive impact on my life? And how could I have acquired the ability to spread the good news to those around me, good news that can potentially bring them everlasting happiness and fulfillment?

Of course, being merely a human, I cannot understand the book on my own; I need help to apply its invaluable teachings in my daily living, in how I conduct myself. And I have no fear of never finding the right teacher, for I am sure to find the greatest and most perfect teacher to guide me: the Author of the book Himself.

Thus, I thank Jehovah God for giving me the highest privilege of reading His most wonderful book, the Bible. I pray for understanding of His Word; I pray for a loving heart; I pray for faith that will assist me in enduring the greatest tribulations; and most importantly, I pray that His sacred name be known among all and glorified for eternity. I pray for worldly knowledge of His Holy Word, that it be taken in as food to feed our spiritual needs, so all His fantastic creations can enjoy His fulfilled purpose, forever and a day. Jehovah is our divine beacon of light and life, and having Him as our King, we shall never be in want. Amen.

The Ultimate Life's Manual

"The fear of Jehovah is the beginning of wisdom; A good understanding have all they that do his commandments..." (Psalm 111:10)

How can we tell right from wrong? Where can we be guided to the straight path to eternal salvation? How can we show our love for God? How can we show our works for our faith? Making decisions can be tough, especially nowadays, when society has promoted individual decisions, saying that there is actually no right or wrong—it is all a matter of personal choice. But is that so? Can we really thrive by doing whatever we want? As we have clearly seen, the answer is no. Countless times, history has proven that human decisions lead to destructive consequences of varying severity. History also shows that people live better under a well-organized government or rulership, where its guidance is from the Divine Source, Jehovah.

In Biblical times, Jehovah intervened to help those who loved Him, to steer them onto the right path, and to prevent or stop plots devised by those who did not fear Him. He guided good kings by either speaking to them personally or sending them messages through His prophets. How wonderful must it have been, to have one-on-one contact with Jehovah! How much would we give now to have such a privilege? But even though we do not have such personal contact with God, He is still guiding any of us who desire to be guided. How? Through His Holy Scriptures, which the Wise Author had written to aid us.

"But was the Bible not written by men?" you ask. Yes, the Bible was physically penned by humans, but it is completely inspired by God, so He is its actual Author. Since all sixty-six books of the Bible have only one Author, the Scriptures are consistent in content and theme throughout, without contradictions. After reading seven versions of this holy book, I find that any "contradictions" cannot withstand real scrutiny. Therefore, we can fully trust in its messages and its ability to deliver us from evil—if we choose to carefully study its infinite wisdom and teachings with our whole hearts, souls, and minds. This means that we must have the desire to study it, think over what we learn with faith and reasoning, and, most importantly, apply what we learn daily.

Although the Bible is thousands of years old, its teachings are timeless and ageless and can endure the toughest trials and tribulations. Here, I will highlight some of the most important teachings found between the covers of this sacred book. Only by following them closely will we become true Christians, followers of Jesus, who, as you know by now, was sent down to Earth to preach his Father's teachings, not his own.

Rest assured that the following Bible principles will lead you to a fulfilling Christian life. But do read the entire Bible to obtain its sacred teaching as a whole, so you will not miss out one bit.

Love Jehovah God

"God is a Spirit: and they that worship him must worship in spirit and truth." (John 4:24)

What more is there to life than love? And what love is more important than love for Jehovah? It is the love upon which all other spiritual love is based and dependent.

Jehovah is the one and only true God Almighty. The most important commandment in life is to love Him. We must worship Him and Him only. We must worship Him by obeying His commandments, which benefit our own wellness in mind, body, and spirit.

Since no human has seen God, other than His Son Jesus, we do not know what He looks like; therefore, we must never create an idol to worship Him. Some wrongly feel that in order to worship God, they have to go to a specific place. But Jesus corrected this notion by reminding us that God is a Spirit, who, although is not everywhere, can be worshipped anywhere. As long as you put your heart, mind, and soul into loving Him, you are correctly worshipping Him. Worshipping Him is listening to Him. Of course, attending a church is crucial, for it connects you and fellow Christians into one body in Christ. But a church is not the only place where God can be found.

When we honor our Heavenly Father, we need to honor the Son. Honoring the Son shows our love for the Father. If you do not respect His Son, how can you truly love the Father? A remarried woman will know whether her new husband really loves her by observing how he treats her daughter. If he loves her, he will love her daughter as well. So show Jehovah you love Him by loving His Son, Jesus Christ, and all His other creations.

Love One Another

> "Beloved, let us love one another: for love is of God; and every one that loveth is begotten of God, and knoweth God." (I John4:7)

The second most important commandment is to love other people as yourself. But Jesus added to this by saying, "A new commandment I give unto you, that ye love one another; even as I have loved you, that ye also love one another. By this shall all men know that ye are my disciples, if ye have love one to another." (John 13:34-35) What is the difference between this new commandment and the original one? To answer this, think about the way Jesus loved us. Did he not put other people's interests and well-being above his own interests and welfare? His sacrifice to cleanse us of our sins shows this more than enough! Most, if not all, of the other teachings and commandments are based on this single commandment, along with the most important commandment. If you do not want something to be done to you, do not do that something to others, such as cheating, killing, and stealing.

Putting other people's interests first, however, does not mean that you should abandon yourself. Take care of your needs, as well. Doing so does not mean that you will turn into a selfish person. Taking care of yourself enables you to continually care for others. If you constantly put the needs of others first and yours last, you will eventually use up all your energy and resources. And guess what happens? You will be unable to care for either others, or yourself. My own mother is a good example of prioritizing the needs of others, always caring for me and others first before caring for herself. As a result, I watch broken-heartedly as her energy and strength waste away. I try to remind her that her own needs are very important, too, and that she should watch over her own health and needs as well.

Serve love starting at home. When family bonds strengthen, our government will strengthen. Happy families make happy societies, and create a stable government. Without a sturdy foundation, civilization crumbles. This is why our world experiences problems from every angle—love is missing among family members. Once we put love into our homes, love will start working from the bottom up.

Do not murder

"Whoso sheddeth man's blood, by man shall his blood be shed: For in the image of God made he man." (Genesis 9:6)

This is probably the most obvious and easily understood teaching for most people. It is not acceptable to shed blood, especially that of the innocent. Killing others will kill you only, for Jehovah can easily resurrect the slain but killing will greatly distance you from Him, who hears the cries of your victims, and who will promptly punish you.

When we think about murder, we often think about the ruthless killing of humans only. But I would also like us to focus on the purposeless ending of animal life. Every living creature is in God's heart. He takes interest in every breathing soul He has made. Just as He hates the evil that humans bring upon other humans, He likewise detests the senseless slaughter and abuse humans inflict upon animals.

We are to imitate God's ways and actions as best we can. We are to be the masters over all other creations in the way God is the Master over us. He shows us love, so we must show animals love. Of course, it is perfectly fine to kill animals for food (God has given His permission in that we do not eat the blood), for clothing, and for other purposes necessary for our survival. Other than that, we must not murder animals for amusement, nor should we condone unkind treatment others bring upon them.

Be they humans or animals, we must not murder them. We must show them our respect, for they all are God's creations. God is holy, and His creations should be kept holy and our ground undefiled by innocent blood.

Keep your marriage holy

> "Let marriage be had in honor among all, and let the bed be undefiled: for fornicators and adulterers God will judge." (Hebrews 13:4)

Besides the covenant between God and humankind, marriage is the most sacred of all vows. After creating Adam, the first man, Jehovah felt that it was not good for him to be alone, so He created a woman to be Adam's helper and keep him company. Thus, Jehovah is the Originator of marriage, and whatever He originates is holy and should not be disturbed by humans.

We should consecrate ourselves to cleanliness at all times, before we enter into a marriage, and remain chaste during our marriage. Sexual relations are blessings God especially grants to a man and a woman in marriage, not outside of it in any form. Therefore, all kinds of fornication—sexual acts outside of marriage—are strictly forbidden. Our bodies are holy temples for Christ, who lives in us; whatever we do, we must do good for Christ's sake, so when we commit immoral sexual acts, we are in turn polluting his sacred dwelling place.

When we say, "I do," we should make sure this statement is an everlasting promise. If you feel that such a vow can be broken, or that it is not one of the most important vows you will ever make, it is best not to utter those words until you are absolutely certain that you will commit to the relationship to the best of your ability. Divorce is prohibited (except in the case of abusive or sexually unfaithful marriages), for it is ruining the art, the oneness and unity of a man and a woman, that God has created: "Whosoever shall put away his wife, except for fornication, and shall marry another, committeth adultery: and he that marrieth her when she is put away committeth adultery." (Matthew 19:9)

Remaining sexually virtuous is only one method of sanctifying marriages. Open communication, empathy, compromises, and honesty, among other elements, are magical ingredients that will lead to true love and a sturdy bond.

Finally, harmony in lifelong partnerships can exist only when leadership is exercised in an orderly and godly way. When people in a society are governed by a firmly established hierarchy, where each member in a rank ungrudgingly lives up to their assigned tasks and responsibilities, perfect harmony will result. This also holds true in the marriage setting, where the Bible lays down the ideal order of headship: the man of the household, the wife, and finally, the children.

Our Creator is naturally the head over all beings. Is this Master aggressive and domineering, seeking only His interests? No, God constantly goes out of His way to do what is best for His subjects, even sacrificing His dearest Son to save His unfaithful children. When the King on the highest seat provides such endless love and care for ungrateful creations, then how much selfless devotion should the man and wife give each other and their children!

Jehovah and Jesus set the best example for us

about what headship in a loving relationship means. Just as God tenderly watches over His flock, the husband should likewise look after his wife and treasure her as his own body. And just as the Christ submitted himself to God, even onto death, the wife should also glorify her husband by honoring his position as the head of their home. When both partners in a marriage value their unique roles and set out to do what is right in God's eyes, achieving and maintaining a happy, holy affinity is not only highly probable but is also likely to extend to the life after our passing world. Meeting each other's needs not only ensures the other person's happiness, but it will make our Father's heart glad even more, for we are not just living for one another—we are living for Jehovah most of all.

Honor your parents

> "A wise son maketh a glad father; But a foolish man despiseth his mother." (Proverbs 15:20)

We honor and love Jehovah because He is our very Life-Giver. For the same reason, we must honor and love our parents, for they have given us our lives, and in turn the privilege to be life-givers ourselves.

Even though your parents may not be the greatest people who ever lived, God has chosen them to be the only two people to become your parents, to rear you. If not for them, you would not be alive to have the privilege to smile, to laugh, to sing, to dance, and to enjoy and experience all the other wondrous gifts life has to offer. Honoring your parents is how you can truly show how much you appreciate this precious gift of life. By giving you your life, they have in turn given you the knowledge of God. For this, you must eternally thank them.

If nothing else, honor your parents because of their position. Even though some parents seem to try hardest to make their children miserable and do not appreciate the privilege of parenthood, you still need to honor them because of their position over you. In general, the elderly should be honored, and parents, being older than you, fit in this category.

By honoring your parents, you honor God. If you can honor your earthly parents, you prove yourself capable of honoring your Heavenly Father, your ultimate Parent, and the Parent of all parents.

Do not steal

"Let him that stole steal no more: but rather let him labor, working with his hands the thing that is good, that he may have whereof to give to him that hath need." (Ephesians 4:28)

How would you feel if someone stole what you love? Even if it is something that you do not need, wouldn't it still be hurtful and cause distrust? Stealing does not steal only material things; but above all, it steals trust, loyalty, and friendship, things that cost far more than any item on Earth. Stealing itself is valueless and worthless, and the thief is even more valueless and worthless.

Moreover, how much valuable is the stolen property compared to the trust God has in you? Do you not agree that Jehovah's friendship is the most priceless of the priceless? Do not break the sacred trust God has placed in you.

Embrace modesty

> "It is not good to eat much honey: So for men to search out their own glory is grievous." (Proverbs 25:27)

A humble heart is a good heart. A modest person is a wise person. If you open the door to arrogance, you will close the door to appreciation and acceptance of others or life in general. A humble soul can readily accept God into his or her heart and is grateful to Him. An arrogant spirit is a foolish one whose love for self is useless when that love does not attract love from others. The proud are also blind — they cannot see or admit their faults, so they will never learn; yet, they easily find or invent faults in others.

Do not look down upon others for any reason. Do not turn your heart away from the disabled — a car accident could send you to a wheelchair, as well. Do not shun the not-so-pretty — you, too, will grow old and lose your looks. Feed the poor as you are fed; warm the homeless as you are warmed.

Arrogance is fruitless. You may be smart, but there is always someone out there who is smarter; you may be handsome, but a handsomer person will always walk on Earth. But if you are pure, no one could humanly be purer. Purity is like white — no other color can be whiter. So aim for purity and start with humility.

Do not be jealous of others

"Jealousy is cruel as Sheol; The flashes thereof are flashes of fire, A very flame of Jehovah." (Song of Solomon 8:6)

Arrogance can be at the opposite end of the spectrum from jealousy, but as with arrogance, the same principles apply—there will always be someone handsomer, prettier, smarter, wealthier, or happier than you, so what good does being jealous of others do you? It will be fruitless and endless, and it costs friendships and even lives, for some crimes of passion are committed by people overwhelmed by jealousy.

The biggest such crime ever committed was the impalement of the perfect man, Jesus Christ.

People get jealous of others when they compare what they do not have with what others have. But, my friend, I tell you—do not compare the surface or materialistic objects, but rather the intangible values. Although your pockets may hold less of value, why would you think that your life itself is worth less than the lives of the rich? You may see a life gilded in gold, but do you know what is underneath? Do you know if all the wealthy are truly happy? Admire those who are happy and good, not simply wealthier or healthier. Follow in the footsteps of those who are happier, not of those who are only more successful or wealthier, unless you know the true ingredients that will make you genuinely happy, not simply wealthy and prominent.

Protect fellow humans

> "He that justifieth the wicked, and he that condemneth the righteous, Both of them alike are an abomination to Jehovah." (Proverbs 17:15)

"Let God take care of justice" is the excuse I often hear from those who fear the bad guys, or worse, those who use it as a weapon to continually do evil. We need to put final judgment in God's hands, but does that mean that we should do nothing to protect the victims and to stop the wicked from repeatedly harming the Earth? No, it simply means that we should not seek revenge. It is our responsibility to do everything we can to help victims and protect our society.

When you are called in as a witness, provide true testimony. Relate what you know truthfully. Never hurt the innocent and never protect the guilty. Do not refuse to testify the truth, for a victim's very life may depend upon your words.

Do not take a bribe, for bribes blind even the so-called wisest men. When someone asks you to keep silent about a crime, do the opposite. If you do not, you become partner to the wicked. Those who protect the evil are more evil than the evildoers. If you see that your friend is in the wrong, promptly correct him so both of you will not be guilty.

Lend a helping hand

"Let each man do according as he hath purposed in his heart: not grudgingly, or of necessity: for God loveth a cheerful giver." (II Corinthians 9:7)

Take care of those who need your help the most. The keyword is "your" help—not their help, not my help, but *your* help. So you should help those who are closest to you—your family, your friends, or any strangers you just met who need immediate help.

When you are available in someone else's life to be helpful, put your kindness to work and lend a helping hand. Do not care for those you have never met over caring for your family. Some people enjoy volunteering in their community while doing little to help out at home. Some would rather donate generously to political parties, churches, and charities than save the money for the needy and the sickly right in their own homes. Many crave public recognition, thinking that good deeds done privately would not shine the spotlight on them (they forget all about God's attention, the most important attention of all). If you can help others behind closed doors, your help is true and honest. Jesus once said, "When thou doest alms, let not thy left hand know what thy right hand doeth: that thine alms may be in secret: and thy Father who seeth in secret shall recompense thee." (Matthew 6:3-4)

Be completely helpful by finishing what you have intended or promised to do for others, and do your best with it. Help is not so helpful if only half complete.

If someone asks for bread, do not give them fish. Sure, you can give fish with the bread (a good idea if you truly believe it is desirable), but not the fish alone. Give others what they ask for. Provide what they need. Something pretty but not useful will not be helpful. Treat others the way they want to be treated.

When you feel that someone needs help, ask that person if this is the case. Not everyone is comfortable asking for help, so step in whenever you feel help is needed.

The most appreciated help is the kind where the recipient truly feels that he or she has been helped, without feeling obligated to return the favor. Although we may ask for benefits in return in a strictly business setting, such as a joint venture or a win-win situation, expecting rewards after helping others in general is not the way to go. Do not make those you help feel as if they owe you something, and in turn, they will feel as if they owe you a ton of thanks! Ask only for the joy that comes with helping others in need.

When given straight from the heart, help brings smiles to both the giver and the receiver. Now that is what I call a win-win situation!

Do not be greedy

> "Better is a little that the righteous hath Than the abundance of many wicked. For the arms of the wicked shall be broken; But Jehovah upholdeth the righteous." (Psalm 37:16-17)

Greed can blind even the smartest people. Greed is often the father of all other iniquities—some people murder others or risk their own lives for money, while others prostitute their bodies for it. Heed what the apostle Paul wrote: "For the love of money is a root of all kinds of evil: which some reaching after have been led astray from the faith, and have pierced themselves through with many sorrows." (I Timothy 6:10)

What can those who succumb to greed possibly accomplish? Greedy people can acquire and store a houseful of gold, but what good will it do them when they are dead? Can they take the gold with them to the grave?

Instead of hoarding worldly treasures—ones that will only rot with our flesh—we need to gather and collect what death can never touch, what we can still enjoy when resurrected. Do not be greedy for the dead things, but be as greedy as you like with the things of life, so you can enjoy them all you want, forever and a day, all in the presence of your loved ones, with the approval of Jehovah.

Control your temper

"But let every man be swift to hear, slow to speak, slow to wrath: for the wrath of man worketh not the righteousness of God." (James 1:19-20)

Many violent crimes start with arguments that escalate out of control. One silly disagreement between two pairs of lips may end up as dead bodies on the ground. But even if no physical harm comes from a hurtful remark, it will still damage the human spirit.

Words can touch a person's innermost essence where no knife or bullet can ever reach, and the resulting wound may last for years, even an entire lifetime. Thus, pay heed to feelings before opening your mouth to speak. If what you intend to say is nothing pleasant, keep your mouth closed so you will spare a soul.

If a situation gets too tense, simply walk away. It is better to lose an argument than it is to lose a life or two.

Jehovah does not approve of violence in any form, be it speech or action. We need to avoid situations that may result in violence.

Even if we do not physically or verbally engage in violence, we should also avoid being unmindful of violence. For example, when we see or hear of violence on the news, we must not turn a blind eye, but detest what we see or hear.

Keeping a distance from any kind of violence will ensure a peaceful spirit. Only when we achieve such a serene state can we connect with God and fully enjoy the privilege and experience.

Avoid a lying tongue

> "The getting of treasures by a lying tongue Is a vapor driven to and fro by them that seek death." (Proverbs 21:6)

God speaks truth in every word He says. He is always faithful in fulfilling His promises. He takes all speeches as seriously as He takes all actions. After all, speaking is a form of action, is it not? Since we are made in God's likeness, we need to love what He loves and hate what He hates. He hates lying, so we must avoid lying to the best of our ability.

Lying seems to be a sin that can be easily avoided, yet it may be the hardest to conquer. What should you do when your friends ask for your opinion on their new outfits or hairdos? Do you often find yourself complimenting your friends when you actually think the opposite, to prevent upsetting them? In times like this, we forget one important principle: we must please God over pleasing anyone else. Once we hold firm to this belief, we will not find it as difficult to avoid lying. So next time you are in such a situation, think twice before resorting to lies. Instead, you can say something to the effect of "That hairdo/outfit does not do you justice."

As far as broken promises go, they do not begin as lies when people believe they will do what they say. But promises that are not fulfilled have the same effects as lies. To avoid breaking your promises, do not make a promise in the first place unless you are certain you can keep it, or unless you will try your best to fulfill it. Do not substitute "I will try" for "I will" if you never intend to "try" — that is just like saying, "I will call you" and not doing so. Phrasing something as a generality does not excuse you from keeping your promise, or make breaking your promise less serious.

Instead, think carefully before you make a

promise. If you cannot do it, do not promise it. If you can, or if you know you will try your best to keep it, then say you will try to do so.

Seek the spiritual, avoid the worldly

> "Ye adulteresses, know ye not that the friendship of the world is enmity with God? Whosoever therefore would be a friend of the world maketh himself an enemy of God." (James 4:4)

Of the many unique characteristics Jehovah has given to us, spirituality is the most important. It is what we use to draw closer to God and to understand what His wishes are for all of His creations. Without spirituality, we would be an empty house full of dust and dirt. Sadly, many people throughout history have abandoned spirituality. As a result, many have become the children of the worldly. Spirituality is from God, whereas the world is from Jehovah's opposing force. The spiritual bring us to God, whereas the worldly take us away from Him.

What is the "world"? Does it refer to what God has created? No—how could it, since everything Jehovah has created is good? The "world" refers to the condition humans have established on their own terms, away from God's rulership. It is the world that was founded after our first two ancestors disobeyed our Father. So when the "world" is mentioned in the New Testament, it is often referring to our chaotic world.

How can you recognize the worldly

belongings? Anything that goes against God's teaching belongs to the world. For instance, wars are worldly—they are the destruction of your brothers and sisters. God is love and we must follow in His example to be love ourselves. Is killing members of your family love? No, so wars are not spiritual but worldly. Therefore, true Christians are against war and all things of the world.

Does staying away from the world mean we should isolate ourselves from the people of the world? No, Christians are told to be *in* the world, not *of* the world. We are to be the salt and light, to gently shine in the world in order to lead others in the right direction and onto the path to salvation.

Are all nonbelievers worldly? No, many people have never had the opportunity to know about God; they include infants and children, the mentally challenged, those who died too early, and those who are isolated from teachings about Jehovah, among others. There are also loving people who have not yet embraced the idea of a Creator. They are either stubbornly ignorant or doubtful, but I do not believe they are worldly—it is not for me to judge or condemn. This is why all people will have a second chance—when Jesus comes again, these nonbelievers will personally witness the Son of God, and I feel that it will be hard for them not to become believers.

Also, keep in mind that not all believers are spiritual. Believers have to love God, not simply believe in Him, as we have already discussed. They need to show their faith through their works. So we cannot always tell who is worldly or spiritual based solely on a person's religious belief. Often enough, religion causes barriers—instead of using love to bind us, "believers" resort to manmade laws that appear spiritual in order to condemn others, building fortresses so impenetrable that they make many frown at even a mere mention of religion. These self-proclaimed righteous people forget that 1) God's laws are to benefit us, not trap us or make our lives difficult, and 2) we are all sinners, so no one has the right to condemn anyone. So in many ways, we may never know who are the true spiritual believers; only God knows, for He can see into the hearts and motives of people. This is why we should leave final judgment to Him.

Is all spirituality good? After all, everything God has made is "very good," but obviously, Satan has managed to turn some into darkness under God's permissive will. Hence, it is up to us to identify good spirituality from bad. To do so, we need to learn what kind of spirituality is good, instead of focusing on all the traits of the bad kind of spirituality.

The main quality of godly spirituality is that it should draw us close to God in mind, body, and spirit, and it should cause us to reflect God's character as closely as possible in everything we do and say. A random act of kindness and a heartfelt prayer are examples of pure spirituality. Therefore, any kind of spirituality that takes our focus away from God, or that lets us do something that goes against God's wishes, is from the source of darkness, and we must keep a great distance between it and ourselves. If someone performs miraculous acts in the name of God yet yields ungodly fruits, stay away from that person, for that one is a wolf in sheep's clothing. The same goes for someone who tells the future in God's name but the foretold signs do not manifest—that one is a lying prophet. On the other hand, befriending someone of little status who lives according to God's wishes will enrich your own spiritual life immensely.

As beings who are created in God's own image, many of us hunger for spiritual materials, and Satan uses this thirst to his advantage. He has been utilizing religion as his means to divert people from God. How many religions do we have? Hundreds? No. Thousands? Not that many, either. In Jehovah's eyes, we have only two religions: the true religion and the false religion. We can argue that many religions contain some common truths, but that is only *some*. Christianity is the only religion that contains all the truths, and nothing but the truths. Hence, all other religions are false, including any versions of Christianity that have been tampered with by Satan. God has combined all the false religions into one body: the great Babylon, the system that the sneaky serpent has taken thousands of years to establish, refine, and spread.

Jehovah has already warned us about this great Babylon: "Come forth, my people, out of her, that ye have no fellowship with her sins, and that ye receive not of her plagues: for her sins have reached even unto heaven, and God hath remembered her iniquities. Render unto her even as she rendered, and double unto her the double according to her works: in the cup which she mingled, mingle unto her double. How much soever she glorified herself, and waxed wanton, so much give her of torment and mourning: for she saith in her heart, I sit a queen, and am no widow, and shall in no wise see mourning. Therefore in one day shall her plagues come, death, and mourning, and famine; and she shall be utterly burned with fire; for strong is the Lord God who judged her. And the kings of the earth, who committed fornication and lived wantonly with her, shall weep and wail over her, when they look upon the smoke of her burning, standing afar off for the fear of her torment, saying, Woe, woe, the great city, Babylon, the strong city! for in one hour is thy judgment come." (Revelation 18:4-10)

God will destroy the entire system suddenly in His due time, without any further warning, so we must not involve ourselves with it; we must get out of it as soon as we can so we will not be destroyed along with it.

When we clean ourselves of the influence of the false religion, we will then need to embrace the true religion. Sheep that are scattered by a pack of wolves must be gathered under one good shepherd; they cannot be on their own lest another pack devours them. Our loving Shepherd has been waiting for us to turn to Him, so let us follow the call of His gentle voice. Allow Him to care for our needs in His green pasture to time indefinite.

Abstain from blood

> "Only be sure that thou eat not the blood: for the blood is the life; and thou shalt not eat the life with the flesh." (Deuteronomy 12:23)

From the very beginning, when Jehovah permitted humans to eat flesh for the first time after the flood in Noah's days, He specifically ordered people, "But flesh with the life thereof, which is the blood thereof, shall ye not eat. And surely your blood, the blood of your lives, will I require; At the hand of every beast will I require it. And at the hand of man, even at the hand of every man's brother, will I require the life of man." (Genesis 9:4-5)

"But does this rule not pertain only to Israelites?" you may wonder. No; although this commandment was included in the Mosaic Law, which governed the agreement between God and the nation of Israel, God first gave this decree to Noah and his family. Since Noah is the forefather to all of us, this statute concerns us. In other words, God set this rule *prior* to the covenant He made with the Israelites, so it applies to the overall human population outside any specific agreement.

What about blood transfusion? Some people, particularly the Jehovah's Witnesses, feel that taking blood into your body, no matter by which method, is not permitted. What does the Bible advise us to do? The earliest apostles said, "That ye abstain from things sacrificed to idols, and from blood, and from things strangled, and from fornication; from which if ye keep yourselves, it shall be well with you. Fare ye well." (Acts 15:29) Note that the word "abstain" is used. While "abstain from blood" means "do not consume blood," the verb is used to modify the other three prohibited actions, so the word is used in more than one meaning. Still, I personally cannot determine whether the broader sense of "abstain" is intended for "blood." We can either interpret it as simply "do not eat blood" or "hold ourselves back from blood." If we accept the broader sense, we would need to deny blood transfusion to save a loved one's life. On the other hand, if we see the command as only "do not eat blood," we would be free to accept and offer transfusions during medical emergencies.

While it is wise to be safe rather than sorry and accept the broader definition, we do have to keep in mind that God's laws are to benefit us. For instance, God told His chosen people in the Old Testament to observe the sabbath by not performing any work on it. During Jesus' days, the religious leaders and Pharisees used this sabbath law to burden their people; they prohibited people from performing anything they deemed as work. When Jesus healed the sickly on the sabbath, it greatly offended the Pharisees, who were even more ruffled when Jesus openly proclaimed their hypocrisy. Jesus asked them, "Is it lawful on the sabbath to do good, or to do harm? to save a life, or to destroy it?" (Luke 6:9)

Do you see the similarity between these two commandments? While people should avoid work on the sabbath, people should not use it to excuse them from helping someone in need. Likewise, I feel that while we should abstain from blood, we should not use this command as an excuse to avoid saving lives.

One other incident in the Bible supports my thoughts. Jesus reminded the Pharisees, "Have ye not read even this, what David did, when he was hungry, he, and they that were with him; how he entered into the house of God, and took and ate the showbread, and gave also to them that were with him; which it is not lawful to eat save for the priests alone?" (Luke 6:3-4) In this unique set of circumstances concerning King David, he ate the bread that only the priests could eat because there was nothing else available to feed David and his men.

Honoring God is our first priority in life. However, some people do not understand what honoring Him truly involves. On another occasion when the Pharisees and the religious scribes confronted Jesus for breaking their "noble" traditions, Jesus said in reply to their accusation, "Why do ye also transgress the commandment of God because of your tradition? For God said, Honor thy father and thy mother: and, He that speaketh evil of father or mother, let him die the death. But ye say, whosoever shall say to his father or his mother, That wherewith thou mightest have been profited by me is given to God; he shall not honor his father. And ye have made void the word of God because of your tradition. Ye hypocrites, well did Isaiah prophesy of you, saying, This people honoreth me with their lips; But their heart is far from me. But in vain do they worship me, Teaching as their doctrines the precepts of men." (Matthew 15:3-9)

Here, Jesus again pointed out their hypocrisy. While seeming to act honorable by dedicating things to God, they dishonored their parents, thus breaking one of the Ten Commandments: Honor thy father and thy mother. To better illustrate this point, let us say you donated all your surpluses to your church, and told your needy parents, "I'm dedicating this money to God, so I'm afraid I can't help you."

What does honoring God mean? Would it be okay to honor God without honoring His works? No, we need to honor God by honoring His creations, just as loving others shows we love God. In everything we do, we need to pinpoint the principle behind each law given by God. Jehovah forbids us to eat blood because He said that the blood is the life. He takes every life, whether a human or an animal, very seriously. Since He cares for the life of a dead animal so strongly, would He not take the life of a needy human extra seriously? If a child requires blood transfusion, would He forbid it? If we refuse blood transfusion that could save someone's life, would we really be honoring God?

I believe that special situations warrant exceptions, especially when they are matters of life and death. I also believe that to honor God, we need to honor His principles behind His laws. We cannot honor Jehovah by dishonoring His works, nor can we honor Him by creating burdensome rules that inhibit others from honoring Him.

However, this is just how I feel, so I do not want you to take my word for it. Ask God about blood transfusions and discuss this important subject with those whose hearts are set in God's ways.

To sum up this chapter, let your love for Jehovah God, fellow humans, and all of God's creations, govern your actions. When you do, you will have done the righteous thing.

Love is the firstborn of Jehovah's principles. If something is not good, it is not from love, not from God, so do keep far away from it.

How Should You Study the Bible?

"The fear of Jehovah is the beginning of knowledge; But the foolish despise wisdom and instruction." (Proverbs 1:7)

How do we study the Bible so as to receive its benefits to the fullest extent possible? Well, how did you study for exams while you attended school? Did you not thoroughly read through the materials given to you, then carefully think about their meaning? And if you did not understand a section, did you not ask your teacher for clarification? Finally, did you not apply what you learned to your best ability so you actually took in the knowledge practically, not just mentally, to prove to yourself that whatever you absorbed actually worked? Studying the Bible primarily involves the same steps: read, question, and apply.

Before I go into those three steps at length, I would like to stress here three points that can help make your Bible reading a pleasant, fully rewarding experience.

First, it is crucial that you read every single word in the Bible, both the Old Testament and the New Testament, and always compare what you learn in the New Testament with the Old Testament, just as Jesus did while he taught his followers—he usually backed up his lessons with quotations straight from the Old Testament. The New Testament did not exist during Jesus' days. The Old Testament was the only Scriptures available to help people verify and support the teaching of Christianity. By reading and comparing both Testaments, you will be able to understand God's Word fully and completely. If you just read the New Testament, you will not receive God's complete messages.

The Old Testament is also important because it tells you about how you came into existence, and it is the only place where you can read about the earliest history of humankind. But again, if you only read the Old Testament, you will be missing out on the vital information about Christianity, which is the only true path to God and salvation.

Second, just as it is important to read and study every word in the Bible, it is vital to obtain a most accurate translation. There are mainly three kinds of Bible translations: the literal, which is translated word for word; the dynamic, which is a translation in accordance with what the translators believe the text means (so this kind can be very biased); and the translation that achieves a balance between the two types. I strongly advise that you use the third kind, but one that leans more toward a literal translation of the Bible. Personally, I look for translations that 1) rightfully and respectfully retain

Jehovah's name and 2) seem to be most accurate.

It is a gross disrespect to remove God's name and then replace it with the title "the Lord." Many false gods and people, including kings, nobility, and even heads of households, are known as lords. It is vital to use Jehovah's name while preaching and spreading His teaching; otherwise, how can people know the God you refer to is Jehovah and not some manmade god or even a king in a faraway kingdom?

If a certain verse or a passage does not conform to the teaching of the Bible as a whole, then something tells me that it has been either mistranslated or purposely added into a later version.

And third, we must take heed to what the apostle John said: "Beloved, believe not every spirit, but prove the spirits, whether they are of God; because many false prophets are gone out into the world." (I John 4:1) No matter what you read or hear, or even see, do not be quick to believe that it is truly from God Almighty. There are plenty of misleading teachings out there, so we must be careful not to be fooled by them. This is especially so since we are living in the last days, where the world is filled with false teachers and magic tricks to cloak your heart and fool your eyes into believing the false. The very best place to see whether what you heard or read is accurate is in the Bible; of course, it has to be an accurate Bible translation that was not translated to conform to a specific doctrine.

We must follow in the example of those noble people who "received the word with all readiness of the mind, examining the Scriptures daily," whether what they were taught "were so." (Acts 17:11)

"Ask, and it shall be given you; seek, and ye shall find; knock, and it shall be opened unto you: for every one that asketh receiveth; and he that seeketh findeth; and to him that knocketh it shall be opened." (Matthew 7:7-8)

Only diligent and regular Bible study can lead us to the true teaching of Jehovah. Never search for a shortcut. If you are given a doctrine or a specific church teaching, study the Bible to see whether the doctrine is from God or from man. Always question what you hear or read. Keep finding the truth in the Bible with your heart.

Friend, I invite you to study what I wrote in this book and compare it with a good Bible and a spiritual heart, to see if what I have shared is true.

As a student myself, I am always learning something new, and I know I cannot possibly understand everything I read, but that does not mean that my Bible reading is fruitless. If I could get closer to God and His truth by even one percent from each study, and I study the Bible often, it means that I could progress far more than before I began my journey.

So with no further delay, let us examine how we should properly study the Bible.

Read God's Word with faith and reasoning

There is a big difference between simply reading the Bible and really understanding what you read, just as there is a difference between simply hearing your friend talk and really listening to that friend with your heart. We may read, but reading brings us no fruits when the words do not enter our hearts or minds. Jesus told his followers to love God with all their minds, meaning that we need to apply mental effort and energy to study Jehovah's Bible. If whatever your eyes take in enters both your heart and mind, you will be able to either see that you understand its meaning or realize that you do not comprehend it. If you do not understand, ask. Never hesitate to question what you do not understand.

Question what you do not understand

When Jesus taught his people about God's forthcoming Kingdom, only his closest disciples asked him questions when they did not understand what he was talking about, unlike all the others, who just heard his talk and focused on the free food he gave them. So learning involves asking questions.

How would you ever gain insight if you did not ask for and receive an explanation? Never play guessing games or use your instincts to fill up the void. This is especially important in this case, where you need to comprehend the Bible as best you can. Do not be shy or afraid to ask for clarification. No question is ever too small or stupid concerning the Bible.

But where can you receive the right counsel? How can you find accurate answers to your questions? The first source you need to seek is, not surprisingly, the Author of the book, so if you need the wisdom to understand, ask Jehovah to help you by sending you the Holy Spirit.

> **"But if any of you lacketh wisdom, let him ask of God, who giveth to all liberally and upbraideth not; and it shall be given him. But let him ask in faith, nothing doubting: for he that doubteth is like the surge of the sea driven by the wind and tossed." (James 1:5-6)**

Second, attend a Bible study class or your local church. It is important to first make sure that whichever group you join conforms to true Bible teachings. Many false Christian teachings exist, so do some research and attend some services before committing yourself to their ways.

And third, find some good Bible study aids and guides that conform to true Bible teachings. I suggest that you get together with spiritually rich Christians as study buddies while you learn and teach one another, building a good and rewarding relationship in the process.

Apply the Bible teachings you have learned

Finally, after familiarizing yourself with the Bible, it is time to apply its teachings and principles to your everyday living. The Bible was not so meticulously written just to be read. What good will its wise teachings do you if you do not use them? If a math teacher gives his students a formula, do the students not use it to solve their mathematical problems? The formula would no doubt make their work much easier; if they did not take advantage of the formula, they would need to figure out a way to solve the problems on their own.

Once you apply Bible principles daily, you will certainly see its rewards spiritually, mentally, and physically, for it is the one and only instruction manual on how to live a good life—written by Jehovah, our Life-Giver Himself! You will never ever again need any other book on how to improve your life. No need to waste your time browsing and trying out various tips from dozens of self-help books that will only frustrate your mind and deplete your bank account.

Go ahead, put this book down and pick up your Bible. Its many pages may be intimidating at first, but once you start reading it, I am certain you will find it to be the most intriguing book there is! Where else could you find the actual story of creation, the history of our very first ancestors, and the true knowledge of the Greatest Creator? Truly, it is a book to be treasured, read, and reread again and again and again, and passed on to future generations to time indefinite.

Wisdom—How Should You Cultivate It?

"For where your treasure is, there will your heart be also." (Luke 12:34)

A long time ago, a wise king ruled a prosperous kingdom, where peace reigned within and from all sides. As a matter of fact, this king was wiser than all men in the East, for God had given him exceeding wisdom and insight "even as the sand that is on the sea-shore." (I Kings 4:29) He wrote 3,000 proverbs and 1,005 songs; he taught botany and biology; he easily administered justice in difficult cases; and he was the God-chosen person to construct the first splendid temple of pure gold in Jerusalem. Kings from faraway nations all sought his profound wisdom and brought him great gifts, making him not only the wisest man but the richest: "The king made silver to be in Jerusalem as stones, and cedars made he to be as the sycamore-trees that are in the lowland, for abundance." (I Kings 10:27)

This king lived a perfect life, with numerous

servants attending to all of his needs. He had everything and everyone he wanted. And "everyone" included one thousand women. Despite all the years of building his wisdom, despite all the time walking in God's ways, and despite all that God had bestowed upon him, this king, in his weakness for women, became a fool. No, he was not a fool for having a soft spot for the opposite sex; he turned into a fool when he allowed his association with women to turn his heart away from God by bowing down to manmade gods, including the detestable god Molech of Ammon, to which people sacrificed children. He, as you have already guessed to be Solomon, committed two sins against God: 1) he married foreign women whom God forbade Israelites to marry, lest they turn their hearts away from God (kings were also not allowed to marry too many wives), and 2) he worshipped false gods other than the one true God.

Although Solomon had greatly faltered in his life, his experience does tell a story of wisdom. What can you learn from his story?

The knowledge of right and wrong is stored in the mind, but wisdom can only be exercised in the heart. No matter how large a library your mind is, if the desire in your heart is but a flicker, you will not be able to put your knowledge to good use. If you have a great mind without a great heart, your great mind is rendered useless. What good would books do if you have no heart to apply their important messages? However, if your heart is great but you lack a great mind, you will become great. No, you may not score a 4.0 grade point average, but what importance is that, really? As long as your heart seeks and applies what is good, you will bring out what is good.

Simply knowing what is wrong and right is not enough for living a good life; if it only required knowledge, then we would have had no trouble establishing a godly world. After all, most humans have an innate knowledge of right and wrong — remember, Adam and Eve ate that fruit from the tree of knowledge, and we are made in God's image. So knowledge is just the ingredient for a good life. A house cannot be built without the necessary materials. But even with the necessary materials, it takes desire and full commitment from the heart to construct the house. Therefore, the search for wisdom starts from the heart. It is then stored up in the mind, where the heart utilizes it to build on and continually bring the best out of it. Without a seeking heart, knowledge is useless.

Solomon had a desiring heart that sought wisdom from God, who graciously bestowed the fullest wisdom upon him, and Solomon stored it up in his mental treasure box. But when his heart lacked a sturdy foundation in God, he quickly forgot about the gift. Instead, his weak heart turned from the knowledge of right and wrong to what was bad. He turned from loving God, took his God-gifted jewels for granted, and loved the darkness. The man who started out as the wisest sadly fell to be one of the most foolish. Do not let this happen to you. Take in the wisdom this story conveys to apply it in your own life. Let your heart focus on our greatest Treasure to cultivate the greatest wisdom. Once you find wisdom, hold on to it tightly, for when you forsake a newfound wisdom, you become more foolish than you have ever been before.

Connecting with Jehovah

"Delight thyself also in Jehovah; And he will give thee the desires of thy heart." (Psalm 37:4)

How can we connect with Jehovah? It is true that interaction with God seems to have greatly lessened since Biblical times, when Jehovah frequently performed miracles and spoke to His people. Even though such occurrences are not the norm nowadays, it is still possible to connect with your loving Creator now.

The first step in spiritually connecting with Jehovah is to learn about Him. Do you not agree that before we can really connect with anyone, we must first get to know that person better? You may use online social networks. I assume that you would first read a person's profile page before you add that person to your friends list or send him or her a message, correct? It is the same with connecting with God. Where can you read about God? You can find the most wonderful and accurate profile of Him in His own Holy Scriptures, the Bible! So if you do not have a copy yet, get one and start your connection.

After you have made yourself better acquainted with Jehovah and the things He likes and dislikes, you can begin connecting with Him more intimately in two ways.

First, pray to Him. Let your prayers be from your heart, not something memorized or untrue. Take heed to Jesus' advice: "When ye pray, ye shall not be as the hypocrites: for they love to stand and pray in the synagogues and in the corners of the streets, that they may be seen of men. Verily I say unto you, They have received their reward. But thou, when thou prayest, enter into thine inner chamber, and having shut thy door, pray to thy Father who is in secret, and thy Father who seeth in secret shall recompense thee. And in praying use not vain repetitions, as the Gentiles do: for they think that they shall be heard for their much speaking. Be not therefore like unto them: for your Father knoweth what things ye have need of, before ye ask him." (Matthew 6:5-8)

Praying to Jehovah is just like talking to a good friend, and this Friend will never get tired of listening to you, so be respectful, but do not be shy. He should be your Best Friend, Confidant, and above all, your Teacher and Advisor. If something is troubling you, talk to Him; if you have had a good day, tell Him and thank Him; and if you need advice or strength, or there is something else you desire, ask Him. Granted, He may not give you everything you ask for, and maybe not immediately, or quite the way you expect, but He will definitely give you what is best for you at the right time, for His time is always the right time.

Always address your prayer to Jehovah and

Him alone, but pray in the name of His Son Jesus Christ, for Christ said, "Whatsoever ye shall ask in my name, that will I do, that the Father may be glorified in the Son." (John 14:13)

Jesus also provided an example of a proper prayer to God. Although we should not use it ritually in our prayers, it is important to carefully study its highlights to guide us in praying with the right motives. Here, we will dissect each line of the prayer, which is found in Matthew 6:9-13.

Our Father who art in heaven, Hallowed be thy name.

- We should address our prayers to Jehovah only, seeking glory for His name, which should be kept strictly holy.

But how do we glorify God's name? Is saying, "Oh, God, let your name be sanctified" all we need to do? No, that is not enough. We can truly glorify God's name only when we perform good works. It is akin to any other relationship we have. If I were to become a publisher, I would publish only good books. Poorly written books would bring down my image. A wandering wife would give her husband a bad name. And disobedient children may make others wonder about the quality of the parenting they received. Likewise, we as creations need to do works that can measure up to God's standards as well as possible. When we stray from God, it means we do not honor His name.

Thy kingdom come. Thy will be done, as in heaven, so on earth.

- We need to pray for Jehovah's Kingdom to come and desire for His will to be fulfilled on Earth, as it is in His heavenly home.

Give us this day our daily bread.

• We should ask Jehovah for our daily needs, not for excess pleasures, though He bountifully provides life's delights as well.

And forgive us our debts, as we also have forgiven our debtors.

• It is wise that before we pray, we achieve a peaceful mind and hold no grudges in our hearts. When we forgive the wrong that has been done to us, we will be able to ask God's forgiveness for our own wrongdoing, for "if ye forgive men their trespasses, your heavenly Father will also forgive you." (Matthew 6:14)

And bring us not into temptation, but deliver us from the evil one.

• We are bombarded by temptations on a daily basis. Often enough, we cannot overcome Satan's schemes, so we must ask God to deliver us from evil's deadly clutches.

Should you end your prayers with "amen"? "So be it" is what "amen" means. Saying it after a prayer affirms all the words you have spoken and shows that you have put your trust and hope in God for Him to act as needed. While saying amen may not be required since the Bible did not say it is necessary, it never hurts to do so. I feel it is a great way to end prayers, so I always conclude mine with amen, as follows: "My prayer is said in the name of Jesus Christ. Amen."

Should you pray in a special posture or place? Some people think that we need to pray in a certain way or go to a particular place to get God's attention. Do we really need to resort to some physical display so that our prayers are heard? Such a belief is not only wrong but degrades Jehovah's sovereign power. No matter where you pray, when you pray, what you pray for, why you pray, and how you pray, as long as you earnestly and respectfully pray to Jehovah, He will hear you. Of course, if you wish to kneel during your prayers, by all means do so. I actually strongly advise that, since it shows your subservience and your honor for the King. But if you are unable to kneel, do not fret over it, for Jehovah can see your heart and grant you your wish if it is within His will for you.

The second step to take if you truly want to connect with God well is to do what He loves and avoid what He hates, just as you would do with your human buddies. I am sure you and your friends share common interests and that you enjoy doing the same hobbies together, and that you also avoid doing the things that bug one another, right? (Well, okay, you may enjoy bugging your pals once in a while, but do not try that with Jehovah!) By fulfilling God's wishes, you are showing that you care about Him and His desires, and that you are not selfish. Plus, doing what He loves is for your own good (so it is selfish in a way, I suppose?).

Now get going—start connecting with God. If you pray to Him tonight, tell Him I said hi!

Your Destiny, Designed?

"Be not deceived; God is not mocked: for whatsoever a man soweth, that shall he also reap." (Galatians 6:7)

Are our lives all planned out beforehand by Jehovah? Many people believe that we are ruled by our fate, which is assigned to each individual upon entering this world, so that everything we do, whether good or bad, is already fixed into our destiny. In this scenario, we live like robots, doing the will of the Creator, not our will. Therefore, we cannot be blamed for whatever we do. If someone murders another, how could he be blamed when he could not have done anything to avoid this fate?

If our lives are controlled by our kismet, would it be fair for Jehovah to punish us for our bad deeds or reward us for our good deeds, if these deeds were long ago programmed into our lives without any participation from us? Is God really that unjust? No, of course not! He is not unjust at all; instead, He is always the Seeker of justice. Since Jehovah is just, that means that the theory of fate holds no ground. What does the Bible, Jehovah's inspired Word, tell us regarding this topic?

When the children of Israel rebelled against God by doing what He hates, ranging from murdering and prostitution to worshiping manmade wooden gods, Jehovah constantly sent His servants the prophets to warn them of the consequences: their lands would be taken by their enemies and they would be captured and taken into foreign nations. Would God ask them to turn from their evildoing if He knew that they could not avoid their fate? Would He so unreasonably punish them for sins He Himself put into their lives?

In Noah's days, the Earth was polluted with people's evil acts, and the cries of their victims reached Jehovah. Saddened that He had ever made humans, Jehovah sent the great flood to destroy all humans, except Noah and his family, and all the living creatures of the lands and skies, aside from the ones God brought into Noah's ark. How could God regret creating humans if He had established their destiny in the first place?

Jehovah also regretted that He had ever appointed Saul to be Israel's first king, for Saul turned from His teachings and instead chose to act according to his own wishes. Again, would God regret something He had already programmed beforehand?

God, an Active Bystander?

Since Jehovah does not create our destiny for us, is He in any way taking part in our lives? Or is He looking on as a bystander? No, the Bible indicates that Jehovah is actively involved in our lives when we require it. Even when we do not seek His help, He will step in to deliver us with His mighty hand and outstretched arms.

Jehovah can accomplish His divine purpose and will no matter what people plan however meticulously. For instance, Joseph was sold into Egypt by his brothers. While his brothers planned to harm Joseph to achieve their self-interest, Jehovah turned their evildoing into a rescue plan to save not only Joseph but the entire land of Egypt and its surrounding countries, including the land of Canaan, where his father, Jacob, and his wicked brothers lived. Joseph became a great governor in Egypt who saved the lands from a severe seven-year famine.

Can Jehovah look into the future to see if something needs change? Yes, of course; when Jehovah so chooses, not only can He look into the future to see what *will* happen, He can see what *could* happen in any given situation. When Jehovah promised Abraham that his descendants would become a great nation, He told Abraham that his children would stay in a foreign country for four hundred years, forced into slavery, but He would bring them out to their promised land in His appointed time. That indeed happened when Joseph was sold and brought to Egypt, and eventually, his whole family followed suit. When the Egyptians forgot Joseph's life-saving deeds, they forced Israel's descendants into hard labor. To fulfill His promise, God then delivered them out of the house of bondage using Moses as a mediator.

Probably the best example we have of God

looking into the future is Jesus Christ's execution. God knew that the Pharisees and religious leaders would hate Jesus enough to kill him. Taking advantage of this situation, so to speak, Jehovah sacrificed Jesus to cleanse us of our sins. Jehovah did not make them kill Jesus—He *let* them. God also allowed Judas to betray Jesus, knowing beforehand what decision Judas would make.

Jesus also foretold the future when he said to Peter that he would deny him three times before the rooster crowed. After Jesus was arrested, Peter did indeed deny that he knew Jesus three times, for he feared for his own life. As soon as the rooster crowed, Peter remembered Jesus' words, so he wept bitterly.

Jehovah does not need to plan years ahead or predestine the entire future; when Jehovah feels it is necessary to intervene in a situation or change manmade plans, He can do so at a moment's notice. For instance, He told King Solomon that if he followed His guidance and did what was right, He would make sure his kingdom lasted forever. King Solomon had many wives, and they all turned his heart from God to worship the foreign gods, angering Jehovah. Because of this, Jehovah told Solomon that He would tear his kingdom from his hand and give it to another ruler, yet He would not destroy his kingdom completely for the sake of the agreement He made with King David. Therefore, Solomon's generation only ruled the one part of Israel that became known as Judah. God's promise is fulfilled, for Jesus was a descendant of Solomon, and he will be the King whose Kingdom will reign to time indefinite.

As you can see, Jehovah generally does not predestine a person's fate or an event in the future; instead, He likes to have situations unfold on their own, without intervening or changing the direction in which things go. When He does intervene in an event, it is only in people's best interest.

Can We Create Our Destiny?

Are we in charge of our lives? Absolutely. Each of us is an agent of free will. That means Jehovah has given us each the freedom to make our own decisions. Therefore, our future lies in our own hands. Our decisions today will impact our tomorrow either positively or negatively, depending on what we decide.

The bottom line is: Fate does not control us—we control our own fate. We are responsible for our own lives, and we should be in charge of our destiny. If you want to gather gems, cultivate the good; but if you choose the wrong road, you hurt yourself or others around you (if you hurt others, it really means you will hurt yourself the most, for Jehovah hears the moans of His children and will promptly sentence those who committed the wrong).

Do we respond to the changes in our environment? This seems to be the next big question people have. What do you think the answer is?

Many people have put their lives on autopilot, going wherever life takes them or doing whatever life asks of them. Many feel that they simply respond to the changes in their environment. But the facts are 1) *we* are actually the environment and again, 2) *we* are in control of our future.

People tend to view their environment and surroundings as uncontrollable and that they are compelled to follow any changes brought about by society. What many do not realize is that *we* are the surroundings. When we are in control of our lives, we in turn change our environment. If we become shoplifters, our society is viewed as a thieves' nest. On the other hand, if we help our neighbors, our society becomes a model community. So there is no environment that is separate from us—we ourselves are the environment. The environment does not mold us—we mold the environment.

Finally, people nowadays often bring up the law of attraction to explain the role we play in creating our future. Is it real or is it an illusion?

Simply put, I believe that we reap what we sow. If we sow good thoughts and actions, we will reap good results. If we bring positivity to others, we will receive positivity in our lives: we will be happy with ourselves for our good actions (near future), we will see people mirroring or appreciating our positivity (future), and we will be rewarded when God's Kingdom comes (at the end of this current system of things). On the other hand, if we commit a petty crime, what we will receive is a jail term and a ruined reputation, and above all, it will grieve our Heavenly Father.

Other than that, I feel the law of attraction is stretching it. Let me briefly define this so-called law before I will tell you why I feel that way. The law of attraction, from what I have gathered, simply means that anything that happens to you in life, good or bad, is a result of the energy you send out, good or bad. Does that mean that my mother somehow attracted juvenile rheumatoid arthritis for me when I was merely an infant? Does that mean I asked for blindness at age seventeen? We cannot answer "why?" using the law of attraction. Some things in life we cannot control, so we cannot use this "law" to explain why some things happen the way they do, or blame ourselves for every negative event in our lives. To say that we have the power to bring every instance of goodness or badness into our lives just through our thoughts, feelings, and actions, puts us at too high a level, as though we are creators of the universe, like God.

If the law of attraction can simply be defined as "we reap what we sow" excluding events we cannot control, then it is real. If it extends beyond this, then it is an illusion. In other words, this law holds true only for events we can control, not events we cannot control.

Yes, I have heard of miraculous stories about people who have achieved fantastic physical or medical feats using this law, but know that any miracles must be credited to God and His permissive will, not any manmade laws. Any credit to any other person or thing besides God is what I call an illusion from the truth. I am able to overcome my multiple physical disabilities and blindness. Is it because of my own strength or the strength God has given me? I am able to do so not because I have the strength within myself, but because Jehovah gave me this strength. I do not rely on myself—I rely on God. To say I am capable on my own is only a lie. I owe credit where credit is rightfully due.

Conclusion? As with the angels, God's heavenly messengers and servants, we have the power of the free will God has given to us. Again, Jehovah allows us to make our own decisions; He does not brainwash us into being robots who do whatever He wishes. All He asks from us is that we live by His guidance, rules, and regulations. It is completely up to us whether we choose His route to bring ourselves bliss, or abandon His support to enter into darkness.

What route will you choose? Will you wisely use your free will to put your faith in Jehovah and Jesus in order to create a truly happy life for yourself and others? It seems to me that you do want to make the best of your free will — otherwise, you would not be reading this book. I congratulate you, for this is the wisest way to use your free will!

Jehovah's Spiritual Image

"And God said, Let us make man in our image, after our likeness..." (Genesis 1:26)

What did Jehovah mean when he decided He and His Son Jesus would make humans in Their "image"? Does it mean that humans physically resemble God's form? No, in Their "image" means that people are spiritually like Jehovah to some extent. He has given humans some of the spiritual aspects He has: the ability to think and reason, an innate knowledge of right and wrong, a conscience, a full spectrum of emotions, and the need for spiritual things in order to be truly happy. On top of all that, Jehovah has also graciously granted us free will, the power to make up our own minds regarding things concerning us.

How have we exercised our free choice? Everyday events we initiate, from cursing one's friends to cheating on one's spouse, clearly tell us that instead of being grateful for such a precious gift, we misuse it. We not only abuse our free will, but abuse it to abuse fellow creations.

Yet, some people blame their genes for the bad deeds they do. They say, "How can we help it if we were made to make mistakes?" Did God really create us with defective genes or genetic codes that compel us to commit crimes and sins? No, after Jehovah made the first couple, He saw they were "very good." Could very good creations have very bad genes? The Bible tells us that the people sinned on their own; their thoughtless actions were not blamed on any genes. However, the pair has passed down their sinful nature to every one of their descendants. Does that mean we do have defective genes and that we are entirely helpless against them?

I believe the answer lies in the power we possess: free will. If our genes are really to blame, then it would make the gift of free will null and void. If we were helpless against any genetic predisposition, Jehovah would not hold us responsible for our actions, good or bad. If God knows that our genes are the culprits, why would He waste time urging us to follow in His ways? Do you believe that the God of Justice would have punished past evildoers if He knew that their genes made them fall? Rather, He knew they, themselves, caused their fall.

But what *was* inherited from Adam and Eve, if not bad genes? I do not know, but it really does not matter. What does matter is that, whatever was handed down, we have control over it. We have our free will, the tool we can use to direct our lives. Because of the sinful nature we inherited, we do have an inclination to steer away from the right path, but we are still in charge, nonetheless. The task is harder but not impossible, so we are far from being helpless with our situation.

Do you know what else? We have sufficient help to aid us in wisely using our free will to combat any fleshly tendency—the Holy Spirit! Therefore, we have no reason to be like those who use our inherited weaknesses as an excuse to continue traveling on the dark road. When they claim, "Since God knows we are weak, He will expect it. So why bother trying to be good? After all, it is beyond our ability to avoid it," we know how dead wrong this line of thought is!

Do you love Jehovah? Your answer determines whether you will use your free will to do good or use it to do harm. As you may realize by now, everything is based on whether we love Jehovah. If we love Him, we will wisely and appreciatively use our free will; if we do not love Him, we will treat our free will as garbage.

In conclusion, our situation is not hopeless; we are not battling in vain with any invincible inheritance from our first parents. Instead, if we turn to God to assist us in correctly using our free choices, we will, with a great certainty, achieve greatness. It is never too late to mend our ways, to carefully exercise our free will to propel us to heights never before imagined.

If you have the desire to change, then now is the time, no matter how many wrong turns you have made in the past. Your rebirth starts with studying the Bible. What are you waiting for? Start now. Let it be the first step you take in wisely using your free will, to truly conform to Jehovah's spiritual image!

Freedom in Free Will

"Now the Lord is the Spirit: and where the Spirit of the Lord is, there is liberty." (II Corinthians 3:17)

Since Jehovah gave us free will, does that mean we have the freedom to do everything we want? Absolutely. But does that mean we *should* do everything we want? If we do not want to repeat history, we should have learned by now that we must definitely *not* do everything we want, for it causes disorder and chaos. We must draw a line between the pursuit of liberty and the preservation of morality. We should never put virtues and morals on the line. We should conform to morality, rather than legality — not everything that is legal is moral, and not every moral deed is viewed favorably in our legal system, for our judiciary is comprised of manmade laws that are not always based on morality.

Why has general courtesy diminished, especially the respect that should be given to the elderly? Where has chivalry gone? Some people blame the disappearance of courtesy on human rights movements, such as the women's liberation movement, but that is not the case. Human rights is simply seeking equality.

A society should treat everyone with equality. That means no discrimination against race, age, or sex, and that people should not be judged by their health, wealth, intelligence, or lack there of. We must treat people according to how the Bible teaches us, not according to our own preferences. Beyond this, equality should not seek freedom at the expense of morality, but rather, compliment morality so people will not be unfairly judged.

The main culprit in the demise of genuine courtesy is the near disappearance of morality in society. Just turn on the TV, or the radio, or flip through a magazine, and you will know what I mean.

If we could restore morality to our society, many of the problems we face on a daily basis would be gone. For one, the sickly and the elderly would not encounter as many problems or as much discrimination as they do today. Children would be taught at a young age to respect the sickly and the elderly, and they would grow up into responsible and loving adults who would in turn pass down these values to subsequent generations.

Instead of embracing a godly way of living, we have sought liberation—liberation that sacrifices morality.

We all want to be free. While freedom is wonderful, we need to draw a line between obtaining freedom and destroying morality. Would it be okay for people to abuse the interests and well-being of others just so they can pursue their own freedom? Is it okay to do whatever we want, no matter the cost? Is it better to show love for others by staying within the bounds of morality than it is to destroy others in the pursuit of our own fleshly desires?

Granted, morality is not completely gone, and it will be fully revived once God's Kingdom comes. Right now, morality lies in our own hands—we need to be responsible and take actions on our own. If you have children, teach them morality based on Bible principles so they can establish firm foundations from which to build a worthwhile life; when you are at work, show love to your fellow employees; and when you are out and about, be the one to lend a helping hand to the disabled. Your good actions will be examples after which others can model themselves. Be the person you want others to be!

Does keeping to morality hinder us in being free? As a matter of fact, it does not. In actuality, what enslaves us is breaking the values God has set for us. As we learned well from our very first two ancestors, going against God's laws took freedom away from them. Humans imposed their will on one another, making everyone crazy and driving everyone wild. When we choose to do whatever our fleshly bodies desire, we put chains around our spirits. When we gamble, we let money rule over us; when we visit pornography sites, we let our lewd vices enslave us; when we drink excessively, we lose the gift of rational thought and feelings; when we practice immoral sexual acts, we are trapped by sexually transmitted diseases or forced into unplanned parenthood; and when we lie and cheat, we have the burden of remembering every excuse we have made in order to hide our ugliness.

Keeping to the moral standards set in Bible principles, on the other hand, frees us. When we do exactly what Jehovah tells us, we will not be trapped by any unwanted fruits of temptation. That allows our spirits to have the kind of freedom we could never experience if we do what we tell ourselves to do.

Having a government with God as the Commander in Chief, we will not be afraid of any sort of imperfection, for God is perfect and His advice is therefore perfect for us. His advice and laws, if adhered to, will not cause any harm, unlike manmade laws or self-made laws and opinions that could cost our lives for eternity.

Since each individual is different, each in turn has his or her own opinions on any given issue. But God is only one God, so there will never be any conflicts. With Him, "yes" means "yes" and "no" means "no." With us, our "yes" will always be a "no" for at least one person out there.

We all must say "yes" to Jehovah's laws in order to pursue real freedom. It is time to abandon our own ways and break away from the chains we have fastened around ourselves. No one needs to be the slave of others, neither for money nor fleshly lust. We must be set free, so let Jehovah abolish our slavery and set us free forever. Let us be willing servants of Jehovah and Jesus; let us serve Them because we love Them, not because we are ordered to. Serving Them will release the bonds of temptation the world has tied around us. We will no longer feel trapped to please others, nor will we face temptations that will bring us to ruin. At last, we will live in a land that is truly for the free!

Do Not Be Stupid!

"Woe unto the wicked! it shall be ill with him; for what his hands have done shall be done unto him." (Isaiah 3:11)

Which people are the stupidest? Picking out the stupidest kind of people involves determining how much harm their stupidity has caused others — the greater the harm, the stupider the people. In your mind, go through world happenings since humans began marking history. Which people have constantly brought the greatest destruction to others and even to themselves? Do you not agree with me that the stupidest group of people that ever existed is evil people?

What does being an evil person mean? Is it the same as being a bad person? Bad and evil people share one thing in common: they do what is bad. But the similarity ends there. What makes them different is that evil people know what they do is bad and do it anyway. Bad people, on the other hand, do bad without really knowing it is bad. When bad people learn that what they do is bad, they can choose one of two routes: turn to doing good, or remain bad. If they remain bad, bad people will become evil people.

If your child takes a toy from a friend, does that make him evil? No, of course not, if you have never told him that stealing is a bad thing. When Adam chose to listen to Eve rather than obeying Jehovah's command, was he doing something evil? Yes, he became the very first evil man. The first evil person is Eve, since she ate the forbidden fruit first, and then convinced her husband to follow in her sinful footsteps.

Are all sinners evil? Some think that "sinners" and "evil people" mean the same thing. What they forget or do not realize is that we are all sinners, every one of us, so when they believe all sinners are evil, they are actually labeling us all evil. Are we all evil? The answer should be obvious. Plenty of sinners unknowingly offend God, so they cannot be evil. Sinners become evil only when they purposely go against what is ethical. We *can* say all sinners are bad. This is why Jesus said that no one is good, only God. However, I know that Jesus is good, too. He is just too humble to admit it!

Why do I call evil people the stupidest group of people ever? Let us use Satan as an example. We all know that he is the number one troublemaker, the father of the lie—the lie that led Eve to sin—so he is the most evil being we have ever known. What caused him to be evil?

In the beginning, Satan, along with many other angels, personally witnessed God creating Earth and all of its inhabitants. It must have been a moment of tremendous happiness and pride, with most angels cheering on and worshipping God. It is safe to guess that Satan felt jealous then—he wanted to be worshipped and he wanted all the glory, so he rebelled against God by disturbing His creations, just as a younger prince might want to conjure unrest in a kingdom to usurp his older brother and take the throne as king himself.

From that time on, Satan became the great opposer, causing trouble however he can. He was an angel that fell, and as he fell, he took with him some of the other angels. They decided to battle with Jehovah for the high seat.

> "Shall the axe boast itself against him that heweth therewith? shall the saw magnify itself against him that wieldeth it? as if a rod should wield them that lift it up, or as if a staff should lift up him that is not wood." (Isaiah 10:15)

What were these fallen angels thinking when they took the route to evil? Were they so terribly stupid that they failed to realize that they, as mere creations, could not possibly prevail over their very Creator, and that going against God would get them into huge trouble? Apparently, they *were* that stupid!

Just as some angels in the mighty heavens embraced stupidity to be evil, we humans on Earth have made the same mistake. We have killed, cursed, cheated on others, and performed many other abominations.

Evil people are too stupid to realize that their victories are only temporary, and that their victims are easily saved by Jehovah. Did they think that their evil effects would last forever? Did they expect to do evil for eternity? Evil people only pay attention to the present—they see they are winning and they celebrate. Obviously, they do not know their celebration is short-lived. After their brief party, they will be sent away forever and a day. Good riddance!

Has their stupidity numbed their emotions to the point they do not even know how to fear? Any sensible person who goes against our legal system will fear being punished, which is dependent only on whether the perpetrator is caught. Jehovah is the Policeman of the universe who catches suspects even before they carry out their crimes. So it is insanely stupid for the fallen angels and evildoers not to fear God for the crimes they commit against others, and ultimately, against God. I have to shake my head in speechless amazement. What else is there to say?

Should evil people really be to blame for their evil deeds? Is Satan not the mastermind behind all evildoing? Many people believe that we cannot be entirely at fault for the wrong we commit—after all, Satan is our great tempter. Well, I have to contradict this common belief. Although Satan tricks us into doing what he wants us to do, he can succeed only when his target is already tainted with prior pollution.

Satan and his followers are merely opportunists. If his target is clean, he does not have the ability to defile it. If it is unclean, he can make it even more unclean. An unvaccinated person will be open to contracting a virus that a vaccinated person can avoid. Therefore, we must be vaccinated against Satan's schemes with a great dose of Jehovah's protection. Let us heartily ask God to deliver us from temptation and give us a heart that will always desire to learn and keep His ways. Rest assured, Satan will have no power to trample down our defensive wall if we do not allow him near. Firmly tell him no, and he will flee, for he knows he cannot waste what little precious time he has left.

So, my friend, when you see the results of sheer stupidity, be sure never to step onto that road, for it is a road that leads to eternal destruction, a black abyss of nonexistence, of nothingness. Would you not rather be under the light and rejoice with God? Then travel on the opposite road, and you will find valleys of gold and streams of silver, where you and your children will call home for generations.

Turn from Evil

"Seek ye Jehovah while he may be found; call ye upon him while he is near: let the wicked forsake his way, and the unrighteous man his thoughts; and let him return unto Jehovah, and he will have mercy upon him; and to our God, for he will abundantly pardon." (Isaiah 55:6-7)

Is there hope for evil people? Can they repent? Of course, I believe anyone can repent when he or she first has the desire to, and sets his or her heart to do so. Satan can repent if he wants to! So there is hope for everyone, including Satan and his fallen angels if they truly desire to change.

Where should we start? What should be the first step we should take to the path of righteousness? Being a virtuous person can be quite hard at times, as we inherited a sinful nature from the first two people. It is especially difficult for us because Satan is our king, and he tries his hardest to tempt us into doing what God hates. We know God is allowing him to win for the time being by what happens daily in our world.

However, Jehovah knows our weaknesses, and He is most forgiving of our sins when we repent.

Therefore, repentance is the first step to becoming good.

What does it take for you to repent? What does repentance really involve?

Let us say you shoplifted at your local Wal-Mart store. To repent for your action, you need to:

1. Admit that shoplifting is wrong.
2. Feel sorry that you shoplifted.
3. And never shoplift again.

When you have truly repented, Jehovah will forgive you. He clearly states in His Holy Scriptures, "I have no pleasure in the death of the wicked; but that the wicked turn from his way and live: turn ye, turn ye from your evil ways." (Ezekiel 33:11) His grace was illustrated in the book of Jonah, where God forgave Nineveh, a great city of over 120,000 people, when they repented.

But you have to truly repent. The keyword is "truly." True repentance means that you stick to this step: never do the wrong again. Sincere repentance involves a change of one's ways, not simply a change of one's attitude. Feeling sorry for the wrong you did is meaningless if that regret does not affect your future actions. If you repeat the same error again, it means you have not repented.

Just because Jehovah is forgiving does not mean that we should abuse His love. And just because He is forgiving does not mean He is not just. This perfect, holy God requires true repentance; anything less will not earn His approval.

Once we turn to the right path, we must be careful to stick to it. To take our old route again will make our travel more arduous than it was before we found the right path. God warned us, "When the righteous turneth from his righteousness, and committeth iniquity, he shall even die therein. And when the wicked turneth from his wickedness, and doeth that which is lawful and right, he shall live thereby." (Ezekiel 33:18-19)

"He loveth righteousness and justice: The earth is full of the lovingkindness of Jehovah." (Psalm 33:5)

When we put forgiveness and justice together, we get a judge-like figure in Jehovah, who judges things fairly. He acquits those who have truly repented and sentences those who claim to have repented but continually repeat the same offenses.

Friend, we must focus on the now for a bright future. It is not too late to say "sorry" for the wrong you did and change your ways. But do not delay; do it before it *is* too late to repent, for Jesus will visit us any day, like a thief—when we least expect it. Be not caught off guard; you may not get the chance to apologize tomorrow. Today is the day that determines your future!

Wash Yourself First

"And why beholdest thou the mote that is in thy brother's eye, but considerest not the beam that is in thine own eye?" (Matthew 7:3)

    Does a sinner have the right to condemn others? What reason does a murderer have when he scornfully calls a thief "sinner"? How could a cheater tell others not to cheat?

    Before you judge others, judge yourself first. Before we fix what is wrong in others, we first must clean up ourselves, and then we can help our neighbors wash themselves. To scorn in others what we have in ourselves makes us liars and deceivers. How could we hate the wrongdoers when we have done worse deeds ourselves?

    In order for people to see the good, we need to set good examples to guide others. Parents who cheat and lie to each other will set bad examples to their children, who may learn the bad behaviors and pass them on to their own offspring. On the other hand, when we exercise wisdom and seek counsel from Jehovah, we can change our own improper behavior and replace it with a mild and loving temperament that will in turn become the model for others.

If we judge others without fixing the wrong in ourselves, Jehovah will do to us the same way we do unto others. So if we want to receive a fair judgment, we need to first exercise fair judgment on others. It is wise to take Jesus' advice: "Judge not, that ye be not judged. For with what judgment ye judge, ye shall be judged: and with what measure ye mete, it shall be measured unto you." (Matthew 7:1-2) What Jesus meant was that we should not judge others as hypocrites, finding other people unrighteous when we are unrighteous ourselves. Moreover, as we do not have the ability to read people's hearts, we cannot determine the real motives behind people's actions. An act may appear righteous when it is otherwise, and vice versa. It is unwise to make quick judgments on others, good or bad. Leave that to Jehovah. However, we need to judge people if what they openly do harms others. Fair judgment is done only to protect our community.

Serve Justice on a Silver Platter

How should we judge fairly? Following the practical guidelines below will help you determine the steps to take when problems arise.

• As already mentioned, we first need to clean up our own acts.

• We need guidance from the Bible to know the difference between right and wrong.

• We need to judge not according to people's skin color, social status, or level of wealth, but according to the severity of their actions.

- Fair judgment is the deliverance of the appropriate sentence to whomever committed the wrong. Do not hold one person responsible for another person's bad deeds—each person is responsible for his or her own behavior.
- We must give true testimony and not welcome false accusations. We must testify as true witnesses when we are asked to do so; otherwise, we would be as guilty as the evildoers we protect.
- Finally, fair judgment includes forgiving others when they have truly repented.

Oh, Give Me Mercy!

Why is it important to forgive? Here is my list of the top five reasons why you need to forgive.
- Every one of us has done something wrong in our lives, both unknowingly and deliberately, but we have hoped for other people's forgiveness. We are relieved when we receive forgiveness. So why can we not extend forgiveness to others, especially when they have done something unknowingly, or of a lesser degree of harm?
- As we have all wronged one way or another, we have no excuse not to forgive others. How could sinners condemn sinners?
- Since we must forgive as sinners, we must forgive more so if we are saints, for forgiveness is one of the godly virtues.
- Forgiving others allows us to move forward. Constantly holding a grudge will make you feel worse than necessary. Wrongdoers have already caused us harm; why have them harm us more by

holding negative feelings toward them in our hearts? Not forgiving others is only treating yourself badly, so be good to yourself and welcome forgiveness into your heart if you have not already!

• Above all, God told us to put wrongful matters in His hands. He is the one who takes care of unjust actions and finds justice. We need to let Him take care of our problems and deal with the bad guys, so we can enjoy our lives to the very fullest.

By judging using God's laws, fewer innocent people will be wrongly sentenced and more criminals will be rightfully brought to justice. Streets will be safer, people will be freer, and governments will run smoother.

It is true that, as with anything else we do, we will not achieve perfect justice, but that is not an excuse for us not to do our utmost to aim for the highest accomplishment we can when we set our heart on the right goals. Just because we cannot receive the gold medal does not mean that the silver medal is unworthy. But do all that you do as if you are going after the gold medal, and do not be surprised when you do hold one in your hands—for remember, God's Holy Spirit will empower you to win a gold medal more precious than any we have ever known.

Serve Love with Justice

"All chastening seemeth for the present to be not joyous but grievous; yet afterward it yieldeth peaceable fruit unto them that have been exercised thereby, even the fruit of righteousness." (Hebrews 12:11)

Timmy stole a toy from his friend Paul's place, and brought it back to his own home. When his mother found out about it, she said nothing but only let him play with it. As Timmy grew older, his first theft became a petty one, for he progressed into stealing frequently. Then one day, he was caught stealing an electronic gadget from a department store and was immediately sent to jail.

Sarah loved the necklace her best friend Kelly had, so when Kelly was not looking, she put it into her dress pocket and took it home. As soon as her mother found out that it was stolen property, she told Sarah to give it back to Kelly immediately, and scolded her for stealing it, explaining why stealing was wrong. She then punished Sarah appropriately and promptly. Sarah never stole again, for she did not enjoy getting caught, and most importantly, she now knew why it was not right to steal.

In these two stories, whose mother loves her child the most? Is it Timmy's mother, who gave Timmy no warning for his action? Or is it Sarah's mother, who disciplined her for her own good?

When proper discipline is absent in the rearing of children, parents are neglecting the role of good teachers necessary to bring up responsible and caring adults. When telling right from wrong based on Bible principles is abandoned, children lack the knowledge and wisdom to make the right decisions, and they do not understand why some things are bad in the first place. Therefore, discipline should consist of the teaching of godly principles and appropriate punishment, which should be just severe enough to get the message across. If Sarah's mother only punished her, Sarah would not understand why. So always answer the unasked "why?" prior to discipline.

> **"For whom Jehovah loveth he reproveth; Even as a father the son in whom he delighteth." (Proverbs 3:12)**

Love is unyielding in the sense that it does not forsake discipline and justice. Children brought up in a loving, disciplinary environment will be able to apply and cultivate whatever they learned early, and they can also use the same principles to teach their own children.

This is why Jehovah gives us a set of rules to follow—He loves us. He wishes us to follow them only for our good. After all, what does it matter to

Him if we do not listen? He is not dependent upon our decisions, just as parents are not dependent upon their children's decisions when they have passed away.

It is, therefore, wise to heed God's rules, so we can spiritually mature into true adults. I repeat: we reap what we sow. So if we sow godly principles, we will gather desirable results from applying those principles.

Show Loving Discipline

How should you discipline your children so that your orders are absorbed and taken seriously? Here are some general guidelines to help you effectively send your children in the right direction in life.

- Teach your children what is right and what is wrong, so they will have no excuse to say they did not know what they did was wrong in the future. Identify right and wrong using stories and proverbs found in the Bible.
- Teach your children why something is good and why something is bad, so they will understand why and how to love the good and detest the bad.
- Inform your children of the consequences if they do not follow your guidance on doing what is good. Match the severity of your punishment with the severity of your children's disobedience. But do not be too harsh on your children; parents should punish with a loving heart. Any discipline that is beyond what is required will only do harm.
- Keep your word—if your children disobey

you, discipline them as you have prescribed. If you fail in this step, your children may learn that your warnings are unsubstantiated, and do not carry any undesirable outcomes. In such cases, they will not get anything from the warning except knowing not to listen to you again.

- From time to time, reward your children for their good deeds—but I advise against rewarding them every time they do something you told them to do. Children should learn to do good for the sake of goodness, not rewards. However, always show your approval by complimenting them on their good work; that will be sufficient reward on your part. Leave it to God to reward them greatly, surpassing any reward you can ever give them.
- Most importantly, always assure your children of your love for them. Like God, always give your children hope. Your children need to know that punishment is not the end of the world; it does not mean you have stopped loving them. Your children also need to know that they are not fully secure when they perform a good deed, unless they continue pursuing the high road.

Realize that, if you do not like to discipline your children, God will discipline them in a more painful way, so it is best that you set them on the right road now. Let them know God as early as possible and start doing good as soon as they can. By doing so, you will not end up receiving discipline alongside them.

Follow the Light

"Walk with wise men, and thou shalt be wise; But the companion of fools shall smart for it." (Proverbs 13:20)

How many disabled people do you know? No, I am not referring to the people who simply have a physical or mental disability. I am talking about the ones who allow themselves to become disabled or let others make them disabled. A person, healthy or otherwise, is spiritually disabled when he or she lets everyday negativity or problems hinder him or her from truly loving the life he or she lives, or from going after his or her heart's desires.

Why do we have so much negativity, specifically the negativity that comes from people? It is because negativity comes in too many forms, easily outweighing the quiet and delicate positivity. Think about it for a minute: pure goodness can come in only one form, one order. I compare it to one specific order in a deck of cards. If you put the cards in order (positivity), and then you drop the deck, it will most likely go out of order (negativity). If you drop the cards five times, it will likely result in five different disorders (negativities). So, as with a deck of cards, goodness has only one face while negativity has many faces. A good person will be good. A bad person may be a liar, a cheater, a thief, or a murderer—bad apples come in all different forms. There is only one way to be good; there are countless ways to be bad. In essence, it is easier to be bad than it is to be good, therefore it is easier to be attracted to negativity than it is to be attracted to positivity. Since God does not control people's hearts, it is easy for many to move to the left a bit, or to the right a bit, rather than staying straight in life. This is why doing bad requires no motivational speakers. Worse yet, books like this one and speakers such as yours truly even have to exert effort to remind others how to be good! Is the Bible not enough for everything we do? It should be.

So how do we ignore the many faces of negativity to live happily, or spiritually ultra-abled, as I like to call it? Just follow these steps.

- Part of the answer lies in the question. You *must* ignore negativity to your best ability. If you truly, seriously, undoubtedly want a positive, spiritually rich life, putting some effort into blocking out negativity will no longer seem hard; it will actually be invigorating. It all depends on your desires—do you desire positivity or negativity?

Your desires are the fuel that get the vehicle—your attitude—going in the right direction. If your desire for moving forward is strong enough, it will conquer your negative feelings. For instance, when I lost my eyesight, my desire for a happy life defeated any feelings of sadness, frustration, or depression—

those feelings did not even get a chance to show their ugly faces before my desires prevailed!

You must have the desire to live positively, to follow in God's footsteps. You need to desire it one hundred percent—ninety-nine percent will not be enough to maintain it. If you are not finding and focusing steadfastly on the positivity, that tells me that your desires are not strong enough, no matter what you say. This is why many people cannot seem to get out of their ruts—their desires are simply not strong enough. They may feel the desire to be positive, but if they are not achieving a positive attitude, their desires are still lacking. You absolutely have to hunger and thirst for happiness and want to move forward. Just like a starving person in search of food, your desires have to propel you forward in search of the light at the end of the dark tunnel.

Use your desires to seek positivity on a daily basis. Positivity brings happiness, and it comes in all forms. You will feel good when you settle conflicts, make compromises, and conquer the cold shoulder. Many people cannot arrive at an agreement or end a conflict because they do not have the strong desire or willingness to do so. For instance, you have probably had lengthy arguments in which each party wants to be the winner. Each party's desire to be right overpowers the desire to end the argument.

Always desire the desirable—the sweet, the pure, the beautiful—and it will lead you to a desirable life.

Are my desires strong? You bet! My desires are as sturdy as they get. My desire for a positive life is steady—I can count on it as easily as I can count on the sun to rise tomorrow. I may be wheelchair-bound and blind, but I am in no way disabled, but ultra-abled. So fire your soul for desires for a positive life, not a negative life.

• Put God's opinions and approval above that of others. Many people tend to let a negative comment ruin their mood for the rest of their day, unable to ignore it and focus instead on the good things they do have. But are people's opinions and criticism really that important? Certainly, it is wise to take heed of the righteous, but when a fool throws a rash comment your way, should you waste your time and emotions on it? When you know that you have done nothing morally wrong, feel good about it, even if others say otherwise.

Jehovah's opinion is the most important of all opinions. If you do not get His approval, no one else's approval matters. If you receive His approval, then you have received a gold medal, and no other opinion can possibly compare.

• Keep in the right crowd. To be enlightened, you must seek a light source, rather than a dark source. Our greatest light source is Jehovah — who else and what else could possibly outshine His glory? He is the light we must follow. But just as it is important to follow Him, it is also prudent to follow and be with the right sources on Earth. We all know that birds of a feather flock together. So we must surround ourselves with the kind of people we want to be like. The sources you seek can determine your direction, or help lead you in the right direction. If you want to be more positive, surround yourself with positive people; if you want to be happy, spend time with happy people; and if you want to be miserable (I highly doubt that), have miserable people as company.

> **"Be not unequally yoked with unbelievers: for what fellowship have righteousness and iniquity? or what communion hath light with darkness?" (II Corinthians 6:14)**

If you want to learn how to be good, you need to befriend those who are righteous. Otherwise, if you have the wicked as your friends, they will take you with them down to the abyss of eternal destruction. King Solomon had many wives; each took his heart away from Jehovah. If he had associated himself with the right women who loved God, he would not have fallen.

Beware that you do not associate yourself with those who can turn your own heart away from Jehovah. Do not be quick to believe what people tell you, for not all are ethical and good. Listen to the Scriptures: "The simple believeth every word; But the prudent man looketh well to his going." (Proverbs 14:15)

Do not go with the crowd just because it is a large group. Just because many people do the same thing does not mean that what they do is morally right. Do not yield to the majority to achieve harmony. If only one person does the Word of God, befriend that person. Gaining such friendship is more precious than gaining the entire world.

We must honor God's Word above any and all human ideas, cultural mores, and customs, no matter how promising, exciting, and rewarding they seem to be. Keeping firm to this principle will help you avoid associating yourself with the wrong crowd and ideas.

Also, we should select what we choose to entertain us, whether television shows, movies, books, music, magazines, or video games, to name a few, with great care. If any source condones ungodly thoughts and actions, it is wise not to partake in its food lest it negatively influence you. The news is generally fine, for it informs us of what is happening around us so we can be prepared in certain situations when necessary. For example, if the news issues a severe weather warning, we will know to watch out for one another's well-being.

• Follow Jehovah's light. Just using our own strength is not enough. We need the support from our Source of life, and that is Jehovah, our Father. When we get stressed and have a lot weighing upon our hearts, does it not feel better when we have someone to whom we can pour out our feelings? Is it not so much better to have a loving arm around your shoulders as you cry than to cry alone? Is it not so much better to talk with someone you love than to talk to someone who does not care about you, or to just keep your feelings pent up inside you? Then how much better would it be to release our cries to Jehovah, to ask for Him to strengthen us!

"Be strong, and let your heart take courage, All ye that hope in Jehovah." (Psalm 31:24)

When you feel alone, when you feel that no one in the world understands you, and when you feel hopeless, pray to God. He knows you more than you know yourself, and this Loving Creator will ignite hope within you to help you overcome life's negativity and challenges.

I find that hope in God is the most rewarding kind of hope there is. When I hope in God, even when the situation I am in seems hopeless, I become all hopeful again.

Although I am blind, I can see far and wide; even though I am disabled, I can climb high mountains. Let the ropes of hope in Jehovah haul you high!

Fruitless Worrying or Fruitful Concerns?

"...I say unto you, be not anxious for your life, what ye shall eat, or what ye shall drink; nor yet for your body, what ye shall put on. Is not the life more than the food, and the body than the raiment?" (Matthew 6:25)

Do you sometimes feel overwhelmed by your worrying? Do you agonize over the future? Do you often wonder how tomorrow will turn out? Do you worry about whether you will have enough money to support you for twenty, thirty, or forty more years? Do you feel trapped by your endless thoughts?

How can we kick back, relax, and enjoy the scenery as we travel along on our journey? Are we even able to?

We are definitely able to put our worries behind us in order to live more lightly. Jesus knows what burdens our hearts, and he desires to take away our load, so let us carefully study what advice he has for us, so we can replace our troubled spirit with peace of mind.

Jesus gently reminded us that the birds of the

heavens do not sow, "neither do they reap, nor gather into barns; and your heavenly Father feedeth them. Are not ye of much more value then they?" (Matthew 6:26) We can fully delight in life's blessings only when we allow God to care for us, for He knows what we need even before we begin to worry ourselves, and He will provide for us just as He clothes "the grass of the field, which to-day is, and tomorrow is cast into the oven, shall he not much more clothe you, O ye of little faith?" (Matthew 6:30)

Yes, I know what you may be thinking right now: "How could we not worry when we know there are millions of people who have literally starved to death? God did not care for their needs, did He?" It does seem that God has forsaken us in our own misery, does it not?

Did God really abandon our needs on Earth? Did people starve to death because God somehow forgot to feed them? We already know that our grand planet is able to produce all the food we could ever need. So what went wrong? Our greed, our lack of neighborly love! It is grossly wrong to say it is God's fault when we, ourselves, are to blame for not meeting the needs of our fellow humans.

So Jesus could accurately conclude, "Be not therefore anxious, saying, What shall we eat? or, What shall we drink? or, Wherewithal shall we be clothed? For after all these things do the Gentiles seek; for your heavenly Father knoweth that ye have need of all these things. But seek ye first his kingdom, and his righteousness; and all these things shall be added unto you." (Matthew 6:31-33)

Take note especially of what Jesus said last.

What should be our focus? As Christians, we need to get our priorities straight. People get overly frustrated when they confuse what is vital with what is fleeting. Once we sort out our agendas and pinpoint the truly important matters and tasks, we will no longer feel as overwhelmed by our daily demands.

Should we solely concentrate our energy on our earthly home? No, we should devote our time and effort to our everlasting home in God's Kingdom. When we seek heavenly riches, we will live in eternal happiness and prosperity, with all of our needs met abundantly and endlessly. Therefore, we must use our strength on what is important to Christians: hope for our needs *after* this world rather than *in* this world. That is our priority; everything else comes after this.

Taking ourselves lightly with our passing troubles in this temporary home, however, does not excuse us to party our days away or pardon us from our responsibilities to live well in every way. When Jesus told us not to worry about tomorrow, for "the morrow will be anxious for itself. Sufficient unto the day is the evil thereof," it is wrongly concluded that he was telling us not to plan for our lives here at all. (Matthew 6:34) Did he mean that we should abandon our concerns and responsibilities for one another? No, quite the contrary. It is our duty to care for ourselves and one another. He simply repeated his advice for us not to let our concern turn to excessive anxiety that would overwhelm and consume our mental and physical energy, for tomorrow will always have its difficulties and we have no need to add to them. After all, would worrying do us any good? Would worrying magically put food on our table? But concern will allow us to diligently work for our next meal. God provides the materials; it is up to us to perform the work.

Next time, when your thoughts exhaust you, ask yourself, "Are they fruitless worries or fruitful concerns?" Fruitless worrying is when you are stressed about the things you have no control over. (Why worry about things you *can* control?) God has your needs in His hands, so why doubt His care?

Would taking life one step at a time be more enjoyable than if you were to fret over your situation thirty years from now? Even if you could plan out your future and determine that you have enough money to support you for the rest of your life, so what? Any calamity could strike you at any time, taking away everything you worked for so diligently. Therefore, put your mind on today; it has enough issues for you to deal with, and only when you focus on today will you create a lasting future — in the Kingdom. Be fruitfully concerned for others, one day at a time, and seek God's Kingdom first, for whenever we seek things of the good, we will receive good in return; whenever we sow whole-heartedly, we will reap fruitfully.

Do You Eat the Smaller Fish?

"He that oppresseth the poor reproacheth his Maker; But he that hath mercy on the needy honoreth him." (Proverbs 14:31)

The big fish eats the small fish, the small fish eats the weak fish, and the weak fish eats the ill fish.

What am I referring to? No, I am not talking about the food chain. This is what I call the bullying chain.

I am pretty sure that, like me, you have witnessed the big guy bullying the small guy as the small guys does nothing to defend himself. Yet, the small guy turns around and bullies the weak guy. Like the small guy who did not have the guts to defend himself, the weak guy quivers with fear. But the next day, the weak guy becomes as much a bully as the small guy when he meets an ill guy, who becomes this weak guy's victim.

Bullying is everywhere, from the schools and hospitals to your own living room. Bullying comes in all sizes and forms — the physical, the mental, and the spiritual, including discrimination and neglect. There is the bullying between coworkers and employers and employees, and there is the unfortunate bullying that occurs in families.

But just because there is bullying does not mean that the bullying chain should continue. You can break the chain in two ways.

• Defend yourself when you are being bullied, and protect those who are bullied. People prefer to bully those who seem easy to pick on. They bully the ones who depend on them. Their bullying worsens when their victims do not fight back. So stand up tall when you are bullied; show them that you are not an easy target, and often the bullies will back down. Trust me, bullies are people—they are scared of trouble and will not want to touch those who can fight back. Have you ever seen the big guy bullying the giant guy? No. So act like the giant guy.

When you witness bullying, defend the victim by either reporting the bullying or showing the victim how to defend himself. Bullies pick on loners, and avoid those who have allies.

> "Judge the poor and fatherless: Do justice to the afflicted and destitute. Rescue the poor and needy: Deliver them out of the hand of the wicked." (Psalm 82:3-4)

• Do not turn around and bully someone smaller or weaker than you. When you see someone who is less wealthy, less pretty, less healthy, or less intelligent, than you, do not think, *I can take advantage of this person!*

> "My brethren, hold not the faith of our Lord Jesus Christ, the Lord of glory, with respect of persons. For if there come into your synagogue a man with a gold ring, in fine clothing, and there come in also a poor man in vile clothing; and ye have regard to him that weareth the fine clothing, and say, Sit thou here in a good place; and ye say to the poor man, Stand thou there, or sit under my footstool; Do ye not make distinctions among yourselves, and become judges with evil thoughts? Hearken, my beloved brethren; did not God choose them that are poor as to the world to be rich in faith, and heirs of the kingdom which he promised to them that love him?" (James 2:1-5)

Treat everyone with equality. No matter who you meet—a prince or a pauper—treat both kindly, and in the same way. Do not look down upon the woman who has not washed her hair for days or has holes in her shirt. Even if you think to yourself, *Yuck!* never let your actions mirror your feelings. Treat her well; give her a generous smile, and make her feel like a princess.

Following these two tips will shatter the bullying chain into a million tiny pieces.

Our Work Not in Vain!

"Except Jehovah build the house, They labor in vain that build it: Except Jehovah keep the city, The watchman waketh but in vain." (Psalm 127:1)

When you admire the beautiful sunset alone, do you not long to have someone you love share the moment with you? An ordinary moment can easily turn into a special memory if shared with those you cherish; even a moment of silence can be savored. If an author creates a masterpiece, what good would the book do if there are no readers to take in its important messages or be enthralled by its suspenseful story line? Writers need readers to give meaning to their works. A house is useless if it does not have inhabitants, just as a life is valueless when it lacks companionship and love.

Yet, even if we live a life filled with love from others, and do whatever we thoroughly enjoy, we will all die someday. No matter how good or bad we were, we will all end up in the exact same place, in the same condition. For those who do not believe in Jehovah, such a life is an empty, valueless, purposeless existence. What good is everything when you will leave it all behind? These individuals put their lives on autopilot, going wherever life takes them and doing whatever life demands at the moment. They lack enthusiasm for what they do or say, and neither look forward to nor dread the future. What is there to hope for when your end is death?

But now, since we know our Creator, the knowledge in Him showers light upon us, giving life true purpose. We will all pass away, but only for the time being. Whatever we do will never go to waste. The good we cultivate will blossom and grow into a great harvest, and whatever bad we do will be burnt and destroyed forever. Thus, whatever we do right now is fruitful: our good deeds will yield good fruits, while our bad deeds will yield rotten fruits; and all the fruits we yield will be for God. He will collect the good ones while tossing away the bad, along with their planters He will treat accordingly.

> "...fear God, and keep his commandments; for this is the whole duty of man. For God will bring every work into judgment, with every hidden thing, whether it be good, or whether it be evil." (Ecclesiastes 12:13-14)

What can you do to create a meaningful life? Is a worthwhile life all about obtaining fame and fortune, fulfilling your heart's deepest desires, or going on a daring adventure? Many people have found that, even after they have achieved their life-long goals, they still feel empty and disappointed. What they had once thought would fill the hole inside turned out to be just another one of their ephemeral undertakings, leaving them as empty as before.

How do you achieve a truly meaningful life? The earthly achievements we accomplish are fleeting ventures; they do not last forever. Therefore, they do not and cannot fill the void. We will last forever when we put our faith in Christ, so we must obtain those gems that will last forever with us. What lasts forever? We learn that spiritual values are everlasting, and the cornerstone of purest spirituality is no other than the greatest Spirit, Jehovah Himself. Thus, knowing and having a relationship with God creates a life that endures, and gives meaning to time indefinite.

With the knowledge of Jehovah, we will always have an audience and a companion. Each writer will have readers, each dancer will have an audience, and every stargazer will have a lover, for Jehovah is our greatest Companion. We will never accomplish tasks in vain, nor sing a song that goes unheard, when we have Jehovah by our side.

> **"Whoso keepeth the fig-tree shall eat the fruit thereof; And he that regardeth his master shall be honored." (Proverbs 27:18)**

With Jehovah as your Best Friend, be sure that whatever you do is a delight to Him. Let whatever you do be for God and be with God, for He is holy and He has made you holy, so be so, just as the apostle Paul urged in his letter to the Romans: "I beseech you therefore, brethren, by the mercies of God, to present your bodies a living sacrifice, holy, acceptable to God, which is your spiritual service." (Romans 12:1)

If you drink, drink in honor of God; if you eat, eat in honor of Him. If you throw a party, throw it in His honor. If you laugh, laugh with Him; if you cry, cry with Him, for He feels your happiness and sorrow, all that human companions cannot. And if you love, love for Him, and love abundantly, for He is love.

Do Not Destroy the Honor!

"For I am persuaded, that neither death, nor life, nor angels, nor principalities, nor things present, nor things to come, nor powers, nor height, nor depth, nor any other creature, shall be able to separate us from the love of God, which is in Christ Jesus our Lord." (Romans 8:38-39)

What is the most destructive consequence if we do not apply Bible principles to our daily living? We know by now that not listening to God's words will bring us calamity. If we steal, we may get caught and locked up behind bars; if we kill, we may receive the death sentence; if we lie, we can lose a good friend; and if we commit adultery, it may ruin our names. Yet, these consequences are far from being the worst outcome we will experience if we commit iniquities. What *is* the worst fruit we would gather after diverging from the straight path?

Imagine your friend repeatedly telling you not to do a certain thing, yet you do not listen—how would your friend feel? Would she feel hurt and upset? Would she feel that you do not love her and cherish your friendship?

When we disobey God's commands, we are hurting more than simply a friend—we are hurting the very Creator who gave us each breath we take, the Originator who lovingly made us in His own image to be like Him. Can you just imagine the extent and the intensity of the pain He experiences when we turn to the left or to the right on our paths? Therefore, the most devastating result of our acts of impurity is ruining the relationship we have with Jehovah. When we sin, the only one we are sinning against is Jehovah. A crime is an offense against the creation; a sin is an offense against the Creator.

Let us imagine that after years of searching, you have finally found your soul mate, who has all the best qualities of which you ever dreamed. Would you not do your very best to keep this sacred union? Would you allow your actions to destroy the treasure you have at last found? No, you would work hard to keep this relationship by showing your love and applying invaluable principles.

The relationship we have with God is the most sacred of the sacred, the highest of the highest, so we must do everything in our power to maintain this sacred relationship with God. When we try our utmost, even if we fail from time to time, He will see our effort and forgive our weaknesses, and that will help us maintain the connection with Him.

Hold on tightly to the privilege, the greatest honor you have—being one of His magnificent creations. Do not allow worldly temptations to take this honor away from you. Be strong, ask for strength, and Jehovah will strengthen this privilege!

The Value of Success

"That which maketh a man to be desired is his kindness; And a poor man is better than a liar." (Proverbs 19:22)

What is success? What is the kind of success that is truly of greatest value in life? To answer this, we first must find out what Jehovah God wants from us. What He desires from us is what makes us truly successful.

What does God wish of us? First, let us think about His intent and purpose in creating us in the first place. The Bible, His holy Word, clearly indicates that He created the world and humans so we can be fruitful and multiply and create a beautiful world, filled with loving, caring, honest, sincere, and trustworthy people. Knowing this, we can see that it is our core values that God cherishes, and, in turn, wishes His human creations to establish and pass on for eternity.

Thus, what constitutes a successful person is a successful human being. It is not about being a successful businessman, a successful doctor, or a successful teacher—that all comes later. Success is successfully realizing, establishing, and holding tightly to the priceless values of life.

A blue-collar man who constantly provides love and care for his elderly mother is a hundredfold more successful than a billionaire who loves only his money. A mother who stands by her disabled daughter's side as opposed to a mother who appreciates only a healthy daughter displays the kind of success that is multiplied countless times.

If you are a parent, would you love your child all the same, no matter how beautiful or ugly, how rich or poor, how smart or stupid, and how healthy or ill he or she was? If yes, then you would be a successful parent.

Are you successful when, no matter how hard you have worked and how you have striven to do your best, you still have not achieved your intended goal, but you have learned many valuable lessons along your journey? Yes, you are successful, and for two reasons: First, you have worked your hardest and have tried your best—the best is all we can ask from anyone. And second, you have been wise enough to learn lessons as you worked. Achieving a goal, without learning much from the process, does not make a person truly successful.

Once you have become a successful human being, you can then become a truly successful businessman, a successful doctor, or a successful teacher. If you do not have good values to start with, what do you have to expand on? A businessman who cheats his clients of their money to become a millionaire is not successful. On the other hand, a man with integrity has that value upon which to build his business. From there, he can become a successful businessman who will earn only honest money and attract loyal customers.

Thus, success is calculated by the spiritual values you can provide to others that can not be physically measured by the amount of money or the level of prestige you achieve. God does not care how much money you make or how much you donate to Him; He cares how much love you provide to His other creations; this will show Him how much of His unconditional love you can return and how much faith you have in Jesus Christ. This is how He measures success, and this is how we should measure success.

I find my mother is the most successful person I have ever known, and one of the most successful people who has ever lived. It is true that she has made many mistakes, but she has learned lessons, has done her utmost to be a wonderful mother and person, and sets an excellent example for others of what being successful is really all about in life. I have learned a lot from her, and the lessons learned can lead me onto my own road to great success.

Life's FAQs: Mysteries, Solved!

"In the beginning God created the heavens and the earth. And the earth was waste and void; and darkness was upon the face of the deep: and the Spirit of God moved upon the face of the waters. And God said, Let there be light: and there was light. And God saw the light, that it was good: and God divided the light from the darkness. And God called the light Day, and the darkness he called Night. And there was evening and there was morning, one day." (Genesis 1:1-5)

Have you ever wondered if science contradicts the process of creation as told in Genesis? Or have you ever wanted to know what happens when people die? Is there really a hell? Why does God permit evil and suffering? In this chapter, I will briefly address these questions with the help of the trusty Bible.

Bang! And out came Earth?

From where did Earth come? What does science say? It theorizes that our magnificent, purposeful planet came to be in a sudden explosion called the Big Bang. Could such a fantastic and complex system as our universe, with its finely tuned laws, suddenly come from nowhere and exist in such perfect harmony?

Even if inanimate objects could pop out of nowhere, could the Big Bang have possibly produced active, living, breathing creatures of various complexities, designs, purposes, and functions? Even if animate beings could indeed arrive from thin air, how could they have the ability to reproduce immediately? If they could not reproduce right away, they would not have had any chance to exist and survive to this date. Reproduction is no small matter; it involves a highly organized system. To come from nothingness, by chance, equipped with such advanced and orderly capabilities is not probable at all, do you not agree?

Even if there were indeed a Big Bang, there had to be a cause for it, for every effect has a cause. This holds especially true for something as fantastic as our universe. Is the Big Bang magic? Then there must be a magician behind it. If your child asks you, "Where did the stars come from?" and you tell her that they just popped out from nowhere, would she fall for that? If even a small child cannot believe it, how could adults be fooled by it? (As, evidently, many adults have somehow been.)

Where science cannot satisfactorily answer, the Bible beautifully and accurately supplies: "In the beginning God created the heavens and the earth." It clearly indicates that we have a Creator who created everything; He is the cause of the effect, the coming into existence of our universe.

Science theorizes that Earth had only water and land in its early, formative stages, followed by organisms in the oceans and then land creatures. The Genesis account in the Bible agrees. So, long before scientists came up with the origins of our planet and life, the Bible already accurately told of our great beginning.

Long before people proved it scientifically, the Bible indicated that Earth hangs in space: "He stretcheth out the north over empty space, and hangeth the earth upon nothing," (Job 26:7) and that Earth is round: "It is he that sitteth above the circle of the earth..." (Isaiah 40:22)

What was the length of time spent on the creation process for everything on Earth and for Earth itself? How long have Earth and its life forms been in existence? According to science, the last dinosaurs existed over sixty-five million years ago. But how could that be when God created our planet in only six days? But read carefully what the Bible says: "And God saw everything that he had made, and, behold, it was very good. And there was evening and there was morning, the sixth day." (Genesis 1:31) God did create everything in stages over a six-day span. But does the Bible indicate how long each day lasted? No, it does not. Sometimes, a "day" in the Bible simply refers to an unspecified period of time, so each day in creation could have been thousands or millions of years long in our human time.

The Bible can be trusted, but can science? Science is always trial and error, especially when it concerns theories, many of which the Bible does not confirm — so the existence of dinosaurs so many years ago may or may not be true. What both the Bible and science agree on is that animals came first, and so the dinosaurs could have died (and they did) before God decided to create humans (for good reasons, I must add!).

Science says that our universe is 13.7 billion years old and Earth is 4.5 billion years old. Does the Bible say otherwise? No, the Scriptures do not state any time frame, so they can neither agree or disagree.

As we can conclude, whatever the Bible mentions, science confirms, such as the case concerning the stages of creation. For whatever the Bible does not verify, scientific theory remains just that — theoretical.

Why do we die and what happens after death?

Jehovah created humans with the intention that they live forever. But when Adam and Eve disobeyed Him, God told Adam, "In the sweat of thy face shalt thou eat bread, till thou return unto the ground; for out of it wast thou taken: for dust thou art, and unto dust shalt thou return." (Genesis 3:19) This is why not a single human being can escape death, for death entered the entire human line through Adam.

What is death? What happens after we die? The following Bible quotations answer these questions.

"For that which befalleth the sons of men befalleth beasts; even one thing befalleth them: as the one dieth, so dieth the other; yea, they have all one breath; and man hath no preeminence above the beasts: for all is vanity. All go unto one place; all are of the dust, and all turn to dust again." (Ecclesiastes 3:19-20)

"For the living know that they shall die: but the dead know not anything..." (Ecclesiastes 9:5)

"The dead praise not Jehovah, Neither any that go down into silence." (Psalm 115:17)

"Whatsoever thy hand findeth to do, do it with thy might; for there is no work, nor device, nor knowledge, nor wisdom, in Sheol, whither thou goest." (Ecclesiastes 9:10)

"Put not your trust in princes, Nor in the son of man, in whom there is no help. His breath goeth forth, he returneth to his earth; In that very day his thoughts perish." (Psalm 146:3-4)

"But man dieth, and is laid low: Yea, man giveth up the ghost, and where is he? As the waters fail from the sea, And the river wasteth and drieth up; So man lieth down and riseth not: Till the heavens be no more, they shall not awake, Nor be roused out of their sleep." (Job 14:10-12)

Yes, the Bible clearly indicates that when we die, we cease to exist. Death is simply a state of nonexistence.

But do righteous people not go to heaven after death? Jesus supplied: "No one hath gone up to the heaven, except he who out of the heaven came down—the Son of Man who is in the heaven." (John 3:13, Young's Literal Translation) Clearly, the answer is no. Moreover, "the heavens are the heavens of Jehovah; But the earth hath he given to the children of men." (Psalm 115:16) Heaven is God's own home—why should we crowd His living space? Are we sinless, that we have the privilege of living in His house?

How about hell—do evil people go to hell after death? After reading the next section in this chapter, you will conclude that the answer is no as well.

Thus, we do not have immortal souls. After we pass away, we do not go on roaming as spirits or ghosts, nor do we enter another world, neither the heavens nor hell. We instead sleep in our tombs until Jesus calls us out for Judgment Day: "They that have done good, unto the resurrection of life; and they that have done evil, unto the resurrection of judgment." (John 5:29) Similarly, the book of Daniel tells us, "Many of them that sleep in the dust of the earth shall awake, some to everlasting life, and some to shame and everlasting contempt." (Daniel 12:2) Like Jesus, we will all be resurrected, except for those who will be alive to witness his second coming.

Death is a punishment given to Adam and all mankind after Adam sinned. If we go on living as spirits after death, would death really be, or feel like, a punishment, especially if some go to heaven? What point could God make if He allowed people to live in another world after death? God punished Adam with death—nonexistence—not another world.

Can you imagine what would have gone through Adam's mind if he had gone down to hell after death? *Hey, where am I? God told me we would surely die if we ate that fruit, but am I not alive and suffering great pain? So God lied, and Satan actually told the truth!* Yes, when we believe that we possess immortal souls, then we are calling God a liar and Satan a speaker of truth!

Think about it: If we indeed enter heaven or hell immediately after death, why would a huge Judgment Day be necessary? To enter another world upon death would mean that we have already received God's judgment, does it not? So why would we need to be judged a second time? The Bible talks about only one-time judgment for the resurrected, not second, or third.

If the wicked souls go to hell, then are judged again, does that mean these people are being given another chance to go to heaven if somehow they could be proven righteous? And what if the righteous souls in heaven were to receive another judgement—would some have new evidence against them to prove their unfaithfulness, which would sentence them to hell? No, the Bible teaches us that each of us receives only one judgment, according to what we have done in our entire lifetime on Earth. We would not be initially judged by entering either heaven or hell, and then judged again in the resurrection.

Take note of what Jesus once said: "When thou makest a feast, bid the poor, the maimed, the lame, the blind: and thou shalt be blessed; because they have not wherewith to recompense thee: for thou shalt be recompensed in the resurrection of the just." (Luke 14:13-14) Yes, the righteous will be rewarded in the resurrection of the just, not immediately after death.

"Fear God, and give him glory; for the hour of his judgment is come..." (Revelation 14:7)

Also, if we do live on as immortal souls, then why does the Bible tell us about a massive resurrection event after the end of the last days? Resurrection is specifically for the dead, to raise them up from their tombs, so how could immortal souls be resurrected? Jesus explicitly said, "No man can come to me, except the Father that sent me draw him: and I will raise him up in the last day." (John 6:44) If people are already in heaven, why would Jesus need to raise them up? Heaven dwellers do not need anyone to "raise them up"!

Most importantly, the idea of humans having immortal souls goes against one of Christianity's main teachings. If we believe that each of us has an immortal soul that lives after our bodily death, then we are calling Christianity a false religion that made up Jesus' death and resurrection! As a matter of fact, the fundamental belief of our Christian faith is the resurrection of Jesus, for it gives us hope that death will be our last enemy once we have accepted Jehovah's grace. His resurrection signifies hope for all humans; those who have died, whether righteous or unrighteous, will be resurrected to be given a second chance not only to live, but live to time indefinite.

Jesus' resurrection proves to us that there is no immortal soul. If we have an immortal soul that can shoot straight up to heaven upon our death, then why would resurrection even be necessary?

Body, Soul, and Spirit

"Soul" in the Bible simply means "living creature" or "self," so any living animal or human is a soul. When the living creature dies, that means the soul dies. Hence, a man is a soul; so is a bird, a butterfly, or a goldfish. "Soul" also means "life" in the Bible. To say that a soul is leaving a person means that life is leaving that person. Soul can also be the entire life you live. So I can say that I love my soul even though it has brought me many challenges.

Besides being a living soul, you have a spirit. To help you better understand the "soul" and "spirit" concepts, I would like you to consider a human being. What comprises a person? A body, yes. But where do the willpower, stamina, love, and mental strength come from? They are elements we cannot see, touch, taste, hear, or smell, yet we know for certain that they exist.

I always say, "People can do whatever they want to you physically, but no one and nothing, except God, can touch your spirit if you do not let them." What do I mean by that? To answer this, let us study how Jehovah created humankind, specifically what ingredients He used in His creation. Genesis 2:7 tells us, "Jehovah God formed man of the dust of the ground, and breathed into his nostrils the breath of life; and man became a living soul."

What materials did Jehovah use to create a human being? He used the dust of the ground and the breath of life, which He breathed into the body. The spirit was the force God breathed into Adam in order to give him life, and what resulted was a living soul. All the intangible elements come from the spirit.

Jehovah owns the breath of life, the spirit of a person. It is true that He owns everything, but only He can touch that spirit. This is why we should not fear people, for they cannot destroy our spirits (life forces) or souls (our entire lives in the hand of God); it is only God who "is able to destroy both soul and body in hell." (Matthew 10:28) Only God can end our lives permanently.

When we die, our life force returns to God—it comes under His control, so each person's fate becomes dependent on God. Whether He wants to resurrect that person is up to Him. So right before Jesus died, he cried, "Father, into thy hands I commend my spirit," and then he "gave up his spirit," entrusting his fate into God's hand; it was then up to God to resurrect him at His appointed time. (Luke 23:46; John 19:30)

Basically, the spirit (breath of life) is what you receive into your body in order to become a living soul (creature) and have a soul (life) and spirit or the "inner self" (everything that is not physical). So each of us is comprised of a body, spirit, and soul, and all of these elements are mortal. When those of us who are cleansed by Jesus' blood are resurrected, we will receive immortality. Simply put, we become immortal after we are resurrected, not immediately after death; and for those who are still alive at Jesus' second coming, they will receive immortality then, as the Bible says: "...in a moment, in the twinkling of an eye, at the last trump: for the trumpet shall sound, and the dead shall be raised incorruptible, and we shall be changed. For this corruptible must put on incorruption, and this mortal must put on immortality. But when this corruptible shall have put on incorruption, and this mortal shall have put on immortality, then shall come to pass the saying that is written, Death is swallowed up in victory." (I Corinthians 15:52-54) We will be raised up owning a different kind of body—a spiritual one, not this physical body we have now.

It is clear to us that the Bible does not teach the doctrine of immortal souls. However, you may still have some questions left unanswered, so I will answer some of the frequently asked questions to help ease any remaining doubts you may have and assist you in obtaining the truth on this crucial subject.

Question: Jesus said, "Whosoever liveth and believeth on me shall never die." (John 11:26) Does that prove that people still live on after physical death?

Answer: No, Jesus was not teaching the doctrine of immortal souls. Prior to resurrection, all people will eventually die. You see, to God, all people are already dead when they do not follow in His ways, whereas those who believe in Him and accept His Son are all living. This is why Jesus said, "God is not the God of the dead, but of the living," and

"Leave the dead to bury their own dead." (Matthew 22:32; Luke 9:60) This is how Jehovah is still the God of Abraham, and the God of Isaac, and the God of Jacob, even though they are in the grave.

The dead are the worldly; the living are the spiritual who will never die. The living who died before God's great war will be raised into an eternal life.

Question: Luke23:43 seems to tell us that people do have an immortal soul that goes to heaven immediately following death. It is what Jesus said to the criminal who was impaled next to him: "Verily I say unto thee, To-day shalt thou be with me in Paradise." Does this indicate that we do have immortal souls?

Answer: No, it does not support the idea of immortal souls. To understand this, we need to take into account a few essential points.

- Notice that Jesus used the word "today." Did Jesus return to heaven that day? No, he returned to God's side forty-three days later. Jesus used "today" as a promise that the man is in his heart from that time onward, and that he will resurrect him to be with him in paradise at God's appointed time.
- Another explanation for "today" is perhaps that the comma was placed in the wrong spot. The old manuscripts of the Scriptures have no punctuation marks, so Jesus might have meant, "Verily I say unto thee to-day, shalt thou be with me in Paradise." If this is the case, then it settles any contradictions, and actually flows much better in

their brief conversation. See for yourself:

The criminal said, "Jesus, remember me when thou comest in thy kingdom."

So Jesus promised him by saying, "Verily I say unto thee to-day, shalt thou be with me in Paradise."

Do you see that by using "today" Jesus was assuring the man that he was making the promise that very moment?

• The man knew that entering God's Kingdom will be a future event, not something that would happen on that day, for note what he said to Jesus: "Jesus, remember me when thou comest in thy kingdom." (Luke 23:42) If he believed that the Christ was returning to God's side that very day, why did he ask Jesus to remember him?

• No room in heaven was yet prepared for the criminal. During Jesus' last supper with his disciples, he told them, "In my Father's house are many mansions; if it were not so, I would have told you; for I go to prepare a place for you. And if I go and prepare a place for you, I come again, and will receive you unto myself; that where I am, there ye may be also." (John 14:2-3) Jesus must ascend into heaven first in order to prepare a place before he can accept people into God's home. If even Jesus' disciples had no room in heaven, how could the criminal have?

Only when Jesus comes the second time will he personally bring to us the reward of his salvation. Until then, no one can enter heaven, no matter when we die.

Question: Can you explain this passage? "And

after six days Jesus taketh with him Peter, and James, and John his brother, and bringeth them up into a high mountain apart: and he was transfigured before them; and his face did shine as the sun, and his garments became white as the light. And behold, there appeared unto them Moses and Elijah talking with him." (Matthew 17:1-3) Does this mean that two of the greatest prophets appeared with Jesus as immortal souls?

Answer: It is my pleasure to answer this question! At first read, this passage does seem to support the notion of immortal souls. However, if you read what Jesus told his disciples, you will see that this occurrence can be easily explained. Jesus commanded them, "Tell the vision to no man, until the Son of man be risen from the dead." (Matthew 17:9)

Yes, what his disciples saw was simply a vision, not an actual event! They saw a glimpse of the future, when Jesus becomes the King in God's Kingdom. This is what Jesus meant when he said this six days previous: "Verily I say unto you, there are some of them that stand here, who shall in no wise taste of death, till they see the Son of man coming in his kingdom." (Matthew 16:28) Truly, some of his disciples indeed saw Jesus coming in his Kingdom, on that mountain.

This prophetic vision was like all the visions the apostle John saw in the book of Revelation concerning the end of this world and the new beginning. He saw horsemen riding forth to carry out their missions and martyred souls crying out to have their blood avenged—did you think he saw events that were actually occurring then? Of course not; if he had, then the end of the world would have come exactly when he saw it happen, and you and I would not still be here on this polluted Earth.

Question: In a letter the apostle Paul wrote, he said: "For to me to live is Christ, and to die is gain. But if to live in the flesh, —if this shall bring fruit from my work, then what I shall choose I know not. But I am in a strait betwixt the two, having the desire to depart and be with Christ; for it is very far better: yet to abide in the flesh is more needful for your sake." (Philippians 1:21-24) Was Paul saying that he could immediately be with Jesus after death?

Answer: Yes and no. When you are sleeping, are you able to tell time? No, you cannot, and this is the same case in death. When people die, their thoughts cease, just as the Bible says. The dead do not know anything; they do not even know they are dead! When the dead cannot tell time, one minute and one million years will feel the same to them when they awaken. So after Paul gets resurrected from his long sleep, he will feel as though he has gone to the Christ right away.

In his letter, did Paul mention that he had an immortal soul and that he would be with Jesus *immediately* after death? No, so we must not add words into his intended meaning. If he did not say something, that means it is not there and he did not support it. He, like any one of us, did not have an immortal soul.

Question: In another letter, Paul wrote: "...whilst we are at home in the body, we are absent from the Lord (for we walk by faith, not by sight); we are of good courage, I say, and are willing rather to be absent from the body, and to be at home with the Lord. Wherefore also we make it our aim, whether at home or absent, to be well-pleasing unto him." (II Corinthians 6-9) What did Paul mean?

Answer: Here, Paul was talking about the two opposing forces I have covered earlier in this book: the spiritual and the worldly. When we are at home in our bodies, it means we are more attuned to the worldly—our fleshly desires. As Christians, we need to be at home with Christ, meaning we need to embrace the spiritual. We need to nourish our spirits within, not focus on our bodies. But even if we, as imperfect humans, cannot live with Jesus all the time, God will see our efforts and save us with His grace. So whether we live in Christ or live in our bodily homes, we always must do our best, striving to love God.

Question: Did Elijah go to heaven? The Bible says, "And it came to pass, when Jehovah would take up Elijah by a whirlwind into heaven, that Elijah went with Elisha from Gilgal. And it came to pass, as they still went on, and talked, that, behold, there appeared a chariot of fire, and horses of fire, which parted them both asunder; and Elijah went up by a whirlwind into heaven." (II Kings 2:1, 11)

Answer: No, Elijah did not go to heaven, or God's home. How do we know? Because years later, King Jehoram received a letter from the prophet: "And there came a writing to him from Elijah the prophet..." (II Chronicles 21:12) Elijah was simply sent to a different location on Earth. "Heaven" here simply means "sky," as do many other Bible verses.

Paul mentioned "third heaven" in one of his letters where he talked about a man being brought to heaven in the visions and revelations he received from God, so it seems as though God's dwelling place is called the "third heaven." (II Corinthians 12:1-2)

Elijah went up to heaven, but not the third heaven. And let us not forget that Jesus said that no one has gone up to heaven. If we believe that Elijah went to heaven, then we would call Jesus a liar! So neither Elijah, Enoch, Moses, Abraham, King David, nor Moses has gone up to heaven. If anyone had the honor to enter the gates of heaven, surely they would be the first to step in, right?

Question: If there is no immortal soul, then how could the dead Samuel have come up to answer King Saul's calling?

Answer: Let us study the passage in 1 Samuel 28 to obtain the truth. I will insert my thoughts in bullet points to bring your attention to the verses that will help us answer this question.

> Verse 6: And when Saul inquired of Jehovah, Jehovah answered him not, neither by dreams, nor by Urim, nor by prophets.
> 7: Then said Saul unto his servants, Seek me a woman

that hath a familiar spirit, that I may go to her, and inquire of her. And his servants said to him, Behold, there is a woman that hath a familiar spirit at En-dor.

• Saul wanted to seek a woman with "a familiar spirit," even though seeking the counsel of such people is strictly forbidden by God. Why does Jehovah forbid it? Psychics, mediums, and anyone who practices spiritism have communications with the deceiving demons. God always desires that we know the truth and all that it is necessary for us to know; if fortune-tellers are like God's prophets, then why would God not allow us to associate ourselves with them? In fact, God had ordered that any people with familiar spirits be put to death.

• When God forbids such practices, would He now really give any inspired messages to Saul through this medium? Would the spirit that the medium conjured up be the actual Samuel?

> 8: And Saul disguised himself, and put on other raiment, and went, he and two men with him, and they came to the woman by night: and he said, Divine unto me, I pray thee, by the familiar spirit, and bring me up whomsoever I shall name unto thee.
> 9: And the woman said unto him, Behold, thou knowest what Saul hath done, how he hath cut off those that have familiar spirits, and the wizards, out of the land: wherefore then layest thou a snare for my life, to cause me to die?
> 10: And Saul sware to her by Jehovah, saying, As Jehovah liveth, there shall no punishment happen to thee for this thing.
> 11: Then said the woman, Whom shall I bring up unto thee? And he said, Bring me up Samuel.
> 12: And when the woman saw Samuel, she cried with

a loud voice; and the woman spake to Saul, saying, Why hast thou deceived me? for thou art Saul.
13: And the king said unto her, Be not afraid: for what seest thou? And the woman said unto Saul, I see a god coming up out of the earth.
14: And he said unto her, What form is he of? And she said, An old man cometh up; and he is covered with a robe. And Saul perceived that it was Samuel, and he bowed with his face to the ground, and did obeisance.

- Did Saul see "Samuel" with his very eyes? No, he only perceived that it was Samuel based solely on the medium's descriptions. Saul believed the medium's words, but should we? Can such people be trusted at all?
- Why did Samuel come "up" from the ground? Should not righteous people come "down" from heaven instead?
- How could Samuel still look old? If immortal souls retain their outward appearance upon death, then it is definitely not good news for millions of elderly out there!

15: And Samuel said to Saul, Why hast thou disquieted me, to bring me up? And Saul answered, I am sore distressed; for the Philistines make war against me, and God is departed from me, and answereth me no more, neither by prophets, nor by dreams: therefore I have called thee, that thou mayest make known unto me what I shall do.

- Again, since God was ignoring Saul through all the mentioned methods, would He have approved this forbidden association with the medium?

16: And Samuel said, Wherefore then dost thou ask of

me, seeing Jehovah is departed from thee, and is become thine adversary?

17: And Jehovah hath done unto thee, as he spake by me: and Jehovah hath rent the kingdom out of thy hand, and given it to thy neighbor, even to David.

18: Because thou obeyedst not the voice of Jehovah, and didst not execute his fierce wrath upon Amalek, therefore hath Jehovah done this thing unto thee this day.

19: Moreover Jehovah will deliver Israel also with thee into the hand of the Philistines; and to-morrow shalt thou and thy sons be with me: Jehovah will deliver the host of Israel also into the hand of the Philistines.

• Samuel told Saul that the king and his sons would be with Samuel tomorrow, but where *was* Samuel? If Samuel was in heaven, how could someone God had rejected be with him in heaven? If Samuel was in hell (how could righteous people go to hell?), then would it be unjust for Saul's son Jonathan to descend to hell to be with Samuel and Saul? Jonathan, as the Bible describes, was a faithful servant of God and King David.

Conclusion? Since God rejected Saul and Saul turned to God-forbidden counsel, he had no protection from the trickery of evil spirits. The Samuel that rose from the ground was an evil demon impersonating Samuel. But then, how could we know for sure that there was indeed an appearance when it was confirmed only by the medium? There might just be the voice without any apparition accompanying it. Hence, this story fails to prove the idea of immortal souls.

Even after all these Scriptural examples to disprove immortality, some will still continue to insist that people do have immortal souls, saying that Jesus died physically but returned to heaven as a Spirit prior to his resurrection. These supporters of immortality forget what Jesus said to Mary from Magdala after his resurrection: "Touch me not; for I am not yet ascended unto the Father." (John 20:17) Would Jesus have said that he had not yet returned to heaven if he indeed had?

If you still doubt, I would like to leave you with one question to mull over: If people could enter heaven on their own as immortal souls, then why did Jesus die for us? If we could receive salvation just by our good works, then Jesus died for no reason!

Misconceptions about the state of the dead have caused many people to falter. Having the wrong beliefs is not only a simple problem of ignorance; it can be quite dangerous. How so?

Any communication with what people believe to be the dead is actually a communication with evil demons. Ghosts are not of the dead, but of the demons, for "he that goeth down to Sheol shall come up no more. He shall return no more to his house, Neither shall his place know him any more." (Job 7:9-10) Hence, people often fall victim to the schemes of demonic spirits, who pretend to be the souls of their loved ones or good angels. When we call out to our loved ones who have long been dead, through our own works or through mediums, we are giving demons a great chance to control us. Any and all forms of spiritism open the door to connect us with the fallen angels, so we must keep away from fortune-telling, palm reading, astrology, horoscopes, numerology, and other related practices that are seemingly harmless but that are actually acts of demon worship, even if we merely engage in them for entertainment. Let us heed Jehovah's warning: "There shall not be found with thee any one that maketh his son or his daughter to pass through the fire, one that useth divination, one that practiseth augury, or an enchanter, or a sorcerer, or a charmer, or a consulter with a familiar spirit, or a wizard, or a necromancer. For whosoever doeth these things is an abomination unto Jehovah..." (Deuteronomy 18:10-12)

If your child tells you that he or she has seen a ghost or an angel, please do not dismiss it or reprimand your child! Children have a wild imagination, but nonetheless, it is vital to take heed to what they share with us in the event their experiences are actual. Children are vulnerable prey for demons, and once they fall into their evil trap, the demons may follow them for the rest of their lives. When we connect with demons, we are losing connection with God. We cannot be the children of God while we befriend demons.

Always pay attention to your child. If he or she reports a supernatural experience to you, be sure to ask all about it. What did the apparition look like? What did it do or say? After obtaining all the details, gently tell your child about the Bible and the truths about the condition of the dead and of demons. Tell your child that if he or she sees a ghost again, next time say, "Scram! In the name of Jesus Christ, I tell you to leave us and never return." And if your child sees an angel, tell him or her to say, "Are you from Jehovah? If not, in the name of Jesus Christ, go away and never return to us!" If you, yourself, have similar encounters, do the same.

Ask your child to keep you updated on any unnatural dealings he or she may have in the future, so both of you can work together to get rid of any demons in your lives. Teach your child the Bible daily so he or she can have constant protection from any underworld harm.

The wrong knowledge about Bible truths can also be deadly. Many crimes have been committed based on or influenced by inaccurate knowledge of God's Word. One crime comes to my mind: a woman, who fatally shot her son in the head before she turned the gun on herself to end her own life, had left suicide notes saying that she would send her son to heaven and herself to hell. Although she had a history of mental illness, the wrong teachings about immortality and heaven and hell added to her delusions (not that they were the sole cause of her action).

In order to live a life free from the trickery of demons, we must obtain and spread the truths the Bible teaches. Only the truth will set us free, so be steadfast in your efforts in learning, observing, and spreading the Word of God!

Is there a hell?

Would Jehovah, God of Love, really torment the wicked in an everlasting fire? Does hell go against God's most forgiving nature? Would He, who forgives even the worst sinners when they repent, really reserve a furnace for the wicked to punish them forever for the sins they committed in their short, eighty-odd years of life? Would Jehovah think that it is a just punishment?

Will sinners be burned forever in a furnace? What does the Bible say?

The Bible states that "the wages sin pays is death" and that "the soul that sinneth, it shall die." (Romans 6:23; Ezekiel 18:4) Do these verses say that sinful people will go to a burning hell? No; instead, they clearly indicate that sinful souls will simply die, entering into a state of nothingness.

The Bible describes hell, or "lake of fire," as the "second death" as indicated in this passage, which describes what the apostle John saw in the revelation given to him by the Christ: "The dead, the great and the small, standing before the throne; and books were opened: and another book was opened, which is the book of life: and the dead were judged out of the things which were written in the books, according to their works. And the sea gave up the dead that were in it; and death and Hades gave up the dead that were in them: and they were judged every man according to their works. And death and Hades were cast into the lake of fire. This is the second death, even the lake of fire. And if any was not found written in the book of life, he was cast into the lake of fire." (Revelation 20:12-15)

Since we now know what "death" means, we can conclude that the "second death," like the first death, will simply be nonexistence, a total destruction, and anyone who enters the second death will never be resurrected, including the devil and "the fearful, and unbelieving, and abominable, and murderers, and fornicators, and sorcerers, and idolaters, and all liars." Their part "shall be in the lake that burneth with fire and brimstone; which is the second death." (Revelation 21:8)

Take special notice of Revelation 20:14, which is especially good for proving to us that hell does not exist: "And death and Hades were cast into the lake of fire. This is the second death, even the lake of fire." Note that Hades, which is also a term for hell, is said to be cast into the "lake of fire." Here, we must ask ourselves a few questions:

- Are death and hell objects that can be cast away?
- How could death burn in a never-ending fire?
- How could hell be cast into hell, the lake of fire?

Can you not see that this verse shows us that the lake of fire is simply eternal destruction?

What about the references to Gehenna? Is Gehenna hell? Gehenna is Greek for the Valley of Hinnon, where evil false god worshippers sacrificed their children by passing them through fire, a practice Jehovah abhors. The great reformer, King Josiah, faithfully carried out God's laws and "defiled Topheth, which is in the valley of the children of Hinnom, that no man might make his son or his daughter to pass through the fire to Molech." (II Kings 23:10) And after the Jews returned from their captivity, they turned this valley into a garbage dump, where they burned all their junk, dead animals, and criminals.

Jesus mentioned Gehenna a handful of times, each time using it as a symbol of hell—like garbage, evildoers will be destroyed for good. If there indeed were a literal burning hell, then why did Jesus use "Gehenna"? Could he have not used a specific term that solely meant "hell"?

As a matter of fact, the entire Bible does not have a single word for "hell." Any and all mentions of "hell" have been incorrectly translated from Gehenna (garbage dump), Hades (the common grave), Sheol (the grave as well), and Tartarus (a spiritual prison for the demons only). If there is a hell, then why is there no word for hell? If none of the Bible writers used any word for "hell," then we should not proclaim that the Bible teaches that there is such a place!

It puzzles me that hell advocates use the following verse to support their doctrine: "...fear him who is able to destroy both soul and body in hell." (Matthew 10:28) This statement actually disproves the popular hell notion in two ways.

1. Jesus said *both* soul and *body*, not just soul, will be thrown into hell. Those who support their doctrine on hell teach us that only the *soul* is burned in hell after the body dies, while they still use this verse to prove their creed. Therefore, if they want us to accept their doctrine, they would first need to revise their teaching to say that we, as flesh-and-blood bodies, will enter hell whole. But they cannot! Do you know why? They know that they would not be able to revise their doctrine accordingly, because Jehovah already told us that our bodies will return to

the dust of the ground when we die, so we cannot possibly enter hell in bodily form.

2. The soul will be *destroyed* in hell, not being burned for eternity. I repeat: God will completely *destroy*—not torment—evildoers, both their bodies and souls, by throwing them into hell, the lake of fire, the second death: "For, behold, the day cometh, it burneth as a furnace; and all the proud, and all that work wickedness, shall be stubble; and the day that cometh shall burn them up, saith Jehovah of hosts, that it shall leave them neither root nor branch." (Malachi 4:1)

To my disbelief, many ministers use the parable about the rich man and Lazarus found in Luke 16 to prove there is a hell. When we study the story told by Jesus, we can see that it would be rather ridiculous and, above all, harmfully misleading, to take it literally. As with the passage about "Samuel" answering Saul's bid, I will include the entire passage about the parable below, with my points in bullets.

> Verse 19: Now there was a certain rich man, and he was clothed in purple and fine linen, faring sumptuously every day:
> 20: and a certain beggar named Lazarus was laid at his gate, full of sores,
> 21: and desiring to be fed with the crumbs that fell from the rich man's table; yea, even the dogs come and licked his sores.
> 22: And it came to pass, that the beggar died, and that he was carried away by the angels into Abraham's bosom: and the rich man also died, and was buried.

- Lazarus went to heaven just because he was a beggar? Does that mean that all poor people will go to heaven, regardless of how good or evil they are? If this parable is taken literally, then we ought to believe that all beggars will enter heaven to be with God.

> 23: And in Hades he lifted up his eyes, being in torments, and seeth Abraham afar off, and Lazarus in his bosom.

• So the souls in heaven and hell will be able to see one another and have a conversation?

> 24: And he cried and said, Father Abraham, have mercy on me, and send Lazarus, that he may dip the tip of his finger in water, and cool my tongue; for I am in anguish in this flame.

• Simply one or two drops of water will be able to ease the torment of hellfire? So I guess that hell is not so hot after all.

> 25: But Abraham said, Son, remember that thou in thy lifetime receivedst thy good things, and Lazarus in like manner evil things: but now here he is comforted and thou art in anguish.
> 26: And besides all this, between us and you there is a great gulf fixed, that they that would pass from hence to you may not be able, and that none may cross over from thence to us.
> 27: And he said, I pray thee therefore, father, that thou wouldest send him to my father's house;
> 28: for I have five brethren; that he may testify unto them, lest they also come into this place of torment.
> 29: But Abraham saith, They have Moses and the prophets; let them hear them.
> 30: And he said, Nay, father Abraham: but if one go to them from the dead, they will repent.

31: And he said unto him, If they hear not Moses and the prophets, neither will they be persuaded, if one rise from the dead.

As you can see, we simply cannot use this story to prove there is a hell. However, this tale does illustrate one important point: if people, like the Jews in the New Testament, could not accept the Word of God by the works of God's Son, even the resurrection of the dead, especially of Jesus, will be unable to move their hearts to accept the truth. This is exactly what has been happening since the founding of Christianity—many blindly refuse to acknowledge Jesus as the Messiah even though he lived a perfectly sinless life. If people cannot accept Jesus, who else could they possibly accept? Who else could be even more perfect and righteous than Jesus?

Anyway, back to our subject: hell.
Clearly, the Bible affirms that there is no hell in terms of a fiery place where sinners are burned for eternity. The idea that there is a hell distorts Jehovah's splendid image of a loving God. Anyone who reads the Scriptures to study God's nature will be able to promptly and undoubtedly conclude that it would be extremely out of character for God to establish, operate, and oversee the function of an everlasting torture chamber for His creations.

However, those angels who came down from heaven to have sexual relations with women have been locked up in their own prison known as Tartarus. In this state, they no longer can appear as real humans.

In conclusion, the first death is temporary

nonexistence, whereas the second death is eternal nonexistence; those who enter this second death will be gone forever, with no hope of a resurrection. We only have two roads from which to choose: eternal life for the righteous, or eternal death for the wicked. In my opinion, eternal death is punishment enough for evildoers. Life is the biggest blessing God can bestow upon anyone; not being alive to experience all the wonderful things life brings is unbearable. Even the life we live now is precious; can you not imagine how much more so life will be in the everlasting paradise?

I end this portion with one nagging question I have always had: If so many people believe in a burning hell, then why are many of them still so evil? Surely, if hell exists, wouldn't simply thinking about such a horrific place make them tremble with the most intense fear? Would it not prevent them from even having an evil thought?

Hell, an eternal spiritual separation?

While most believe in a fiery hell, many others believe that hell is an eternal spiritual separation from God. No wonder people are not worried about going to hell! Do you not agree that many people right now are living without God in their lives? In their hearts, they are separated from God. So when they go to hell after death, they would continue to live so. "Without God, we could do all we want!" is probably what goes through some of these people's minds. They could go on sinning all they want, partying their days away in their hell, which seems to be a sinners' paradise.

The Bible does not teach any concept of hell, other than an eternal death that encompasses both spiritual and physical destruction.

Where did evil come from?

Long before Jehovah created Earth and humankind, He created spirit beings known as angels who lived with Him in the spiritual realm He calls home. He gave angels the freedom to make their own decisions, just as He has given us free will. One of the angels abused His gift and chose to rebel against Him. This angel is Satan, who is the father of the lie, which he spoke to Eve in the Garden of Eden to trick her into eating the forbidden fruit. Subsequently, other angels and humans followed in Satan's footsteps. This is where evil came from.

Jehovah did not create evil itself; evil results only when His principles are not followed. Evil is the absence of Jehovah, just as darkness is the absence of light, and as chaos is the absence of rules.

Why does God allow suffering?

Before we examine why God allows suffering, let us understand why we suffer in the first place. Here, I will outline the main reasons why we suffer. Understanding the reasons for our tough times will also answer another crucial question: Is suffering all that bad? Are we unlucky each time when we suffer, or are we somehow blessed enough to suffer?

- Suffering strengthens and prepares us. The trials and tribulations we face daily, some more often and severe than others, are exercise machines for our spirits. A sanitary person who has never experienced the cramps, aches, and sweat of exercise would likely be less strong and toned than one who exercises. Therefore, this person may have less energy and ability to perform certain physical feats when required in the future. On the other hand, those who regularly exercise will have the strength to face and overcome physical challenges when necessary. Life is filled with challenges, and it is partly through suffering that we are strengthened and prepared for tougher obstacles ahead.
- We learn through suffering. If you tell a child who has never been burned not to play with fire, do you think he will learn why? Sure, he would know that it will burn him, but if he has never felt the burning sensation, how would he truly know what being burned actually is? If he disobeys your command and touches a candle flame, do you think then he will find out why you told him not to play with fire? You bet! Because of this experience, he learns to stay away from fire in the future. The mistakes we make in life teach us not to repeat the same error again, or show us how to deal with the same kind of situation, should it come up again. Life is all about living and learning. Going through life without learning anything, no matter how many accomplishments one has achieved, does not make the person a true achiever. What makes a person successful is the number of lessons learned and things experienced.

- We are disciplined when we suffer. The same child who touches that candle flame has received discipline through his throbbing finger. His unpleasant experience tells him that he should not take your command too lightly next time. The famous King David in the Bible was disciplined after he committed adultery and then murder. God brought similar kinds of atrocities upon his own family to show the severity and effects of such crimes. It showed David that not only had his actions brought pain to others, but they were hated by God. Therefore, he knew that it was wise never to turn from the path of righteousness again. It has also been used as a good example for us not to mirror the king's ways, or else we will be disciplined the same way.
- Suffering can be a form of punishment for our sins. Everything that happens to us is the effect of our actions. If a man robs a bank and is caught and sent to jail, his prison sentence will be the punishment he brought upon his own head. We reap what we sow. If we do get away with a crime we commit, be sure that it did not escape the keen eyes of Jehovah, who will promptly punish us if we do not repent.
- We suffer when we are in the wrong place at the wrong time. Imagine that you are under a tree when a bolt of lightning suddenly strikes, electrocuting you. Is there any particular reason why you had to suffer? No, it was simply an accident. Accidents can happen anytime and anywhere to anyone. God and diligent people cannot possibly be held responsible for mishaps.

- We suffer for glory when we battle against evil. Often enough, when we oppose the worldly desires, the world will mock, scorn, criticize, or hate us enough to end our lives. But know that the world hated Jesus before it hated us, so we are in very good company, and therefore, we must not lose heart in fighting our battle against sin. We are glorified when we endure persecution for the sake of righteousness and godly causes. Remember, Jesus suffered greatly when he was impaled; he suffered for the sake of goodness, and we must do likewise. As a matter of fact, Christians are expected to suffer. Innocent suffering is a blessing to refine our faith so it can endure the roughest seas and highest peaks. Therefore, let us joyfully take up Jesus' pole on our path to glory. Let us be victors of suffering for our salvation and give the losing hand to Satan. Jesus suffered for us, and was glorified for us. Let us suffer for him, and be glorified for him and with him.
- Suffering draws us closer to Jehovah. When we go through tough times and heartaches, we realize that our mere human strengths are simply not enough to protect us. It is then that we will call upon God for help and power to assist us in getting through the dark tunnel to the light at its end. But friend, we must not wait till the day of trials and tribulations to call to God; we must do so daily, to better prepare ourselves for any challenges and traumas ahead.
- Finally, we suffer because we are imperfect. We all have inherited imperfection from the first pair of humans. We get ill, grow old, and fall asleep in death. It is true that animals grow old and die, but they were made that way. They were not made with the spiritual capacity to

know right from wrong, so they technically do not commit sins, and therefore, they did not inherit death. But for us humans, we were created in God's image. God never intended for humans to die. Our death is our own doing.

So now that we know why we suffer, we can answer, "Does God cause suffering? Is He to blame for our suffering?" No, we cause all of our suffering, not God. Even when God disciplines us, it is only because we have strayed, so we are the sole cause of the rod of correction we receive. If we drive intoxicated and get into a car accident, can we blame God for it? Again, it all gets down to we reap what we sow. If we choose to sow unwisely, we cannot blame God for our resulting suffering. You must know by now that such a loving Father will not purposely cause us harm.

Yet, why does God permit suffering caused by wicked people? "God is love," wrote the apostle John. How could the God who represents love allow evil to afflict us? The prophet Habakkuk once asked Jehovah the same thing: "You who have purer eyes than to see evil, and who cannot look on perversity, why do you tolerate those who deal treacherously, and keep silent when the wicked swallows up the man who is more righteous than he, and make men like the fish of the sea, like the creeping things, that have no ruler over them?" (Habakkuk 1:13-14, World English Bible)

"Why does God allow evil and injustice?" is probably among the most frequently asked questions ever, and unfortunately, many never receive a satisfactory answer. Where can we receive the accurate answer? From God Himself, of course!

In reply to Habakkuk's question, Jehovah said, "Write the vision, and make it plain upon tablets, that he may run that readeth it. For the vision is yet for the appointed time, and it hasteth toward the end, and shall not lie: though it tarry, wait for it; because it will surely come, it will not delay." (Habakkuk 2:2-3)

What is included in the vision God referred to? "Woe to him that buildeth a town with blood, and establisheth a city by iniquity!" is the judgment Jehovah will sentence upon the evildoers, and "the earth shall be filled with the knowledge of the glory of Jehovah, as the waters cover the sea" is the peaceful, everlasting life under Jehovah's loving rulership for the righteous. (Habakkuk 2:12, 14)

Jehovah by no means enjoys seeing His creations suffer; far from it. Even though He is permitting darkness now, He will not tolerate it for too long. Instead, He long ago appointed the time when He will destroy all fruits of evil, leaving no root or seed for evil to sprout ever again. Then pure good will rule for eternity.

God allows events and people to develop, to give the wicked the chance to change their ways. He does not want to wipe everyone off the Earth without giving them enough chances to realize that what they are doing is wrong. As we know by now, He does not enjoy killing anyone. Rather, He constantly hopes for people to repent and turn to Him; His deepest desire is for every person to embrace a good way of living, so He can save all. This is a main reason why He lets evil go on for a while longer.

Jehovah also allows some time for us to exercise our free will, to show us that our independence from His rule is costing us, and it will also help prove Satan wrong. The devil cajoled the first two humans to disobey God, saying that they would know right from wrong just like God, meaning that they would no longer need God's guidance; instead, they would be able to be on their own. Yes, Satan challenged God's very right to be our Ruler, as if Jehovah were not good enough for the job and as if we would be better off without Him!

Satan also, in front of other angels in heaven, indicated that the righteous Job would no longer be God-fearing if God took Job's good health away: "But put forth thy hand now, and touch his bone and his flesh, and he will renounce thee to thy face." (Job 2:5) Did Job denounce God after Satan made him ill? Absolutely not. True worshippers of God will endure Satan's testing to the end, thus proving him wrong and giving glory to God.

Without providing the time required to answer Satan's challenges, humans will never obtain the truth—that Jehovah is the best King for us—on their own. If God had destroyed Satan on the spot and re-established His kingship over us, stubborn humans would always go on wondering whether they could indeed live successfully without God's guidance. But now, since Jehovah has allowed Satan to exercise his rule over the world and given us the freedom we wanted, it has become quite clear to us that Satan is a horrible liar and that we desperately need God to rescue us from the troubles we have brought upon our own heads.

> **"And I saw, and behold, the Lamb standing on the mount Zion, and with him a hundred and forty and four thousand, having his name, and the name of his Father, written on their**

foreheads." (Revelation 14:1)

Finally, Jehovah lets some time pass in order to fill the 144,000 seats in the heavens. These seats are reserved for 144,000 highly righteous people who will co-govern the rest of the human population alongside Jehovah and Jesus during the forthcoming life of sheer bliss. "These are they that follow the Lamb whithersoever he goeth. These were purchased from among men, to be the firstfruits unto God and unto the Lamb." (Revelation 14:4) Such immense privilege these people will have!

While this small heavenly flock of co-rulers will govern the Earth from the heavens, people on the newly restored Earth paradise will have priests and princes living among them to guide them. Just as with the celestial governors, the terrestrial government body will be appointed by God through the sacrifice of Jesus: "Worthy art thou to take the book, and to open the seals thereof: for thou was slain, and didst purchase unto God with thy blood men of every tribe, and tongue, and people, and nation, and madest them to be unto our God a kingdom and priests; and they reign upon earth." (Revelation 5:9)

At Last, an End to All Evil!

"...death shall be no more; neither shall there be mourning, nor crying, nor pain, any more: the first things are passed away." (Revelation 21:4)

When will all suffering end? How will the righteous be saved? When will the last days of this evil system of things come? And what are the signs to tell us that our days in this world will soon end? These are among the most important questions, and our very lives depend on the answers—each and every one of us, past, present, and future. Fortunately, the Bible gives clear answers and guidance. Let us examine what the Bible has to say.

When will suffering end?

Suffering will end when the great day of Jehovah concludes, after God destroys those who are laying waste to the Earth, spirits and humans alike. Not only will there be an end to suffering but to all that is evil, and death will be our last enemy. All righteous people from all nations and all backgrounds, will delight in a just rule under God's Kingdom for eternity: "And a throne shall be established in lovingkindness; and one shall sit thereon in truth, in the tent of David, judging, and seeking justice, and swift to do righteousness." (Isaiah 16:5)

What will the Kingdom be like?

• People will no longer be victims of human imperfection. There will not be any illnesses, diseases, or discomforts. "Then the eyes of the blind shall be opened, and the ears of the deaf shall be unstopped. Then shall the lame man leap as a hart, and the tongue of the dumb shall sing; for in the wilderness shall waters break out, and streams in the desert." (Isaiah 35:5-6)

• Earth will be restored into a paradise, with no more air, land, or water pollution. "And the glowing sand shall become a pool, and the thirsty ground springs of water: in the habitation of jackals, where they lay, shall be grass with reeds and rushes." (Isaiah 35:7)

• Abundant food and water will nourish all. "They shall not hunger nor thirst; neither shall the heat nor sun smite them: for he that hath mercy on them will lead them, even by springs of water will he guide them." (Isaiah 49:10)

• People will no longer work in vain. Instead, they will enjoy the fruits of their labor and be filled by the crops their fields yield. "And they shall build houses, and inhabit them; and they shall plant vineyards, and eat the fruit of them." (Isaiah 65:21)

• Animals will all be tame and friendly; none will eat or harm anyone. Little children can freely play with wild animals. "And the wolf shall dwell with the lamb, and the leopard shall lie down with the kid; and the calf and the young lion and the fatling together; and a little child shall lead them. And the cow and the bear shall feed; their young ones shall lie down together; and the lion shall eat straw like the ox. And the sucking child shall play on the hole of the asp, and the weaned child shall put his hand on the adder's den. They shall not hurt nor destroy in all my holy mountain; for the earth shall be full of the knowledge of Jehovah, as the waters cover the sea. And it shall come to pass in that day, that the root of Jesse, that standeth for an ensign of the peoples, unto him shall the nations seek; and his resting-place shall be glorious." (Isaiah 11:6-10)

• Happiness, peace, and love will be the main components of everyday living. Sorrow and misery will be only memories from a past that will never be relived again. "...and the ransomed of Jehovah shall return, and come with singing unto Zion; and everlasting joy shall be upon their heads: they shall obtain gladness and joy, and sorrow and sighing shall flee away." (Isaiah 35:10)

• Any kind of discrimination will vanish. People of all nations and ethnicities will live together harmoniously. "...the time cometh, that I will gather all nations and tongues; and they shall come, and shall see my glory." (Isaiah 66:18)

• Finally, death is swallowed up forever.

(Isaiah 25:8)

What a wonderful world it will be! But before it comes, we need to make sure that we will be the ones who are saved, not ones who will be eternally destroyed. Remember, we will be saved only when we have faith in Jesus Christ and exercise our faith. If you say you have faith, but do not show it through your works, your faith is as good as dead. Faith in Jesus is doing what is good by obeying Jehovah's commands, meaning that our top priority is to love God and fellow creations abundantly.

How will the Kingdom of God come?

> "...the sun shall be darkened, and the moon shall not give her light, and the stars shall fall from heaven, and the powers of the heavens shall be shaken: and then shall appear the sign of the Son of man in heaven: and then shall all the tribes of the earth mourn, and they shall see the Son of man coming on the clouds of heaven with power and great glory." (Matthew 24:29-30)

Riding upon a cloud (though not literally as we may understand it now), Jesus the Messiah will make a grand entrance into our Earth's atmosphere from the heavens. It will be at the conclusion of this evil system of things. Jesus is to carry out his mission assigned by God. He will also accept the 144,000 righteous people into heaven to rule our Earth paradise with him.

Jehovah has given His beloved Son the duties

as the righteous King to rule over us, for "worthy is the Lamb that hath been slain to receive the power, and riches, and wisdom, and might and honor, and glory, and blessing." (Revelation 5:12)

However, before Jesus can come, our world will need to enter into the phase of the last days, a time of lawlessness and lovelessness.

When will the last days come?

When Jesus' disciples asked him for the signs of the last days of the system of things, Jesus answered, "Nation shall rise against nation, and kingdom against kingdom; and there shall be great earthquakes, and in divers places famines and pestilences; and there shall be terrors and great signs from heaven. But before all these things, they shall lay their hands on you, and shall persecute you, delivering you up to the synagogues and prisons, bringing you before kings and governors for my name's sake." (Luke 21:10-12)

Jesus also said, "There shall arise false Christs, and false prophets, and shall show great signs and wonders; so as to lead astray, if possible, even the elect." (Matthew 24:24) As Jesus had predicted, numerous antichrists—false religious leaders and Christians, and those who refuse to believe that Jesus is the Messiah—have indeed arisen since the first century, while true Christians have been persecuted for spreading the good news of God's Kingdom. Yet, the good news has been preached all over the world, which has also been foretold as a sign of the last days.

Besides catastrophic wars, famines, natural

disasters, deadly diseases, and a general sense of disorder, the apostle Paul wrote that people will be "lovers of self, lovers of money, boastful, haughty, railers, disobedient to parents, unthankful, unholy, without natural affection, implacable, slanderers, without self-control, fierce, no lovers of good, traitors, headstrong, puffed up, lovers of pleasure rather than lovers of God; holding a form of godliness, but having denied the power therefore." (II Timothy 3:2-5)

Does it seem that we are living in the last days? Even though humans have exhibited such lawlessness throughout history, these characteristics of immorality are now worse than ever. We have mothers drowning their own children; children having children; and profanity has become the norm in our world. If we are indeed living in the last days, then I have good—no, make it excellent—news for you!

Even though wars, famine, and natural disasters have been more numerous and deadly than ever before, they will all reach a horrifying climax at the day of God's great wrath, the Armageddon, when they will draw to a close for eternity. Replacing their terror are never-ending love, happiness, peace, and prosperity for all.

The Great Armageddon

What pops into your head when you think of Armageddon? Missiles, nuclear bombs, and dead bodies on the ground? Although it will be the most grievous war in history, no physical weapons of mass destruction will be used. Armageddon is the time when Jehovah will pour out His great wrath upon the wicked polluters of Earth. There will be only a few survivors, those who love and are faithful to Jehovah to the last minute.

Besides the monstrous disturbance of peace, false religions and human government will be wiped from the face of the Earth. Those who support their evil human governments and false religions will be destroyed along with them.

Afterward, all the dead will be resurrected: the faithful to receive their rewards, and the unrighteous to hear their judgment from Jesus. Those whose names are not found in the book of life will be eternally destroyed, whereas those who pass his judgment will live in the Earth paradise under Jesus' heavenly rule with Jehovah and their 144,000 servants who comprise the governing body of the Kingdom of Heaven.

Moreover, Satan will be locked up in the abyss for one thousand years. After the thousand years is up, he will be released for a short time to tempt people. Those who follow in his lead will be destroyed forever, along with the devil himself. So Armageddon itself will not completely destroy evil; only after one thousand years of peace following this global battle will evil be abolished for eternity. Once perfection is achieved on Earth, Jesus will return the rulership to his Father to be our eternal King.

Armageddon is the war that will end all wars. It is the end of misery and the beginning of happiness for the righteous. It is the destruction of the polluted Earth and the rebirth of a new Earth. It is the beginning of a brand new life, a brand new Kingdom, whose reign will never end or be replaced. Although it is a passing period of great confusion, it is something wonderful to which the righteous should look forward.

When will Armageddon come?

When will the current world system end? That remains a mystery for humankind; only God knows when His great war will begin. It will come as a thief, so Jesus advised: "Take ye heed, watch and pray: for ye know not when the time is." (Mark 13:33) It means that we must do good and exercise our faith in him at all times.

While we are waiting for this evil way of things to end, what else must we do besides exercising godly principles? When we receive good news, should we not share it? Therefore, do not be selfish and keep this good news of God's Kingdom all to yourself—get out there and shout to the whole world that the most wonderful paradise we could ever dream of is coming! I quote Jesus: "What I tell you in the darkness, speak ye in the light; and what ye hear in the ear, proclaim upon the house-tops. And be not afraid of them that kill the body, but are not able to kill the soul: but rather fear him who is able to destroy both soul and body in hell." (Matthew 10:27-28)

One last question you may have is: Can we depend on Bible prophecy? You bet; most of the prophecies in the Bible have already been fulfilled or are being fulfilled, such as the ruining of Babylon:

"And Babylon, the glory of kingdoms, the beauty of the Chaldeans' pride, shall be as when God overthrew Sodom and Gomorrah. It shall never be inhabited, neither shall it be dwelt in from generation to generation: neither shall the Arabian pitch tent there; neither shall shepherds make their flocks to lie down there." (Isaiah 13:19-20) What was once a great city lies in ruins to this day.

Again and again, time has proved to us that we can put our entire trust in the Bible. It is the most accurate account of humankind; if it were not a religious text, people would have used it as the most trustworthy textbook of human origin and history. Archeologists have uncovered plenty of artifacts and the ruins of cities where people and events the Bible has talked about were located, further showing us that the Bible is accurate and trustworthy.

However, the best reason to trust the Bible is the fact that this holy book is from Jehovah! He is the God of truth, who never lies and always fulfills His words: "For as the rain cometh down and the snow from heaven, and returneth not thither, but watereth the earth, and maketh it bring forth and bud, and giveth seed to the sower and bread to the eater; so shall my word be that goeth forth out of my mouth: it shall not return unto me void, but it shall accomplish that which I please, and it shall prosper in the thing whereto I sent it." (Isaiah 55:10-11) Keeping this fact in mind will help wipe away any doubts about the Bible we have ever had, and strengthen our faith in God's promises and plans. The faithful Jehovah will never forget us: "Can a woman forget her sucking child, that she should not have compassion on the son of her womb? yea, these may forget, yet will not I forget thee." (Isaiah 49:15)

Your Sacred Mission

"Know ye not that they that run in a race run all, but one receiveth the prize? Even so run; that ye may attain. And every man that striveth in the games exerciseth self-control in all things. Now they do it to receive a corruptible crown; but we an incorruptible." (I Corinthians 9:24-25)

Friend, what do you truly want out of life? The answer you provide will determine which road you choose next—that to happiness, or misery. I suppose you would want happiness, as most of us do. But how long would you want your happiness to last? We all know that happiness can often be fleeting, lasting mere weeks or even days; such happiness can leave us feeling more unhappy and unfulfilled than even before we were briefly happy. If you truly want happiness that lasts forever—and you should know by now that I do actually mean *forever*—embracing virtuous living right now will help you achieve just that.

If you truly want to be happy forever, you will not find it in the worldly belongings, all of which will be things of the past. What will lead to forever bliss is the knowledge of Jehovah and Jesus Christ; They are the only two Beings who will give you all that you ever need and desire. By following Jehovah's guidance in the Bible, you will not only create a much better life right now, but it will set you on the road that leads to the Kingdom of God.

The decision lies in your hands. If you are not a Christian already, I cannot tell you to embrace Christianity; I can only gently but firmly nudge you, which, hopefully, this book has succeeded in doing. But, no, I am not suggesting that you make a hasty vow to become a Christian. You have to be certain that you will commit to a Christian way of living before you make any promise, for such promises are to God and should not be broken.

Living a bad life is easy; living a Christian life is not. People are constantly inundated with temptations of every kind. The more people you meet, the more temptations you will face. The more places you visit, the more temptations you will meet. Christians have to endlessly seek help from God in order to fight off these temptations. They have to dedicate their entire lives to serving goodness. It is not something done for a few months or a few years; it lasts an entire lifetime. Being a Christian does not ensure that you will live a temptation-free life. It does not protect you from suffering; it actually guarantees suffering.

Would you be able to withstand the enticements of the world? Would you be willing to submit yourself to Jehovah to have Him guide you? Would you keep your temple clean at all times so that Jesus can live in you?

Friend, do not become a Christian or do good

for the sake of the promise of paradise. True good comes willingly from the heart, not grudgingly, and any good that comes forth with an eye to gain is not truly good; such worthless good will not last long. Remember, Jehovah sees people's hearts and will know whether your good comes from your heart or from your head. A truly diligent student will do her best in school, not for paper awards but for spiritual rewards. A good student can look forward to certificates of achievements, but those will not be her primary focus or goal; instead, the goal of the student is a good and fulfilling future life, one that will not only bring happiness to her, but to as many people around her as possible. So let your heart focus like the good student; let your good be from your heart for the spiritual things, not from your head for the worldly things. And let the cornerstone of your spiritual goal be loving Jehovah God Almighty and Jesus the Messiah, His beloved Son, who would be your Righteous Everlasting Father and Prince of Peace in God's Kingdom, the place you could call home for eternity.

I implore you to carefully make the most important decision you will ever make, from the depths of your heart. Your very existence depends upon it. What will you decide?

However, before you make up your mind, let us define "Christian." What does being a Christian mean? Is it just accepting that Jesus Christ is God's Son who is our Savior? If it is simply that, then we can call Satan a Christian! After all, he personally knows both God and Jesus, so much more than we know them. Just as we discussed earlier in this book, being a true believer means being a lover of God's ways: "This is love, that we should walk after his commandments." (II John 1:6) Hence, being a Christian means being a follower of Jesus' ways, which are God's ways: "Whosoever goeth onward and abideth not in the teaching of Christ, hath not God: he that abideth in the teaching, the same hath both the Father and the Son." (II John 1:9) Christians are Christians only when they are Christ-like; they are false Christians if they only acknowledge Jesus' existence and sacrifice without showing Christian love. Moreover, Christians have to draw strength from God to fully and completely follow Jesus' guidance to the best of their ability; they should not pick and choose which commandments they want to adhere to—breaking one rule would mean they have broken all the rules.

Above all, Christians must keep in mind that their works alone do not give them salvation—it is Jesus' selfless sacrifice that has granted salvation to Christians. If we could save ourselves just by performing good works, then Jesus died for no reason! Yet, Christians need to remain faithful in order to keep the gift. In short, Christians are those who accept Jesus' sacrifice, his salvation, and his ways.

After you have decided to convert to Christianity, act. A plan is no good when it does not lead to action. Once you have made your decision, make it your life's most important mission to always act upon it. How should you follow through and act upon a mission that conforms to Bible teachings? Let us quickly recap what we ought to do.

First, we must get to know Jehovah personally. Such a task requires that we read the Bible completely and understand it to the best of our ability.

Second, we must do what the Bible tells us. This will ensure that we are doing what Jehovah loves. What Jehovah loves is what Jesus loves, so when we listen to God, it means we are living an honest Christian life. Above all, this means that we love Jehovah and Jesus in return.

And third, we must share the happiness and good news with others.

> **"He that hath my commandments, and keepeth them, he it is that loveth me: and he that loveth me shall be loved of my Father, and I will love him, and will manifest myself unto him." (John 14:21)**

So go ahead, get a start on your wonderful mission! I do wish you all my very best while you go on your journey. May Jehovah give you a heart that will always seek His ways and the strength to move forward and never give up; may the Holy Spirit give you understanding and wisdom for the Bible; and may Jesus Christ give you everlasting happiness and peace.

Now get ready, set, go! Run for the brightest, boldest, and biggest gold medal there is! Do not be discouraged in your race, for the best pair of Cheerleaders any team could ever ask for will cheer you on and toast you at the finish line!

Personal Experiences

"A wise man is strong; Yea, a man of knowledge increaseth might, For by wise guidance thou shalt make thy war; And in the multitude of counsellors there is safety." (Proverbs 24:5-6)

Jehovah: Secret to Spiritual Championship

How One Blind Individual Continues to See

"...thou shalt remember Jehovah thy God, for it is he that giveth thee power to get wealth..." (Deuteronomy 8:18)

How does being spiritual help you conquer negativity or challenges in life?

Overcoming negativity is not necessarily about making a physical difference. Many times, we cannot physically change our situation. I lost my eyesight, and I cannot magically make myself see again. Conquering negativity is about making a psychological difference for your spirit. By being happy when I am blind, I am successfully conquering negativity.

A method of spiritually conquering negativity is finding the positive side to a negative situation. I know it can be quite difficult to find the good side of something bad every time; you will have to look at your situation from every angle. While at times, the good thing does not come out of the bad until some time has passed.

In life, there are always something good and something bad happening at the same time, and there is always a positive side to the negative, and even a negative side to the positive. And there are times where the bad actually become the good and vice versa. So in actuality, it can be too hard at times for us to judge what is truly good or bad. What we can do is always try to look on the bright side and do our best to live our best, and put all faith in God—that is the secret that gets me going; everything else is just strategy! Yes, it all boils down to receiving the greatest help from God!

Are most barriers real?

I believe many barriers are real, but I also believe that many are based on unfounded beliefs and a fear of the unknown. Often times, when we first encounter a problem, we let our emotions turn it from a hill into a mountain. Whatever size you perceive your problem to be is whatever size problem you will have. If you believe your trouble is too big to handle, it will be too big to handle. But if you think otherwise and put your faith in Jehovah, you will be able to overcome it. For instance, my blindness is a real roadblock to many things; for one, I cannot draw and paint now as I loved to do before. But I am still able to conquer my blindness by focusing on other creative avenues I can take. I focus on what I am able to do, not what I am unable to do. So I turned to writing to continually express my artistic nature. Yes, I lost my eyesight, but I am still able to hear, I am still able to type, so I use whatever gifts I have to make the most of my situation.

Have you ever come to the brink of giving up, when things seem too overwhelming to handle?

No, not in the least, ever. I am too much madly in love with life to give it up. Life is my best friend, a family member. We all have silly arguments with our family and friends, but do we give up on them afterward?

Have you ever been angry at God?

No, of course not; I would never get upset at Jehovah. How could I possibly feel resentful toward Him? To be angry at God is beyond my understanding. What if He had never given me my life? What if I never existed? I would miss all of life's privileges. Thus, I am too grateful to God to have any negative feeling toward Him! Being angry at God is simply out of the question!

I feel that whenever we get angry at someone, not just at God, it stems from a lack of gratitude. We get unhappy only when we do not realize or appreciate the good things people do for us. The first woman, Eve, disobeyed God because she was ungrateful to Him for all of His care and gifts. Instead, she became resentful of the fact that she was not allowed to eat from one tree amidst a grove of plentiful fruit trees. She focused on what little she could not have and ignored everything she did have.

Did you ever ask, "Why me?"

Of course, but never in a negative way. I believe that everyone and everything serves a specific purpose in life, no matter how significant or insignificant. Everything in the universe is designed and created to fulfill a unique purpose. The sun provides us with light and warmth during the day. The rain waters our planet. Plants give us oxygen, while we give them carbon dioxide in return. Just as God has made our bodies to regulate themselves, He has made life to regulate itself. We should put our faith in our lives, even though we cannot always understand why things happen the way they do. Having faith in life is having faith in our Creator. When we go out shopping, many of us buy products made by companies we trust. So when we have faith in our lives, then we are having faith in the Creator who created them.

God works mysteriously, and I am often curious about His plans for me, so this is where "Why me?" comes in.

What explains your strong drive to achieve followed with action?

My strong drive to achieve has to do with my passion for life, for doing my best to live my best. I believe that to love and accept life is to love and accept God; I love life because I love God, and, again,

I am so grateful to Him for my life. Why ruin His gift of life by not achieving and doing my best? When you buy an expensive set of furniture (or anything you love), would you not take good care of it? Would you not love your children with all your heart, soul, and might?

They say that attitude is everything. What do you say?

I say that your desires are everything. You need desires to help you conquer negativity. You may say, "Of course, that is easy." But the key in effectively using desires is to use the *right* kind of desires. We all have desires, but we need to use the good ones and let them rule over all other desires. And the best desire is the desire to know God, to follow in His ways.

What does it mean to be truly successful? And can you share with us some of your tips to success?

To me, success does not mean wealth and fame; success is all about being a successful human being. In order to be truly successful in life, you need to first establish your values.

What qualities do you hold highest? What traits do you want to have and be associated with? Think of what qualities are important to you and hold firm to them. Your values are what you will base your life's decisions on. You will make goals around your core values. For example, my value is goodness, so I make goals that will accomplish my value. I will be satisfied with having achieved that value if nothing else.

Two plus two equals four. If you believe that two plus two equals everything and anything, then you are bound to encounter problems in your life. Your values create a lasting, enduring spiritual environment. Nothing you gain materially is ever guaranteed; everything you own—your car, your house, and even your friends and family—can be taken away from you. But no one and nothing can take away your values if you do not let them. Nothing can destroy your values unless you destroy them yourself. Your values are what will guide you onto the right paths in life.

How can you establish firm values that guarantee success? Pick up the Bible, read and study it. That is where you will obtain true values to propel you to the greatest heights!

Besides establishing your firm values, my golden rule to be truly successful is: Do your best in everything you do. Many people do a mediocre job and expect to be successful; they depend on luck to get them successful. But in the long term, luck will not bring you far.

In life, no matter what position you are in—a parent, a child, a teacher, a doctor—do your best in being your best. And make the most of what you have. If you have only a spoon and a fork, use the fork to comb your hair and use the spoon to play music. Hey, some people do not even have a spoon and a fork!

What is the greatest value?

Love. Love is the most crucial, fundamental aspect of humanity. If you have love, you will have all other good elements. If you do not have love, you have nothing at all. All beauties are the fruits of love, and love comes from God, for God is love, so all goodness comes from God. When we have love, we come from God.

It seems that your greatest strength comes from God, does it not? What are your thoughts on how He works in our lives?

Absolutely! Jehovah is my Power, my Hope, my Strength.

God works in mysterious ways, and all for our benefit, though we may not understand this at first. For instance, I believe the loss of my eyesight was a divine turn of events. Why a divine turn?

If I had not lost my eyesight, I would not have become an author and motivational speaker in order to touch as many people as I possibly can by bringing humor, hope, and healing into their lives. I would have simply gone to college, have gotten my degrees, and become a scientist, and as a consequence, I would not bring the kind of spiritual food to others that far surpasses any other worldly achievements and influences.

God has opened the door for me to make a positive, spiritual difference in others' lives. He has also opened the door for me to deepen my relationship with Him.

The Bible says, "It is necessary to pass through many troubles on our way into the kingdom of God." (Acts 14:22, Holman Christian Standard Bible) The loss of my eyesight is simply another challenge that strengthens my faith and spirit, and draws me closer to God in various ways. Like a child in need, I call on God for strength. And in the meantime, I am spreading the messages of God to others. So the loss of my eyesight helps both me and others around me.

God accomplishes His divine plans through His earthly subjects, no matter how weak they are; this brings out the faith in the people and glorifies God at the same time.

All my works are to glorify God, just as all of Jesus' works are to glorify God. When I am able to overcome my blindness, I glorify God. When I learn about Him, I glorify Him. When I spread His Word, I glorify Him. But I do not do all this on my own — He helps me with everything.

When I count on God to provide the best for me and others, I am strengthened. This is how I can overcome my blindness and all other challenges. I do not question God; I know whatever He does is in our best interest. Therefore, I remain a happy and grateful blind and physically disabled individual who continues to see the beauty in the world, from her heart.

Jehovah will present anyone, if he or she so desires, with the cup to become a spiritual champion!

A Blind and Disabled Gal... Happy?

"...happy is the people whose God is Jehovah." (Psalm 144:15)

Do you know that I am the happiest girl you will ever meet? Okay, maybe one of the happiest, but I tell you, you will not find many people happier than I.

Why am I so happy, you must wonder? Do I have ten bank accounts, each filled to the maximum FDIC-insured amount? Does my countenance radiate such beauty that every guy drools whenever he simply glances my way? Or do I have the happily-ever-after marriage that girls dream of? No, none of those; for one, I am not married—yet. (Psst, do you happen to know a chap whose happiness matches mine?)

I am an individual who is both blind and physically disabled, with the severe juvenile rheumatoid arthritis that decided to call my body home for good when I was a mere infant twenty-four years ago. A blind and disabled gal, happy? Is being blind and disabled the secret to my happiness? Well, not exactly, but it is what helps confirm the most important life lesson I have ever learned, received, and observed, so it makes me a very happy blind and physically disabled lady.

I have gathered and experienced firsthand that in life, everything is divided into mainly two compartments: the spiritual and the worldly. What belong to the spiritual realm are everlasting—they do not know time; they do not know age. They withstand all trials and tribulations. Those who welcome the spiritual elements—longsuffering love, unconditional gratitude, undemanding hope, unwavering faith, and invaluable values—will achieve true success and happiness that will last well beyond life in this world, while leaving a legacy.

The worldly, on the other hand, give you only earthly success: wealth, power, and fame. When you die, they die with you. What good is a roomful of money when you are dead? When we live, we need to collect treasures that will last forever so we can enjoy happiness forever. Many times, we are so focused on achieving what our flesh wants, we forget that whatever our flesh achieves will die with our flesh.

I also learned from the wise Teacher that the darkness, pain, and suffering of the worldly will all be things of the past, and death will be our last enemy. It brings no fruit to those who dwell upon the passing trials and tribulations, but it will be rewarding for those who use challenges as exercise machines for their minds and spirits. So being a spiritual person, embracing the spiritual aspects, will lead you to an enduring, fulfilling life. We are here to strengthen our spirits, to learn what Heavenly Father wants from us, so we can return His love and live by His almighty rule, eternally.

Therefore, I have enthusiastically embraced the spiritual realm of life with my whole heart and soul, and it has been the foundation of my happiness despite all the high mountains I have had to scale. Specifically, the cornerstone of my bliss lies in my deep faith in Jehovah God; it has allowed me to love and appreciate the life He has graciously given me, in turn, enabling me to conquer fiery oceans and thorny jungles to come out with stars in my arms.

Jehovah has been the most essential part of my life in many different ways, and I am more than grateful to Him for everything He has gifted to me. I am constantly reminded of His infinite love in my every waking minute.

I am immensely grateful for the life He has bestowed upon me. It is one of the two greatest presents I have ever received. I am so honored to be alive; I am so honored that He has chosen me to live, so I want to show Him how much I truly cherish and love the life He gave me. Because of my life, I am privileged to know, discover, and experience all the wonderful things life has to offer. True, I have lost the ability to walk and see, but I am never bitter. Instead, I am grateful for having owned these powers before. I am still the owner of so many other wonderful gifts. I can still talk, I can still hear, I can still type, and I am still alive; I have utilized all these great powers to become an award-winning author, poet, motivational speaker, and self-empowerment expert, and to continue loving the life I live.

The other most precious gift, which is no less than the gift of my own life, is my beloved mother, Juliet Cheng. She is the cornerstone and light of my life; the foundation of my happiness, strength, and success—besides God, of course. She has saved my life numerous times, pulling me from the grasp of death. I would have been long gone if it had not been for her. Maternal love is definitely the greatest love that God has ever created, and I will be forever grateful to Him for this wondrous jewel.

Besides blessing us with our lives, God has played a major role in them. We have deep, unwavering faith in Him, and it is this faith that has allowed us to take one sure step at a time forward, as we know He is always there, loving us, guiding us, and supporting us.

If your best friend gave you a special present, would you not do your very best to care for it? My life is the most precious present God has ever bestowed upon me (besides my beloved mother, of course), so I do not want to give it up. I cannot give it up. I must not give it up. I have the responsibility to make the most of my situation, to embrace all life has to offer, to return Heavenly Father's unconditional love by accepting a virtuous way of living, and to share the good with others. And fulfilling my responsibilities, as you can see, makes me the happiest gal you will ever meet!

The Divine Dream of Love & Light

"...we rejoice in hope of the glory of God. And not only so, but we also rejoice in our tribulations: knowing that tribulation worketh stedfastness; and stedfastness, approvedness; and approvedness, hope: and hope putteth not to shame; because the love of God hath been shed abroad in our hearts through the Holy Spirit which was given unto us." (Romans 5:2-5)

From out of nowhere, a young man suddenly appeared before me, yet only his upper body was in my field of vision. I took a cursory look at his apparel — an off-white robe with no collar or hood. Impatient to identify this man who had appeared so suddenly, my eyes ignored any other details and went straight to his face.

He was looking at me. His eyes bored into mine, yet his gaze was not intrusive; it was like the gentle, assuring look a friend would give me. If one met him, one would instinctively trust him on the spot, for his eyes shone with kindness and care. Matching the color of his peaceful eyes was his wavy, brownish hair that framed his face and touched his shoulders.

Then I noticed something else, something quite out of the ordinary—even more extraordinary than the sudden vision—and I was surprised at myself for not noticing it earlier...or had I? What distinguished this man from any other man, or any other living creature, for that matter, was the light that emanated from his entire being. It was a soothing, yellow-white light, not blinding or piercing. This pervasive light blanketed the air around him as if enclosing him in a translucent cocoon, and radiated peace toward me. Despite the fact that he was completely engulfed by this light, it did not veil his crystal-clear features.

He was motionless and wordless, simply gazing at me as if he were a painting, a male version of the Mona Lisa. I was not sure if I was disappointed or relieved, puzzled or curious. Did I want him to speak to me? It was as though my emotions had fled as soon as he appeared. All I felt was serenity. All was calm and still, as if time had stopped.

A moment later, I woke up.

Despite being awake, I could still see his kind countenance in my mind's eye, though not as vividly. Immediately, I knew who had appeared in my dream. I lifted my head, and saw that my mother was awake. "Mom, I just dreamed of Jesus Christ!" I said almost breathlessly.

"Really?" I could hear it in her voice—she was as astounded as me. She propped herself up on one elbow and looked at me.

I saw surprise, curiosity, joy, and yes, some weariness, in her eyes. She was often tired, I knew, being a single parent who had to care for a daughter severely disabled with juvenile rheumatoid arthritis. I thought about our last trip to China to seek treatment of the crippling disease that had made a home in my body since I was an infant, and of the daily hardships we experienced as a team. I could not help but feel a surge of gratitude and pride—gratitude toward her, not only for saving my life so many times but for the endless love she provided me daily, and pride because I was blessed enough to have such a wonderful mother.

My thoughts quickly returned to my dream, and I nodded. "He was young," I paused, thinking. "Seventeen, I believe." That age had not been told to me in my dream, as there had been no sound; I simply knew it, with conviction.

"Seventeen? That is strange, fantastic..."

"Yes, strange," I echoed. But in a good way, I knew. And fantastic—yes, of that there was no doubt.

What did my dream mean? What did Jesus want to tell me? What hidden message did the vision convey? I found out eight years later.

At age seventeen, I lost my eyesight.

Was the divine sign a warning or support? I feel it was both.

After all these years, it still sends shivers down my spine just to think that my dream was that of Jehovah God Almighty giving me a message through His beloved Son, the Christ. I am terribly honored and humbled that Jesus Christ would appear in my dream. How often could I have such a high honor? It has got to be the best, the most special, and the most stunning, dream I have ever had, and I will always treasure it in my heart as long as my soul is in existence. Whenever I think back to the young Christ in my dream, I instantly feel safe and secure. Yes, I am being watched and protected!

Through the years, I have known God has been watching over both Mother and me. We have had to climb many steep mountains and cross numerous deep oceans, yet we faltered not a step, for His loving Being has always been there, supporting us, guiding us, and loving us. Thus, neither of us ever feels alone, and it is our deep, unwavering faith in Him that has allowed us to take giant steps forward, one sure step at a time.

For instance, faith in Him gave my mother great stamina and courage to fight for my life during two custody cases. She lost custody of me twice in America only after disagreeing with doctors' recommended treatments—treatments that could have sent me to my grave, or worse, paralyze me. (In America, parents risk losing custody of their children forever if they disagree with doctors' recommended treatments or even when they want a second opinion.) She knew she would win both cases because she found strength in Him, and because she had the power of reasons in her hand.

With God and Jesus Christ always in my heart, I remain strong in mind, and I will continually love the life I live. They are my strength!

Traveling on the Road to Ultra-Ability

"Jehovah is nigh unto all them that call upon him, To all that call upon him in truth." (Psalm 145:18)

Do you know that I could have been Ms. Grumpy who locked herself in a dark room, feeling sorry for herself and complaining about life being unfair? But because I did something absolutely ingenious, I am quite the opposite.

You see, five days after a needle pricked my arm, I lost my power to walk. No, this is not a fairy tale, but it does have happiness, though not yet a happily-ever-after ending, since my story will not end for another sixty years, at least. When I was eleven months old, I contracted severe juvenile rheumatoid arthritis after receiving a tuberculin skin test. I developed a very high fever five days later, and, as they say, the rest is history, but mine makes for an interesting one, I have been told.

My loving mother, Juliet Cheng, like a fairy godmother always by my side, stood tall, or as tall as her petite frame could manage, when she learned this bad news from my doctor. It did not cause her love for me to wither even a single ounce; it only strengthened her resolve to be the best mother possible. Six times in the next ten years she took me to China, her native country, to seek treatment for my crippling disease. She saved my life numerous times by doing so, for I was knocking on death's door.

I spent my early years in constant pain; some days, I could not even sit up or move a muscle. But in China once, when I was four, I was able to walk for one whole year while receiving effective Western shots combined with massage therapy. For the first time, I could run and dance with the wind. Sadly, my walking days ended when the medicine was put under mass production and the quality of the shots went downhill as a result.

When I was eleven, my health finally stabilized, as if someone had waved a magic wand over me. But I know it was the unwavering, tender care my mother has endlessly and tirelessly given me that did the trick. Now, without the constant, debilitating pain, I had the energy to learn. I started schooling in a special education class in elementary school. Prior to that, I had had no form of education, so just imagine this: I only knew my ABCs and very simple English; I knew that two plus two equaled four and that three times five made fifteen. I had no idea where rain came from or why a beautiful rainbow followed it.

Wanting to learn as much as I could as quickly as possible, I absorbed all that was taught in class, and mostly self-taught myself how to read; like the

Cookie Monster, I devoured one book after another as if they were chocolate chip cookies, and always hungered for more.

After about 180 days of attendance, my special education teacher told my mother, "She is ready to go to a regular sixth grade class, and she will do very well there."

Thus, I eagerly swam into the mainstream system, fishing out numerous awards along the way. I entered high school with a smile that spoke a thousand words.

Unfortunately (did you see that coming?), I lost my eyesight at the age of seventeen and I had to stop attending school. I received home-tutoring with the tutors my school district sent, and I completed my schoolwork using strictly cassette tapes and tape recorders (I recorded my answers and essays for my teachers to grade). I wrote and calculated long chemistry formulas and equations in my head without Braille (I cannot use Braille because of my severe arthritis). To my dismay, I could not accumulate enough credits to graduate (but of the credits I earned, my grade point average is a ninety-seven), so I received a GED diploma instead. I took the entire GED test, including mathematical calculations and problem solving, graphs, and an essay—again, without Braille or vision—and scored an exceptional 3,280, for which I received a special recognition award. I was a student speaker at my graduation ceremony and received a standing ovation for my speech.

Since I no longer could express myself through my artwork (I had been a visual arts artist), I turned to writing to share with others my imagined worlds and creations. I became an author at age twenty, completing three books within the first year.

Can individuals who are both blind and physically disabled with limited mobility be happy and content? Can they still love the lives they live and be grateful simply to be alive? And can they extend their successes to positively impact those around them?

The answer is, of course! Now that I am a motivational speaker and an award-winning author with twenty book awards and nine books to my name (not to mention the more than a dozen books to which I have contributed), I am more than glad to prove it. So go ahead, study me to see how I am able to be happy, but do skip the microscope!

Well, okay, I will let you in on my secrets, so you will not have to sweat to discover them on your own...

There are always two roads to choose from in life: the road to ability and the road to disability. People are truly disabled when they allow challenges to hinder them from going for their hearts' desires and going after their gold medals. You have the power to disable yourself or enable yourself, so which road would you choose? I have chosen to be ultra-abled. Yes, I am not disabled—I am ultra-abled. And choosing that road is one smartest thing I ever did.

What steps have I taken on the road to ability? What is my secret to ultra-ability? Whenever I meet a new mountain, I take the following steps to scale it.

- I calm down in order to focus on what I want

to achieve. I focus my energy on how to improve my situation, not on how I am reacting to it. I will not let negative emotions turn my hill into a mountain.

When I lost my eyesight at age seventeen, I focused first on making the most of my situation and moving forward. I did not let any negative emotions rule me. I knew that it was not the end of my life, and that succumbing to misery would not help me in any way. In fact, it would make my situation worse. Imagine that you are marooned on a deserted island. Would you simply stand there, stomp your feet, pull your hair, and cry, "Oh, poor, poor me!"? Or would you instead calm down to think?

- I fight negativity with negativity. My situation could be a lot worse. I imagine something worse than what I am going through now, and then I compare these situations—with which situation would I rather be dealing? Losing my eyesight does not mean I have lost my vision. I may not be able to paint or draw now, but I am still able to love the life I live.
- I conquer negativity with positivity. I think about something I am grateful for, something that makes me happy, someone I love, and then I replace any negative thought with the positive one.

Whenever stress threatens me, I think about my Heavenly Father and my beloved earthly mother, and I become so grateful and happy to have them that I no longer find my situation stressful; I am then able to endure the negative circumstances so much better.

- I keep these points in mind as I face my obstacles:

a) There is always someone who is facing a problem worse than mine, so I am thankful for my own situation, for all that I have and for the people around me.

b) I am not enduring adversity alone. Untold millions of people are also suffering this very minute, from starving children in Africa, to the homeless on the streets, to abused women behind closed doors. And there may well be people going through the same difficulty I am now experiencing.

c) Everything passes, and so will my current negative situation. Why should I waste my energy on something that will be gone tomorrow? It is true that a negative event can affect one's entire life, but one cannot control or predict life when it shouts "Surprise!" in an unpleasant way. So I simply have to prepare for any challenges and make the most of what I have. For instance, the tuberculin skin test I received when I was eleven months old caused the severe juvenile rheumatoid arthritis that will remain with me for the rest of my life. I know that life moves on no matter what happens to me, so it is wise to move along with it and make the best of what I have. Would sulking and worrying do any good or turn my situation around?

- Above all else, I have deep, unwavering faith in Jehovah God Almighty, and this is the ultimate secret to my success, the most important step to take on the road to ultra-ability. Choosing to have faith in Heavenly Father is the one and only smartest thing I ever did; other smart things I have done pale in comparison. It is faith in God that has allowed me to move forward. I put all my hopes and dreams in His hands. I let Him take care of my problems as I enjoy life. I am a sheep in His green pasture, and He is my Savior, my Protector. When I keep my faith in God strong and steady, my steps in life are strong and steady in turn.

As you can see, I am in control of what happens to me when negativity suddenly boos in my face. I do not have to be the victim of my troubles — let my troubles be victims of my faith and positivity! If I do not let problems stop me, they cannot and will not stop me. It is completely up to me — do I want to be stopped, or unstoppable? You already know which path I chose; do you not agree with me that it is indeed the smartest thing I ever did for myself?

A Note from the Author

"Whoso loveth correction loveth knowledge; But he that hateth reproof is brutish." (Proverbs 12:1)

Before I began writing this book, my first thought was, "How could I possibly write about the most important subject? I am the least likely candidate!" However, the urge to write it was so strong that I could not possibly ignore it, so, soon afterward, I completed the project. I feel that God first gave me this urge and then guided me throughout my writing process. I would not have been able to write it without Him!

Why did I write this book? I wrote it to provoke thinking, to help my own learning, but above all, to urge people to at least pick up the Bible and study it, so they can start a fulfilling relationship with God. A relationship with Jehovah is the most sacred of all relationships, but we can start it only by studying the Bible. I cannot stress enough how vital it is to carefully examine the Bible with our entire hearts. The only way we can obtain accurate knowledge of God is by learning from Him directly, without any middleman, except Jesus, who is the one and only true mediator between God and humans.

When the Jews witnessed Jesus resurrecting his friend, Lazarus, many developed faith in him. But some of them reported the event to the Pharisees, who, upon receiving the news, began plotting along with the chief priests to kill not only Jesus but Lazarus as well. This incident illustrates that even the very best news is unwelcome among evildoers, and that people can see any given situation quite differently — one group might rejoice, while the other might sulk. Like Lazarus' resurrection, the Bible is a straightforward book, yet people interpret it in various ways, some going so far as to distort its simplest messages, confusing whomever they teach. Because of this, it is best to learn the Bible on our own, without letting any religious bias influence our minds and hearts.

My book is the fruit of my reading the Bible seven times, using a different version each time. I have also read quite a few articles about Christianity, and compared what people say with what the Bible says to determine the accuracy of any materials I read. I always try to find and study both sides of any argument, using the Bible as my sole guide to determine which party may be correct. This book is my conclusion. I will never say I am one hundred percent correct. If people can use the Bible to correct me, I will be more than ready to accept it; I will not stubbornly hold on to my beliefs if they are wrong.

The Bible says, "Whoever knows the right thing to do and fails to do it, for him it is sin." (James 4:17, English Standard Version) Since I feel it is of utmost importance to lead others in the right direction to obtaining Biblical truths, to the Bible itself, if I were not to do so, it would be terribly wrong of me. Hence, that is why I wrote what I wrote in this book, including the seemingly tiresome but necessary topics on the doctrine of the Trinity. We often do not realize the true worth of a lesson or experience until the time comes when it is crucial to have such knowledge, or when it is too late to do anything about it. I do not want that to happen to anyone. We need to be prepared to the best of our ability in as many aspects of life as we can. When spirituality based on the Bible is the foundation of life, it is of the essence to fully learn, think, meditate, absorb, share, and teach about the Word of God. What many do not realize is that the Bible is the ultimate and only truth—it is not an alternative belief. So when we are able to grasp the full extent of this fact, it will be much easier for us to embrace its teachings to completely receive its benefits.

Should people automatically accept the mainstream teachings of Christianity without performing their own careful study of the Bible? It seems that many people just go to church and accept whatever they are taught. We need to take the time to really think about the Bible, not blindly accept what we hear. It is always the best idea to examine the Bible on our own and compare it with what other people tell us. Just because many people teach the same thing does not mean the teaching is correct. The road to the truth is narrow, so we must always look for that narrow path.

Knowing God's truths is especially important

now because we are living in the last days prior to Jesus' final return. The last days are marked with "the falling away" of believers, antichrist activities, great "deceit of unrighteousness," and the absence of the Holy Spirit. (II Thessalonians 2:3-10) We must be careful that we will not be counted among those who "might be judged," who "believed not the truth, but had pleasure in unrighteousness." (II Thessalonians 2:12) I echo the God-inspired words of the apostle Paul: "For yourselves know perfectly that the day of the Lord so cometh as a thief in the night. When they are saying, Peace and safety, then sudden destruction cometh upon them, as travail upon a woman with child; and they shall in no wise escape. But ye, brethren, are not in darkness, that that day should overtake you as a thief: for ye are all sons of light, and sons of the day: we are not of the night, nor of darkness; so then let us not sleep, as do the rest, but let us watch and be sober. For they that sleep sleep in the night: and they that are drunken are drunken in the night. But let us, since we are of the day, be sober, putting on the breastplate of faith and love; and for a helmet, the hope of salvation. For God appointed us not into wrath, but unto the obtaining of salvation through our Lord Jesus Christ, who died for us, that, whether we wake or sleep, we should live together with him. Wherefore exhort one another, and build each other up…" (I Thessalonians 5:2-11)

  I fervently hope my book will stimulate people's brains to really think about the Bible. I want people to think, not necessarily to accept my thoughts. I want people to know the truth. I do not want people to quickly accept my messages without thinking and studying the Bible first. After all, I am imperfect, and my way of thinking may be in error. I want my book to be a blessing, not a curse!

I am always open to different opinions. I always allow people to challenge me. I believe challenging is beneficial; this way, both parties will have the opportunity to learn from either side. I thought I would initiate the challenge.

If you have long-held beliefs, I do not expect you to change them overnight. What I urge you to do is examine your beliefs using the Bible to see whether they are grounded in Scriptural truths. If they are not, I fervently hope that you will adopt beliefs that are Bible-based.

What are your personal interpretations of the Bible? Do you have specific questions about anything I have written in this book? I welcome you to share your thoughts with me, and correct me if I am wrong about any issue. Life is a giant school, and we are all together in this learning process. We are both students and teachers to one another, so I invite you to teach me. Let us learn together, and, hand in hand, may we realize our brightest dream as one heart beating in the same rhythm to the song composed by the greatest Composer!

Spotlight Reviews

"Let another man praise thee, and not thine own mouth; A stranger, and not thine own lips." (Proverbs 27:2)

This is an inspirational, motivating and thought provoking book with Shirley Cheng's understanding and look at what Jehovah intended His creations to be like. *Do You Love Jehovah?* gives an in depth look at the Scriptures, while at the same time, giving us a modern day interpretation of His meaning. It is thought provoking, fills you with serenity and makes you look forward to the future.

The examples of daily living, the tribulations and doubts that we feel, are intertwined with Scriptures relating to our feelings. The Scriptures that are used, also give us the answers to why we feel this way and what Jehovah tells us to do about it. Shirley Cheng has made it exciting to read the Bible and to learn more about Jehovah's plan for us. As you are reading the Bible passages in this book and understand how this relates to your life, you can see how Shirley Cheng has made you feel like you are sitting next to Jehovah and He is telling you what to do in your life to make things easier for you.

Even those that believe the scientific explanation of the creation will see that they are in many respects, emulating the words of the Bible and agree with its teachings. This is explained in such a simple and down to earth way, by using life circumstances as examples.

If you are one of the countless millions that feel that your life is missing something, that there should be more to it and that you do not know your purpose in life, read this book. Not all of your answers are in the book, but it sends you in the right direction to find them. It will make you look at life and its trials and tribulations in a new light, help you to cope better with the small stuff and give you the fortitude to overcome the big.

It is little wonder, this book deserves to sit on the shelf next to the Bible, the book that was written by the first Author of this universe. I am sure that Jehovah is very proud of a particular creation of His.

Shirley Cheng has all of the properties, emotions, logic and spiritual being that He was hoping to instill in each one of us. She explains the passages that she uses in the Bible and relates them to our lives, in such a way that we feel like we should have understood it right from the start. The way it is written makes us feel like this is the first time that we have really understood the words that we have read so often.

Shirley may be in a wheelchair, but has walked the universe. She may be blind but see's the true color and beauty in the world, the people and in life. Shirley has found a way in her writing, to open our eyes to the world around us, the blessings bestowed upon us, the path to follow and the life that is yet to come.

There is not one word that can describe this book. My description may say, "Small miracles to guide us happen to us everyday and this book is one of them."

— Jan Hayner, Professional Organizer, Motivational Speaker, Personal Coach, www.OrganizingAndCleaning.com

From what I perceive about Shirley Cheng; she does not hold a sense of fear. Her ability to express her feelings, knowledge, and passion come through so clear in her writing—it is obvious she was born to teach and change people's lives. In Shirley's new book: Do You Love Jehovah? is a true testament of how serious and dedicated she is to God and to leading others toward their personal best through the guidelines and Golden Rule mandates set forth by God. Her grassroots story telling makes this book an excellent read for individuals who haven't made the time to read the Bible. She has clear and concise ability to pin-point the most meaningful and beneficial points to live by through the word of God.

As an individual who works with those afflicted by addiction; this book is a valuable asset to reveal the inner faith and reasoning God has embodied within us.

Shirley's courage is contagious and I am envious of her passion and simplicity to explain her thoughts of faith in such a crisp and knowledgeable fashion. Shirley is a true leader where so many individuals fear to walk; a courageous teacher, her wisdom is fraught with urgency to reach others and spread her given talent. Where people lack to express their true feelings of God; Shirley's courageous soul is free to articulate her acknowledged belief system without judgment. I honor her experience of the Bible and respect her aptitude to express her commitment to God.

This book would benefit anyone who has feelings of loss, loneliness, anger, selfishness, and low self worth. Great for children to learn the foundation their life was built upon.

As always, I look forward to what Shirley Cheng teaches us next. Thank you wise one.
— *Trish Lay, Life Coach, Speaker, Founder of Souls At Play Productions, www.SoulsAtPlayProductions.com*

In her new book *Do You Love Jehovah?* highly acclaimed, award winning author, Shirley Cheng offers answers to the age old questions: Why am I here? Where am I going? Is there a God? How can I make a difference? Cheng introduces the concept that Jehovah God is the beginning of wisdom, the fulfillment of completeness, and the originator of life. She presents Jesus as Son of God, Messiah, and savior, our life sustainer.

In poetic prose Shirley describes the nature of God and the character of Christ with clarity, emotion, and passion. She boldly addresses traditional church doctrine giving her own personal insight and interpretation logically, using a common sense analysis. She includes foundational doctrines for living the spiritual life courageously with determined intention. Because Cheng refutes the arguments of

Trinitarians, her interpretation will not be readily acceptable by Evangelical and Catholic theologians.

In a concise, yet complete, Bible summary, Cheng covers important events and a review of the important themes of the entire Bible from Genesis through Revelation.

Cheng goes on to discuss the image of God, the creation of the world, and man's free will. I personally became intrigued with the way she approached each of the Ten Commandments presented in the scriptures to incorporate them into what she named "The Ultimate Life's Manual." The chapter on "How Should You Study the Bible?" was especially practical and helpful. Cheng's answers in the selection of frequently asked questions are provocative, articulate, and informational.

Shirley Cheng's writing is motivational and inspirational, infusing the reader with high aspirations for personal accomplishment. In *Do You Love Jehovah?* Cheng introduces practical principles for finding empowerment and self fulfillment. Cheng's writing is a source of direction, purpose, and challenge.

— *Dr. Richard R. Blake for Reader Views, Doctor of Ministries Former Instructor at Bay Cities Bible College*

Do You Love Jehovah? is a Christian inspirational guide encouraging readers to look towards God for the guidance and help in their lives, like Shirley Cheng, blind, and with several other medical problems... *Do You Love Jehovah?* is well worth considering for Christian readers.

— *Midwest Book Review, Small Press Bookwatch*

A dear friend of mine, Iris, mentioned to me the night before her death that as Christians, "We are all just vessels through which God's spirit flows—in and through us to others." As I read Shirley's book, *Do You Love Jehovah?* I thought once again of these vessels. Luke 6:45 tells us that "out of the abundance of the heart his mouth speaketh." Shirley's heart is abundant and she is clearly a vessel of faith, gratitude, strength and love from above. This emanates as you will see from each page. Her intellect and reasoning for truthful answers reminds me of yet another Scripture: "But sanctify in your hearts Christ as Lord: being ready always to give answer to every man that asketh you a reason concerning the hope that is in you, yet with meekness and fear." (I Peter 3:15) We are living in turbulent times calling for real answers; you hold in your hands a treasure of real answers that offer each of us a wonderful hope. It is a compelling read to move us to our part in the Divine purpose.

It will be a blessing to all who open its pages and a thorough witness to our Grand God, Jehovah.
— *Susanne Morrone, C.N.C., Author, Consultant*
www.NaturalHealthChat.com

Shirley Cheng introduces YHWH (Jehovah or Yahweh) in her own unique way: not some distant entity but the Father of all, that created all, and loves all. Her common sense analysis of the Bible will shock mainstream Christianity. Jesus Christ is not perceived as God. She arouses logical questions and presents answers based on the Bible Scriptures. Her title question: Do You Love Jehovah? in reality means Do you love LOVE? So no matter what each reader might believe, Shirley's path is full of Love for every creation and incident. And also this path has transformed her from a perceived blind and physically disabled woman to an ultra capable, inspiring person which has changed other peoples' lives around the world. And preaches the Golden Rule "Thou shalt love thy neighbour as thyself." (Mark 12:31) Read this book and overflow your life with LOVE!

— *Maria D. Georga, MBA, Author of* Killing the Cancer Beast, *Greece, www.FreeSpiritWay.blogspot.com*

Shirley Cheng writes in the same manner she lives life: courageously. She is not afraid to tackle the tough questions we ask when we study the Bible, and she is not afraid to present the answers she finds therein. She doesn't worry about popularity or critics; she is all about the questions, the logic, and the Scriptures, as she understands them. (And isn't that all any of us can do?)

The first questions Cheng addresses are about who Jehovah God is, who Jesus is, and what our response should be. She challenges the reader to take an in-depth look at the Scriptures — not from the viewpoint of any religious group or sect, but purely from the viewpoint of one seeking truth.

She goes on to address other mysteries such as: Where did the earth come from? What happens after death? Is there a hell? Why is there evil? Why does God allow suffering? When will suffering end? When will the last days come?

This is good reading for anyone who wants to explore these spiritual issues, no matter what their own viewpoint is. Shirley Cheng shares a little about her own life and spiritual journey at the end of the book, inspirational reading you won't want to miss. She is a remarkable woman who has beat incredible obstacles and lives life to the fullest.
— *Carolyn Warren, Author, Mortgage & Credit Expert*
www.AskCarolynWarren.com

As I finished reading Shirley Cheng's book I thought of the second chapter in The Song of Solomon. The dedication, the love, the joy and happiness which radiates from Shirley Cheng's writing is so pure, so inspiring, so enchanting that I must compare it to the beauty in The Song of Solomon. It is a beauty of spirit in a woman who does not allow physical difficulties to stop her on the road to ultra-ability.

Shirley touches on many things in her book, and through it all her faith in God shines like a beacon, her gratitude for life is wonderful to watch.

People unfamiliar with Christianity will find guidance in this book as Shirley takes us through the Bible and refers to Scripture throughout. And for those who already know the Bible Shirley comes as a loving friend pointing out the importance of the commandments that we must love God and love our neighbor as we love ourselves. She teaches us to show gratitude for the life God has given us and to accept what God sends our way and never worry or complain when difficulties meet us. It is a book that will speak to young people and help them find God.

She truly acts out her Faith and it has been a joy to read her book.
— Ragnhild Munck, Author of Days of Goodbyes
www.DaysOfGoodbyes.com

Shirley Cheng's book is elegantly written. With simplicity and competence she answers the most important questions every human being sooner or later asks him/herself. Her faith in God, who she teaches us to call Jehovah, and her deep knowledge of the Bible, guides her pen and offers explanations to colossal mysteries such as the purpose of life, the place of worry, the value of success, the meaning of death, what is destiny. But most of all, I would recommend this reading, because of the joy of life and the gratitude she transfused in the book. At times, I felt the need to kneel in front of such total deep happiness, coming from a person that knows suffering very well. Now, in times of crisis, we only hear lamentations. Read this book and you will learn how to thank God for every breath we take each day. And each day is worth thanking and living.
— Maria Caterina Capurro, Life, Business & Sports NLPTM Coach
Italy, www.CoachingServices.it

Do You Love Jehovah? is an honest and spiritual account of Shirley Cheng's personal understanding and interpretation of Jehovah's guidance in the Bible. In Shirley Cheng's book she also shares with you the meaning of happiness and how it is only created when Love is Served. She introduces Armageddon and the Last Days according to Scriptures. She reveals to us the difference between our Life-Giver and our Life-Sustainer. There is so much we think we understand in reference to heaven and hell when we really have no clue. Shirley offers this knowledge freely, out of the goodness in her heart. She asks for nothing in return other than that we too can gain the insights that she has.

Shirley has very carefully chosen Scriptures in order that we can find clear meaning to what the messages in the Bible are telling us. Jehovah is not about a new shiny car or winning a political election, Jehovah is about eternal love and goodness for all. He wants nothing more for this world that He created than a spiritual balance and harmony.

Shirley Cheng's hopes are in passing to her readers an insight to a deeper knowledge of God's Word and Plan and also just maybe answer questions we all have pondered such as these: Have you ever wandered about the Bible and its meaning? Do you think we are predestined? Do you value your gift as it was meant to be valued? Is there really a hell or a devil? Who is Satan and his fallen angels? What is the meaning behind the 10 Commandments? Are you prepared to challenged temptation each step of the way? Why is there so much suffering allowed in this world? Why should I follow Jehovah's guidance and not some other religion? Who is really Jesus and what is his purpose? If Jesus already died for us, then why are we still being told we have a judgment day?

Shirley Cheng has overcome her day to day challenges through a heart of love, discipline, understanding and forgiveness. She blames no one nor holds anyone responsible for her many physical

challenges. What she does do, is challenge them back through her ability to understand the meaning of God, Life, Love and Accepting the goodness that Life does offer her. Blind to the world we see, yes, but Shirley's insight to the real meaning of God is as clear as the day which God has created!
— *Dorothy Lafrinere, Women's Self-Esteem Expert*
www.WomensSelfEsteem.com

Cheng has a solid knowledge of the Bible.

She makes her most impressive arguments when she challenges the Trinitarian view. In spite of Cheng's keen intellect, the quality of reasoning wavers a bit throughout the rest of the book. While she makes a stellar case against the Trinitarians, other arguments hold water and others do not.

An example of one jump in logic begins with her claim that love starts in the home. We are to love others around us. This will strengthen our family bonds. True enough. Further, Cheng believes strong families will strengthen the government. Although I agree that strong families do provide a good foundation (with the possibility) for a just government, I do not agree that a stable government is an automatic product from strong families.

No matter what you think of Cheng's views, if you read her book you feel in the presence of a prayerful and thoughtful soul. She could preach a sermon with the best of the 18th century preachers.
— *Laura Evans, United Methodist Church Pastor's Wife, Certified Instructor, Journal to the Self®, www.JournalJoy.com*

During this time in life with so many

challenges people are searching for the answer, many turning to sources that lead to a dead end. Shirley Cheng's book *Do You Love Jehovah?* is a wonderful source of direction for those seeking truth. Shirley has written with great compassion and direction holding nothing back. She has searched God's Word, the Bible for the truth and gives a beautiful statement right up front, "It is time to get to know Him personally."

I love the fact that Shirley shares from her heart and backs her stand by using God's Word. Shirley's great passion and love for her Savior Jesus Christ is evident in her writing and I applaud her marvelous efforts to put it in writing, backed by the Bible. Thank you for your willingness to share and touch lives, be blessed, Shirley.

— Robin Hardy, Business Consultant, Motivational Expert
www.RobinHardy.net

Shirley Cheng has written a fascinating book about her life and the storms she has weathered. She has done a masterful job in exploring the meaning of spirituality as it relates to her life and does not hesitate to show the importance of a spiritual connection for her life. Shirley makes ANYTHING seem possible with faith, determination, integrity, and perseverance.

Being blind and physically disabled has not stopped Shirley from living life out loud with passion, enthusiasm and above all JOY.

I highly recommend this book to anyone who is feeling sorry for themselves and without hope. This book is a "How to" manual for overcoming adversity and reaching ones goals and dreams in order to lead an extraordinary and fulfilled life, despite obstacles. Shirley's book certainly provides the inspiration to embrace whatever challenges you are faced with. She has invited the reader into her world of possibility, hope and joy by giving freely to us her wisdom and opening up our minds to unlimited possibilities.

Anyone facing life's adversities, uncertain and looking for encouragement, hope, a pathway to faith and a spiritual connection, MUST read this book.
— Gladys M. Anderson, M.Ed., CTACC, LMFT
Empowerment Coach, www.CoachForYourDreams.com

Shirley has written a compelling book where she let's you know up front these are her conclusions and thoughts on certain religious and some being hot-button topics. I love the personal facts she relates about her own life journey. She has such a wonderful outlook on life that it should make all of us look at our lives in a special way. When it comes to religion, one thing is for certain: you won't ever get everyone to totally agree, especially with our various takes and personal experiences in life. What I love about this book is how Shirley will cause you to at least think about what you believe, evaluate it, and you can argue your point within yourself to see if what you believe is as solid as you may have thought. Seeing that I wrote a novel entitled *Blessed Trinity* one can only imagine my internal discussion when I came to the section where she discussed her thoughts when it comes to the "Trinity." Then again, one might not agree with my conclusion on this topic in my book.

Shirley has been diligent in her pursuit of the things discussed an touched on. And I applaud her

for following her dreams and I believe that no matter where you land in your thoughts on what you believe, this book will challenge you to at least think more deeply on a few things.
— *Vanessa Davis Griggs, Author of* Strongholds, If Memory Serves, *www.VanessaDavisGriggs.com*

Shirley Cheng provides a solid foundation for understanding the Christian doctrine in a clear and easy to understand way, dispelling many of the misunderstandings people commonly have about the words of our Lord. Moreover, she stands as a beacon of light, a shining example to everyone, that no matter what excuses we may think we have, we can still walk in the path of righteousness.
— *Bill White, The Synchronicity Expert*
www.SynchronicityInYourLife.com

Cheng's book outlines and explains in a very easy-to-read manner, the foundation of the spiritual realm and the significance of living a truly spiritual life. Her explanation of the two components of life — the spiritual and the worldly — is very enlightening, and will help readers see that wealth, power and success are of little value after death, whereas, love, hope, and faith are everlasting.

Cheng deftly makes her points and gives advice on how to be a better person. I highly recommend this book for anyone who wants to know how to form a more lasting relationship with their Creator.
— *Jessica James, Award-Winning Author of* Shades of Gray
www.JessicaJamesBooks.com

Shirley Cheng in deciding to write about a sometimes difficult subject to get the regular person to read about, has done so in a simple yet powerful way. Anyone wondering about Scripture or going through reading the Scriptures themselves can benefit by experiencing Shirley's views. The reader whether agreeing or not can feel this author's heart.
—*Liz Cosline, Author, Life Ownership Coach*
http://SongOfOneUnexpectedLife.info

About the Author

"For God gave us not a spirit of fearfulness; but of power and love and discipline." (II Timothy 1:7)

Shirley Cheng, born in 1983, a blind and physically disabled award-winning author (with twenty-six book awards), motivational speaker, self-empowerment expert, poet, and author of nine books and contributor to twenty-two, is a miracle survivor with tremendous talents, an exceptional, tenacious spirit, and a colorful personality. She was diagnosed with severe juvenile rheumatoid arthritis at only eleven months old. She spent her early years in constant pain, confined to a wheelchair, and was hospitalized for many years while living between China and America until 1994. Unable to receive any form of education until her health was stabilized, Shirley started attending school at age eleven in a special education class in elementary school. Back then, she knew very little English, and her knowledge on other subjects was non-existent. Miraculously, she mastered grade level in all areas after approximately 180 days of attendance, and she immediately entered a regular sixth grade class in middle school.

Shirley has a voracious appetite for books, reading an average of six hundred pages (three books) daily, and has read over a total of two thousand books. Since sixth grade, she has received 100 on every NYS essay test, and stayed at the top of the class ever since. She was awarded for achieving the highest grade of 97 in Earth science in her eighth grade class. She was the Student of the Year and the Student of the Month, as well as a three-time winner of the National Reflections Program in visual arts. She has a passion for writing both prose and poetry. One of her short stories, *Mary Miller, the Elusive Lady*, received Honorable Mention and was published by the *Poughkeepsie Journal* in 1997, and her poem, *The Colors of the Rainbow*, earned merit status and was published in *Celebrate! New York Young Poets Speak Out* in 1999.

Shirley was a contributor to her high school newspaper, providing artwork in tenth grade. She received a standing ovation when she delivered a speech as a candidate for student body vice president in ninth grade.

When her eyesight began to deteriorate at the beginning of tenth grade, she had to use two magnifying glasses, holding one on top of the other, on enlarged print to do her work throughout the year, including the artwork she provided for the school newspaper. In classes, she learned only by listening to her teachers, even with chemistry and math, as she was unable to see the blackboard; still she maintained excellent grades.

Unfortunately, Shirley completely lost her

vision in April of tenth grade. She then received home-tutoring, and successfully completed all her schoolwork by using cassette tapes and tape recorders. She wrote and calculated long chemistry formulas and equations without vision or Braille (she cannot use Braille because of her severe arthritis). Her high school overall average was 97 (a 3.9 GPA without any advanced placement classes). But Shirley could not accumulate enough credits to receive a high school diploma from her school due to her vision loss. In 2002, she received her high school equivalency diploma. She took the entire GED test, including mathematical calculations, graphs, and an essay, in her head, and received a special recognition award for scoring an exceptionally high 3280. She was a student speaker at the GED graduation ceremony, and received a standing ovation for her speech.

Shirley became an author at age twenty, completing three books within one year. She wrote her books using a screen reader on her computer, typing with her two index fingers at the speed of about sixty words per minute. She successfully completed every self-publishing task, including formatting her manuscripts, on her own.

In January 2006, Shirley tied for first place in Be the Star You Are! Second Annual Essay Contest founded by New York Times bestselling author, TV/radio personality Cynthia Brian, garnering her a third appearance on Cynthia's live radio show. Shirley's winning entry, titled *The Jewel from Heavenly Father*, is dedicated to her beloved mother Juliet Cheng. In the following January, Shirley won Honorable Mention in the same contest for her essay,

I Hold the Power, her personal story of overcoming blindness at the age of seventeen. In January 2008, Shirley was yet again one of the winners in the contest, earning Honorable Mention for her essay, *My Mother: A Fighter, a Victor, a Lover*, which applauds her stellar mother for being a courageous and loving fighter to protect her life at all costs.

Shirley has an immense passion for life and is full of life and vigor. Despite her severe disabilities, Shirley has striven to overcome overwhelming obstacles and she is living the life she loves, while she empowers, inspires, and motivates others to do the same.

Shirley has extraordinary goals with the aspiration of attending college at Harvard University, where she plans to earn doctorates in microbiology, zoology, astronomy, physiology, and pathology, after a successful eye surgery.

Shirley is a true magical gift, a star with endless shine.

Shirley As an Advocate

Shirley is also an advocate of parental rights in children's medical care. "When doctors ask yes or no, parents should have the right to say no," says Shirley, whose mother, Juliet Cheng, lost custody twice in the US only after refusing unwanted and harmful treatments for her. The last case in 1990 made international headlines; Juliet appeared on *CBS This Morning* show with host Paula Zahn as she fought to save Shirley's life.

Other Books by Shirley

Shirley is also the author of:
- *Daring Quests of Mystics*
ISBN: 978-1-4116-5664-2
- *Embrace Ultra-Ability! Wisdom, Insight & Motivation from the Blind Who Sees Far and Wide*
ISBN: 978-0-6151-5522-7
- *Dance with Your Heart: Tales and Poems That the Heart Tells*
This book is available in Vietnam, published by the Women Publishing House in 2008 and translated into Vietnamese by Nguyen Bich Lan.
ISBN: 978-1-4116-1858-9
- *Waking Spirit: Prose & Poems the Spirit Sings*
(with foreword by New York Times bestselling author Cynthia Brian)
ISBN: 978-0-6151-3680-6 (trade paperback)
978-0-6151-3893-0 (hardback)
- *Parental Rights in Children's Medical Care: Where Is Our Freedom to Say No? A Look at the Injustice of the American Medical System*
    ISBN: 978-0-6151-4994-3
- *The Revelation of a Star's Endless Shine: A Young Woman's Autobiography of 20-Year Victories over Victimization*
(foreword by Cynthia Brian)
ISBN: 978-0-6151-5044-4
- *The Adventures of a Blind and Disabled Award-Winning Author: Inspiration & Motivation to Empower You to Go for Your Own Gold Medals*
ISBN: 978-0-6151-7515-7
- *First-Step Guide to Self-Publishing and Promotion: Tips*

from a Blind and Physically Disabled Award-Winning Author
ISBN: 978-0-557-00212-2

With highly acclaimed experts, like Dr. Wayne Dyer, Tony Robbins, and Jack Canfield, Shirley co-authored *Wake Up...Live the Life You Love: Finding Life's Passion* and *101 Great Ways to Improve Your Life, Volume 2*.

Book Awards

Waking Spirit: Prose & Poems the Spirit Sings is the recipient of:
- 2009 Silver Recipient of Mom's Choice Awards in Inspirational/Motivational
- The Avatar Award for Spiritual Excellence in Literature (2008)
- Best book in three categories of Reader Views 2007 Annual Literary Awards: First Place in Poetry Nonfiction, and Second Place in both New Age Nonfiction and Spirituality/Inspiration
- Finalist in the national Indie Excellence 2007 Book Awards
- Honorable Mention in the 2007 New York Book Festival Competition in Poetry
- Honorable Mention in the 2007 DIY Book Festival in Poetry

Embrace Ultra-Ability! Wisdom, Insight & Motivation from the Blind Who Sees Far and Wide is the recipient of:
- Nine Parent to Parent Adding Wisdom Awards, including Adult Health & Well-Being, Books – Inspirational/Christian, Gifts for Mom, Gifts for Dad, and Unique Products
- Reader Views 2008 Literary Awards – Honorable Mention for Body/Mind/Spirit
- Finalist in the 2008 Next Generation Indie Book Awards in Motivational
- Finalist in the National Best Books 2008 Awards in Philosophy

Shirley at www.ShirleyCheng.com

Visit Shirley on the Web at www.ShirleyCheng.com to learn more about her, her books, listen to some of her radio show interviews, E-mail her, and subscribe to her monthly newsletter, *Inspiration from a Blind*, to receive words of inspiration, special news and events information, and exclusive offers for members. Her newsletter issues are archived on her blog, http://blog.shirleycheng.com to which people can subscribe via E-mail or RSS.

Personalized autographed copies of all of Shirley's books are available from her Web site.

Her books are also available through Ingram, from Amazon.com (and their international sites) and BN.com, and also available through brick-and-mortar bookstores (ask your local bookstores and libraries to carry them).

Shirley is available for interviews, speaking engagements, book signings, and inspirational events. Contact Shirley via her site at www.ShirleyCheng.com

www.ingramcontent.com/pod-product-compliance
Lightning Source LLC
Chambersburg PA
CBHW020347170426
43200CB00005B/81